SAFETY SYMBOLS

	HAZARD	EXAMPLES	PRECAUTION	REMEDY
DISPOSAL	Special disposal procedures need to be followed.	certain chemicals, living organisms	Do not dispose of these materials in the sink or trash can.	Dispose of wastes as directed by your teacher.
BIOLOGICAL	Organisms or other biological materials that might be harmful to humans	bacteria, fungi, blood, unpreserved tissues, plant materials	Avoid skin contact with these materials. Wear mask or gloves.	Notify your teacher if you suspect contact with material. Wash hands thoroughly.
EXTREME TEMPERATURE	Objects that can burn skin by being too cold or too hot	boiling liquids, hot plates, dry ice, liquid nitrogen	Use proper protection when handling.	Go to your teacher for first aid.
SHARP OBJECT	Use of tools or glassware that can easily puncture or slice skin	razor blades, pins, scalpels, pointed tools, dissecting probes, broken glass	Practice common-sense behavior and follow guidelines for use of the tool.	Go to your teacher for first aid.
FUME	Possible danger to respiratory tract from fumes	ammonia, acetone, nail polish remover, heated sulfur, moth balls	Make sure there is good ventilation. Never smell fumes directly. Wear a mask.	Leave foul area and notify your teacher immediately.
ELECTRICAL	Possible danger from electrical shock or burn	improper grounding, liquid spills, short circuits, exposed wires	Double-check setup with teacher. Check condition of wires and apparatus.	Do not attempt to fix electrical problems. Notify your teacher immediately.
IRRITANT	Substances that can irritate the skin or mucus membranes of the respiratory tract	pollen, moth balls, steel wool, fiberglass, potassium permanganate	Wear dust mask and gloves. Practice extra care when handling these materials.	Go to your teacher for first aid.
CHEMICAL	Chemicals that can react with and destroy tissue and other materials	bleaches such as hydrogen peroxide; acids such as sulfuric acid, hydrochloric acid; bases such as ammonia, sodium hydroxide	Wear goggles, gloves, and an apron.	Immediately flush the affected area with water and notify your teacher.
TOXIC	Substance may be poisonous if touched, inhaled, or swallowed	mercury, many metal compounds, iodine, poinsettia plant parts	Follow your teacher's instructions.	Always wash hands thoroughly after use. Go to your teacher for first aid.
OPEN FLAME	Open flame may ignite flammable chemicals, loose clothing, or hair	alcohol, kerosene, potassium permanganate, hair, clothing	Tie back hair. Avoid wearing loose clothing. Avoid open flames when using flammable chemicals. Be aware of locations of fire safety equipment.	Notify your teacher immediately. Use fire safety equipment if applicable.

 Eye Safety Proper eye protection should be worn at all times by anyone performing or observing science activities.

 Clothing Protection This symbol appears when substances could stain or burn clothing.

 Animal Safety This symbol appears when safety of animals and students must be ensured.

 Radioactivity This symbol appears when radioactive materials are used.

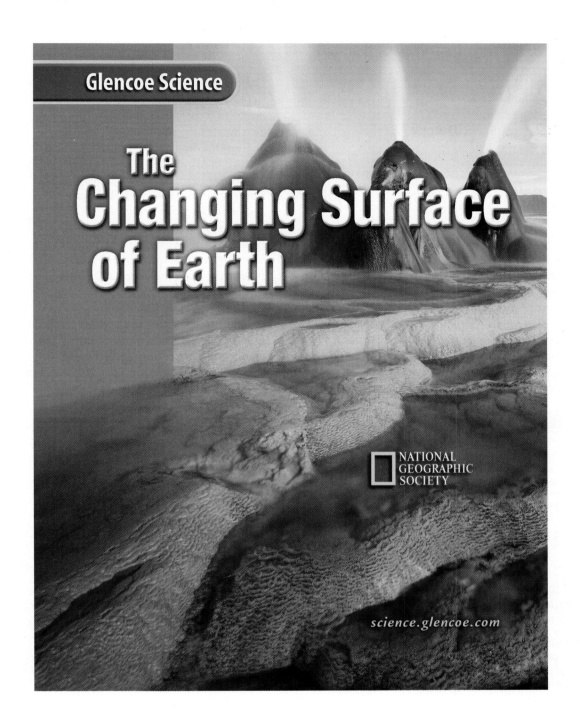

Glencoe Science

The Changing Surface of Earth

NATIONAL GEOGRAPHIC SOCIETY

science.glencoe.com

Glencoe McGraw-Hill

New York, New York   Columbus, Ohio   Woodland Hills, California   Peoria, Illinois

Glencoe Science

The Changing Surface of Earth

Student Edition
Teacher Wraparound Edition
Interactive Teacher Edition CD-ROM
Interactive Lesson Planner CD-ROM
Lesson Plans
Content Outline for Teaching
Dinah Zike's Teaching Science with Foldables
Directed Reading for Content Mastery
Foldables: Reading and Study Skills
Assessment
    Chapter Review
    Chapter Tests
    ExamView Pro Test Bank Software
    Assessment Transparencies
    Performance Assessment in the Science Classroom
    The Princeton Review Standardized Test Practice Booklet
Directed Reading for Content Mastery in Spanish
Spanish Resources
English/Spanish Guided Reading Audio Program
Reinforcement

Enrichment
Activity Worksheets
Section Focus Transparencies
Teaching Transparencies
Laboratory Activities
Science Inquiry Labs
Critical Thinking/Problem Solving
Reading and Writing Skill Activities
Mathematics Skill Activities
Cultural Diversity
Laboratory Management and Safety in the Science Classroom
Mindjogger Videoquizzes and Teacher Guide
Interactive Explorations and Quizzes CD-ROM with
    Presentation Builder
Vocabulary Puzzlemaker Software
Cooperative Learning in the Science Classroom
Environmental Issues in the Science Classroom
Home and Community Involvement
Using the Internet in the Science Classroom

THE PRINCETON REVIEW

"Study Tip," "Test-Taking Tip," and the "Test Practice" features in this book were written by The Princeton Review, the nation's leader in test preparation. Through its association with McGraw-Hill, The Princeton Review offers the best way to help students excel on standardized assessments.

The Princeton Review is not affiliated with Princeton University or Educational Testing Service.

Glencoe/McGraw-Hill

A Division of The **McGraw·Hill** Companies

The "Visualizing" features found in each chapter of this textbook were designed and developed by the National Geographic Society's Education Division, copyright ©2002 National Geographic Society. The name "National Geographic Society" and the yellow border rectangle are trademarks of the Society, and their use, without prior written permission, is strictly prohibited. All rights reserved.

The "Science and Society" and the "Science and History" features that appear in this book were designed and developed by TIME for Kids, a division of TIME Magazine.

Cover Images: Cones and Tufa terraces at Fly Geyser, Nevada

Send all inquiries to:
Glencoe/McGraw-Hill
8787 Orion Place
Columbus, OH 43240

ISBN 0-07-825538-4
Printed in the United States of America.
1 2 3 4 5 6 7 8 9 10 027/043 06 05 04 03 02 01

Authors

Ralph M. Feather Jr., PhD
Science Department Chair
Derry Area School District
Derry, Pennsylvania

Susan Leach Snyder
Earth Science Teacher, Consultant
Jones Middle School
Upper Arlington, Ohio

Dinah Zike
Educational Consultant
Dinah-Might Activities, Inc.
San Antonio, Texas

Content Consultants

William C. Keel, PhD
Department of Physics and Astronomy
University of Alabama
Tuscaloosa, Alabama

Homer Montgomery, PhD
Department of Geosciences
University of Texas at Dallas
Richardson, Texas

Robert Nierste
Science Department Head
Hendrick Middle School
Plano, Texas

Safety Consultants

Aileen Duc, PhD
Science II Teacher
Hendrick Middle School
Plano, Texas

Sandra West, PhD
Associate Professor of Biology
Southwest Texas State University
San Marcos, Texas

Math Consultants

Teri Willard, EdD
Department of Mathematics
Montana State University
Belgrade, Montana

Field Guide

Skill Handbooks—192

Reference Handbook

English Glossary—222

Spanish Glossary—227

Index—233

Interdisciplinary Connections/Activities

Feature Contents

Activities/Science Connections

EXPLORE ACTIVITY

Problem Solving Activities

Math Skills Activities

Skill Builder Activities

Science Skill Handbook

Math Skill Handbook

Technology Skill Handbook

Science INTEGRATION

SCIENCE Online

THE PRINCETON REVIEW

Land Use in Floodplains

I magine what it would be like to watch water rise higher and higher in your house, threatening all your possessions. That's what happened to some people in the midwest in June and July of 1993. The upper Mississippi River basin, with the land already soaked from a wet winter and spring, received almost 14 inches of rain. Even though people struggled desperately to protect their homes and businesses, whole towns were flooded and entire farms were lost, resulting in billions of dollars of damage and loss of life. And yet, after the water receded, the people moved back, homes and businesses were repaired or rebuilt, and new crops were planted.

Living on a Floodplain

Floods are the most common natural disaster in the world and occur when there is persistent heavy rainfall and the soil is waterlogged. The excess water swells a river, which eventually spills out onto the surrounding flatlands. Science is limited to offering options instead of solutions to those who choose to live on floodplains—areas prone to floods. It is the task of individuals and government to develop solutions to the problem of flooding.

Almost ten million homes and businesses in the United States are situated on floodplains. When floodplains are not under water, their flat, fertile soil and proximity to water make them popular sites for towns, farms, and industrial transportation.

Figure 1
Major floods devastated entire communities, such as Jefferson City, Missouri, during the Great Flood of 1993.

Figure 2
Although rivers usually stay within their channels, rivers cover floodplains when heavy rainfall increases their flow.

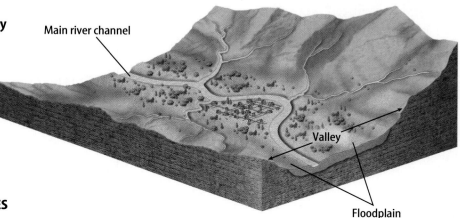

Main river channel

Valley

Floodplain

However, when rivers flow onto floodplains, they also wash through the homes, businesses, and farms that are located there.

How have scientists and engineers tried to deal with the problems of flooding on developed floodplains? One method is to use human-made structures to block or divert the flow of rivers. An estimated 60,000 dams have been built to block water from flowing downstream during heavy rains, forcing it instead into human-made lakes. More than 8,000 miles of levees, or artificial embankments, have been built along rivers to keep water contained in channels.

Limitations

These efforts have proven to be only partly successful. Human-made systems only can contain and direct water to a certain extent. Dams have overflowed and artificial conduits, or pathways for water, have caused flooding downstream. Levees have caused drying of sponge-like, absorbent wetlands, creating land even more prone to flooding.

Because of these problems, many environmental scientists are in favor of leaving floodplains undeveloped and moving floodplain communities to higher ground with the help of the Federal Emergency Management Agency (FEMA) which provides financial assistance to owners of homes and businesses that have been flooded and wish to relocate. The United States Department of Agriculture's Wetlands Reserve Program also is working to keep floodplain wetlands from being developed and to return developed floodplains to wetlands. But, in many cases, the program only can afford to pay prices far below estimated property values.

Figure 3
A wetland can absorb flood-waters more effectively than developed land can.

Figure 4
The floodgates on this dam had to be opened after weeks of heavy rain.

The Limits of Science

Society often asks scientists to solve problems. But there are times when the role of a scientist is limited to offering options. Science deals with facts, but there are questions it cannot answer. For example, people want answers to questions about how to prevent flooding or how to protect the homes, businesses, and farms in floodplains. When answering these questions, however, personal, political and economic factors all must be considered.

Figure 5
A system of levees is designed to keep the Mississippi River from pouring into developed areas.

What Does Science Do?

Science helps people solve problems and answer questions. By experimenting, analyzing data, and forming conclusions, people use science to gain an increased understanding of nature. The procedures used by scientists must be carefully planned to produce reliable results. Scientific methods must be observable, testable, and repeatable.

Scientists can apply scientific methods to the problem of living on floodplains. Identifying the problem of flooding is straightforward. Floodwaters are a danger to people and structures on floodplains. Scientists propose and test various solutions to the problem. Controlling the flow of river water through dams and levees can be beneficial, but it will not completely avoid flooding.

Testing Ideas

Scientists often can perform experiments in a laboratory to test ideas about a problem. For example, they might test how water flows through different types of soil or test the reliability of various levee designs. Other times scientists must rely on observations of real-life situations, and observations of past flooding, in order to reach conclusions. When studying floodplain development, scientists cannot accurately predict how water will flow on developed floodplains.

Sometimes mistakes are made in the process of applying scientific methods to solve a problem. When original hypotheses are proven inaccurate, the experience gained through experimentation can help refine or restructure ideas.

For example, engineers who constructed early dam and levee systems did not do so carelessly. While designing systems to control the flow of water, workers cannot predict all the shortcomings and adverse effects that dams and levees might produce. What is now known about rivers and their floodplains largely comes from earlier attempts at flood control.

Figure 6
This home in Rhineland, Missouri, was moved to higher ground after the Great Flood of 1993.

What Doesn't Science Do?

Science deals with facts, but it can't tell people how to think or feel. Science exposes the dangers of flooding, but the decision of whether to accept the risks of living on a floodplain remains with those who wish to stay or move there. One solution to the problem of flooding is to leave floodplains undeveloped and to move communities out of floodplains that already have been developed. Science is not qualified to make this decision. Solutions to the problem of flooding must be balanced among different viewpoints.

Moving communities to higher ground removes them from a river—a fertile agricultural site, a scenic area, and perhaps even an industrial work site. By moving entire communities, neighborhoods are lost and historic sites could be destroyed. In addition, people might not wish to lose government funding that maintains development of floodplains.

People ultimately must make the difficult decisions concerning floodplain development. Although science can be applied to help offer possible solutions, it cannot provide the answers to philosophical and political questions that arise from the problem of flooding. Science can make recommendations but it cannot and should not dictate behavior.

Think of an important land use decision that your community faces now, or faced recently. Research both sides of the issue. What part did science play in the debate? What about politics and economics? Take a position, and then participate in a class panel discussion of the issue.

Figure 7
These students are using debate as a way to learn about both sides of an issue.

Views of Earth

Viewing Earth from satellites, often called remote sensing, is a powerful way to learn about Earth's landforms, weather, and vegetation. This colorful image shows the metropolitan area of New York City and surrounding regions. Vegetation shows up as green, uncovered land is red, water is blue, and human-made structures appear gray. In this chapter, you will learn about studying Earth from space. You'll learn about Earth's major landforms, and you'll learn how to locate places on Earth's surface.

What do you think?

Science Journal Look at the picture below with a classmate. Discuss what you think this might be. Here's a hint: *It can keep you from getting lost on land or at sea.* Write your answer or best guess in your Science Journal.

EXPLORE ACTIVITY

Pictures of Earth from space are acquired by instruments attached to satellites. Scientists use these images to make maps because they show features of Earth's surface, such as mountains and rivers. In the activity below, use a map or a globe to explore Earth's surface.

Describe landforms

Using a globe, atlas, or a world map, locate the following features and describe their positions on Earth relative to other major features. Provide any other details that would help someone else find them.

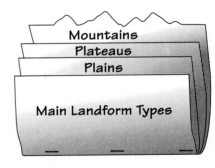

1. Andes mountains
2. Amazon, Ganges, and Mississippi Rivers
3. Indian Ocean, the Sea of Japan, and the Baltic Sea
4. Australia, South America, and North America

Observe

Choose one country on the globe or map and describe its major physical features in your Science Journal.

Before You Read

FOLDABLES
Reading & Study Skills

Making a Main Ideas Study Fold Make the following Foldable to help you identify the major topics about landforms.

1. Stack two sheets of paper in front of you so the short side of both sheets is at the top.
2. Slide the top sheet up so about 4 cm of the bottom sheet show.
3. Fold both sheets top to bottom to form four tabs and staple along the fold. Turn the Foldable so the staples are at the bottom. Cut mountain shapes on the top tab.
4. Label the tabs *Main Landform Types, Plains, Plateaus,* and *Mountains.* Before you read the chapter, write what you know about each landform under the tabs.
5. As you read the chapter, add to and correct what you have written.

Mountains
Plateaus
Plains

Main Landform Types

Landforms

Figure 1
Three basic types of landforms are plains, plateaus, and mountains.

Plains

Earth offers abundant variety—from tropics to tundras, deserts to rain forests, and freshwater mountain streams to salt-water tidal marshes. Some of Earth's most stunning features are its landforms, which can provide beautiful vistas, such as vast, flat, fertile plains; deep gorges that cut through steep walls of rock; and towering, snowcapped peaks. **Figure 1** shows the three basic types of landforms—plains, plateaus, and mountains.

Even if you haven't ever visited mountains, you might have seen hundreds of pictures of them in your lifetime. Plains are more common than mountains, but they are more difficult to visualize. **Plains** are large, flat areas, often found in the interior regions of continents. The flat land of plains is ideal for agriculture. Plains often have thick, fertile soils and abundant, grassy meadows suitable for grazing animals. Plains also are home to a variety of wildlife, including foxes, ground squirrels, and snakes. When plains are found near the ocean, they're called coastal plains. Together, interior plains and coastal plains make up half of all the land in the United States.

Plateau

Mountains

Plain

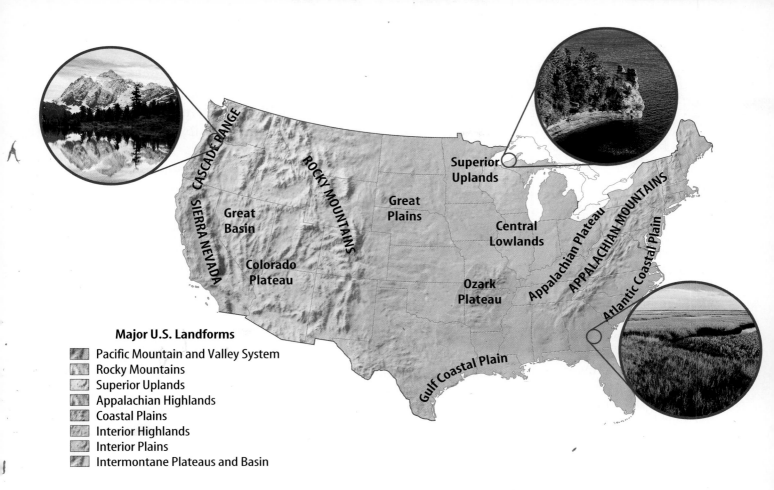

Major U.S. Landforms

- Pacific Mountain and Valley System
- Rocky Mountains
- Superior Uplands
- Appalachian Highlands
- Coastal Plains
- Interior Highlands
- Interior Plains
- Intermontane Plateaus and Basin

Coastal Plains A coastal plain often is called a lowland because it is lower in elevation, or distance above sea level, than the land around it. You can think of the coastal plains as being the exposed portion of a continental shelf. The continental shelf is the part of a continent that extends into the ocean. The Atlantic Coastal Plain is a good example of this type of landform. It stretches along the east coast of the United States from New Jersey to Florida. This area has low rolling hills, swamps, and marshes. A marsh is a grassy wetland that usually is flooded with water.

The Atlantic Coastal Plain, shown in **Figure 2,** began forming about 70 million years ago as sediment began accumulating on the ocean floor. Sea level eventually dropped, and the seafloor was exposed. As a result, the coastal plain was born. The size of the coastal plain varies over time. That's because sea level rises and falls. During the last ice age, the coastal plain was larger than it is now because so much of Earth's water was contained in glaciers.

The Gulf Coastal Plain includes the lowlands in the southern United States that surround the Gulf of Mexico. Much of this plain was formed from sediment deposited in deltas by the many rivers that enter the Gulf of Mexico.

✔ Reading Check *How are coastal plains formed?*

Figure 2
The United States has eight major landform regions, which include plains, mountains, and plateaus. After looking at this map, describe the region that you live in.

Profiling the United States

Procedure

1. Place the bottom edge of a piece of **paper** across the middle of **Figure 2,** extending from the west coast to the east coast.
2. Mark where different landforms are located along this edge.
3. Use a **map of the United States** and the **descriptions of the landforms in Section 1** to help you draw a profile, or side view, of the United States. Use steep, jagged lines to represent mountains. Low, flat lines can represent plains.

Analysis

1. Describe how your profile changed shape as you moved from west to east.
2. Describe how the shape of your profile would be different if you oriented your paper north to south.

Interior Plains The central portion of the United States is comprised largely of interior plains. Shown in **Figure 3,** you'll find them between the Rocky Mountains, the Appalachian Mountains, and the Gulf Coastal Plain. They include the Central Lowlands around the Missouri and Mississippi Rivers and the rolling hills of the Great Lakes area.

A large part of the interior plains is known as the Great Plains. This area lies between the Mississippi River and the Rocky Mountains. It is a flat, grassy, dry area with few trees. The Great Plains also are referred to as the high plains because of their elevation, which ranges from 350 m above sea level at the eastern border to 1,500 m in the west. The Great Plains consist of nearly horizontal layers of sedimentary rocks.

Plateaus

At somewhat higher elevations, you will find plateaus (pla TOHZ). **Plateaus** are flat, raised areas of land made up of nearly horizontal rocks that have been uplifted by forces within Earth. They are different from plains in that their edges rise steeply from the land around them. Because of this uplifting, it is common for plateaus, such as the Colorado Plateau, to be cut through by deep river valleys and canyons. The Colorado River, as shown in **Figure 3,** has cut deeply into the rock layers of the plateau, forming the Grand Canyon. Because the Colorado Plateau is located mostly in what is now a dry region, only a few rivers have developed on its surface. If you hiked around on this plateau, you would encounter a high, rugged environment.

Figure 3
Plains and plateaus are fairly flat, but plateaus have higher elevation. **A** This short-grass prairie in Kansas is part of an interior plain. **B** The Colorado River has carved the Grand Canyon into the Colorado Plateau.

Mountains

Mountains with snowcapped peaks often are shrouded in clouds and tower high above the surrounding land. If you climb them, the views are spectacular. The world's highest mountain peak is Mount Everest in the Himalaya—more than 8,800 m above sea level. By contrast, the highest mountain peaks in the United States reach just over 6,000 m. Mountains also vary in how they are formed. The four main types of mountains are folded, upwarped, fault-block, and volcanic.

> ✔ **Reading Check** *What is the highest mountain peak on Earth?*

Folded Mountains The Appalachian Mountains and the Rocky Mountains in Canada, shown in **Figure 4,** are comprised of folded rock layers. In **folded mountains,** the rock layers are folded like a rug that has been pushed up against a wall.

To form folded mountains, tremendous forces inside Earth squeeze horizontal rock layers, causing them to buckle and fold. The Appalachian Mountains formed 250 million to 350 million years ago and are among the oldest and longest mountain ranges in North America. The Appalachians once were higher than the Rocky Mountains, but weathering and erosion have worn them down. They now are less than 2,000 m above sea level. The Ouachita (WAH shuh tah) Mountains of Arkansas are extensions of the same mountain range.

SCIENCE *Online*

Research Visit the Glencoe Science Web site at **science.glencoe.com** to learn how landforms can affect economic development.

Figure 4
Folded mountains form when rock layers are squeezed from opposite sides. These mountains in Banff National Park, Canada, consist of folded rock layers.

Figure 5
The southern Rocky Mountains are upwarped mountains that formed when crust was pushed up by forces inside Earth.

Upwarped Mountains

The Adirondack Mountains in New York, the southern Rocky Mountains in Colorado and New Mexico, and the Black Hills in South Dakota are upwarped mountains. **Figure 5** shows a mountain range in Colorado. Notice the high peaks and sharp ridges that are common to this type of mountain. **Upwarped mountains** form when blocks of Earth's crust are pushed up by forces inside Earth. Over time, the soil and sedimentary rocks at the top of Earth's crust erode, exposing the hard, crystalline rock underneath. As these rocks erode, they form the peaks and ridges.

Fault-Block Mountains

Fault-block mountains are made of huge, tilted blocks of rock that are separated from surrounding rock by faults. These faults are large fractures in rock along which mostly vertical movement has occurred. The Grand Tetons of Wyoming, shown in **Figure 6,** and the Sierra Nevada in California are examples of fault-block mountains. As **Figure 6** shows, when these mountains formed, one block was tilted and pushed up, while the adjacent block dropped down. This mountain-building process produces majestic peaks and steep slopes.

Figure 6
Fault-block mountains such as the Grand Tetons are formed when faults occur. Some rock blocks move up, and others move down. *How are fault-block mountains different from upwarped mountains?*

Figure 7
Mount Shasta is a volcanic mountain made up of layers of lava and ash.

Volcanic Mountains **Volcanic mountains,** like the one shown in **Figure 7,** begin to form when molten material reaches the surface through a weak area of the crust. The deposited materials pile up, layer upon layer, until a cone-shaped structure forms. Two volcanic mountains in the United States are Mount St. Helens in Washington and Mount Shasta in California. The Hawaiian Islands are the peaks of huge volcanoes that sit on the ocean floor. Measured from the base, Mauna Loa in Hawaii would be higher than Mount Everest.

Plains, plateaus, and mountains offer different kinds of landforms to explore. They range from low, coastal plains and high, desert plateaus to mountain ranges thousands of meters high.

Section Assessment

1. Describe the eight major landform regions in the United States that are mentioned in this chapter.

2. How do plains and plateaus differ?

3. Why are some mountains folded and others upwarped?

4. How are volcanic mountains different from other mountains?

5. **Think Critically** If you wanted to know whether a particular mountain was formed by movement along a fault, what would you look for?

Skill Builder Activities

6. **Concept Mapping** Make an events-chain concept map to explain how upwarped mountains form. **For more help, refer to the** Science Skill Handbook.

7. **Using an Electronic Spreadsheet** Design a spreadsheet that compares the origin and features of the following: *folded, upwarped, fault-block,* and *volcanic mountains.* Then, explain an advantage of using a spreadsheet to compare different types of mountains. **For more help, refer to the** Technology Skill Handbook.

② Viewpoints

As You Read

What **You'll Learn**

- **Define** latitude and longitude.
- **Explain** how latitude and longitude are used to identify locations on Earth.
- **Determine** the time and date in different time zones.

Vocabulary

equator   prime meridian
latitude   longitude

Why **It's Important**

Latitude and longitude allow you to locate places on Earth.

Figure 8
Latitude and longitude are measurements that are used to indicate locations on Earth's surface.

Latitude and Longitude

During hurricane season, meteorologists track storms as they form in the Atlantic Ocean. To identify the exact location of a storm, latitude and longitude lines are used. These lines form an imaginary grid system that allows people to locate any place on Earth accurately.

Latitude Look at **Figure 8.** The **equator** is an imaginary line that wraps around Earth exactly halfway between the north and south poles, separating Earth into two equal halves, called the northern hemisphere and the southern hemisphere. Lines running parallel to the equator are called lines of **latitude,** or parallels. Latitude is the distance, measured in degrees, either north or south of the equator. Because they are parallel, lines of latitude do not intersect, or cross, one another.

The equator is at 0° latitude, and the poles are each at 90° latitude. Locations north and south of the equator are referred to by degrees north latitude and degrees south latitude, respectively. Each degree is further divided into segments called minutes and seconds. There are 60 minutes in one degree and 60 seconds in one minute.

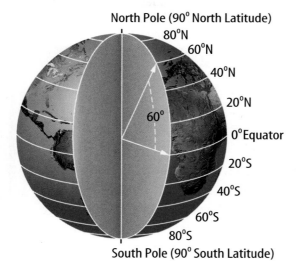

A Latitude is the measurement of the imaginary angle created by the equator, the center of Earth, and a location on Earth.

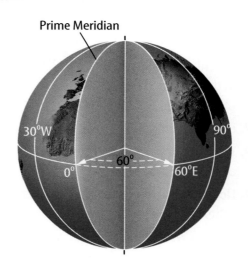

B Longitude is the measurement of the angle along the equator, between the prime meridian, the center of Earth, and a meridian on Earth.

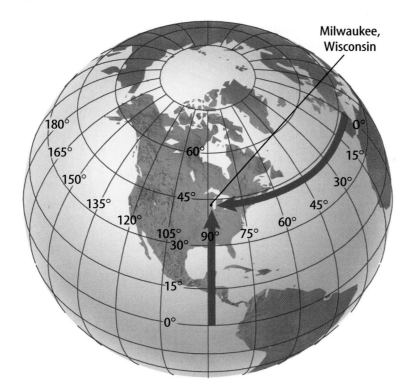

Milwaukee, Wisconsin

Figure 9
The city of Milwaukee, Wisconsin is located at about 43°N, 88°W. *How is latitude different from longitude?*

Longitude The vertical lines, seen in **Figure 8B,** have two names—meridians and lines of longitude. Longitude lines are different from latitude lines in many important ways. Just as the equator is used as a reference point for lines of latitude, there's a reference point for lines of longitude—the **prime meridian.** This imaginary line represents 0° longitude. In 1884, astronomers decided the prime meridian should go through the Greenwich (GREN ihtch) Observatory near London, England. The prime meridian had to be agreed upon, because no natural point of reference exists.

Longitude refers to distances in degrees east or west of the prime meridian. Points west of the prime meridian have west longitude measured from 0° to 180°, and points east of the prime meridian have east longitude, measured similarly.

Prime Meridian The prime meridian does not circle Earth as the equator does. Rather, it runs from the north pole through Greenwich, England, to the south pole. The line of longitude on the opposite side of Earth from the prime meridian is the 180° meridian. East lines of longitude meet west lines of longitude at the 180° meridian. You can locate places accurately using latitude and longitude as shown in **Figure 9.** Note that latitude position always comes first when a location is given.

✔ **Reading Check** *What line of longitude is found opposite the prime meridian?*

Figure 10
The United States has six time zones.

B But students in Seattle, Washington, which lies in the Pacific time zone, are eating dinner. *What time would it be in Seattle when the students in Washington, D.C., are sleeping at 9:00 P.M.?*

A Washington, D.C., lies in the eastern time zone. Students there would be going to sleep at 9:00 P.M.

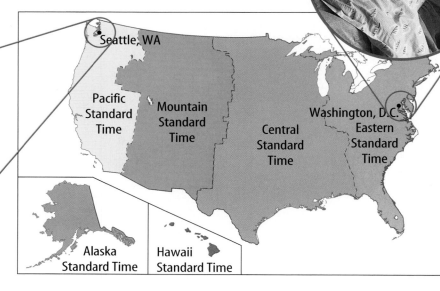

Seattle, WA

Pacific Standard Time

Mountain Standard Time

Central Standard Time

Washington, D.C.
Eastern Standard Time

Alaska Standard Time

Hawaii Standard Time

Life Science

INTEGRATION

If you travel east or west across three or more time zones, you could suffer from jet lag. Jet lag occurs when your internal time clock does not match the new time zone. Jet lag can disrupt the daily rhythms of sleeping and eating. Have you or any of your classmates ever suffered from jet lag?

Time Zones

What time it is depends on where you are on Earth. Time is measured by tracking Earth's movement in relation to the Sun. Each day has 24 h, so Earth is divided into 24 time zones. Each time zone is about 15° of longitude wide and is 1 h different from the zones on each side of it. The United States has six different time zones. As you can see in **Figure 10,** people in different parts of the country don't experience dusk simultaneously. Because Earth rotates, the eastern states end a day while the western states are still in sunlight.

✔ Reading Check *What is the basis for dividing Earth into 24 time zones?*

Time zones do not follow lines of longitude strictly. Time zone boundaries are adjusted in local areas. For example, if a city were split by a time zone boundary, the results would be confusing. In such a situation, the time zone boundary is moved outside of the city.

Calendar Dates

In each time zone, one day ends and the next day begins at midnight. If it is 11:59 P.M. Tuesday, then 2 min later it will be 12:01 A.M. Wednesday in that particular time zone.

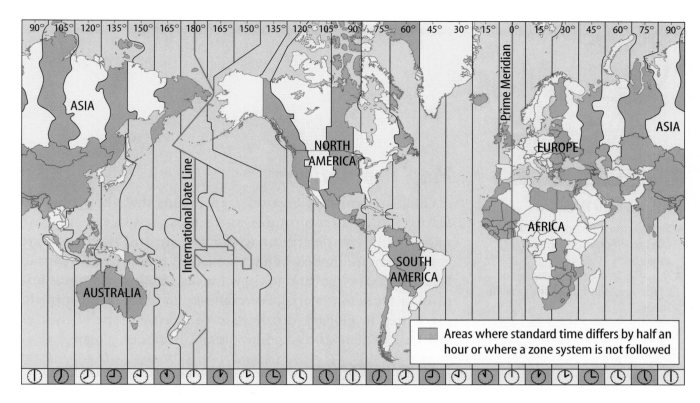

International Date Line You gain or lose time when you enter a new time zone. If you travel far enough, you can gain or lose a whole day. The International Date Line, shown on **Figure 11,** is the transition line for calendar days. If you were traveling west across the International Date Line, located at the 180° meridian, you would move your calendar forward one day. If you were traveling east when you crossed it, you would move your calendar back one day.

Figure 11
Lines of longitude roughly determine the locations of time zone boundaries. These boundaries are adjusted locally to avoid splitting cities and other political subdivisions, such as counties, into different time zones.

Section 2 Assessment

1. What are latitude and longitude?
2. How do lines of latitude and longitude help people find locations on Earth?
3. What are the latitude and longitude of New Orleans, Louisiana?
4. If it were 7:00 P.M. in New York City, what time would it be in Los Angeles?
5. **Think Critically** How could you leave home on Monday to go sailing on the ocean, sail for 1 h on Sunday, and return home on Monday?

Skill Builder Activities

6. **Interpreting Scientific Illustrations** Use a world map to find the latitude and longitude of the following locations: Sri Lanka; Tokyo, Japan; and the Falkland Islands. **For more help, refer to the** Science Skill Handbook.

7. **Using Fractions** If you started at the prime meridian and traveled east one fourth of the way around Earth, what line of longitude would you reach? **For more help, refer to the** Math Skill Handbook.

As You Read

What **You'll Learn**

■ **Explain** the differences among Mercator, Robinson, and conic projections.
■ **Describe** features of topographic maps, geologic maps, and satellite maps.

Vocabulary

conic projection   map scale
topographic map   map legend
contour line

Why **It's Important**

Maps help people navigate and understand Earth.

Figure 12
Lines of longitude are drawn parallel to one another in Mercator projections. *What happens near the poles in Mercator projections?*

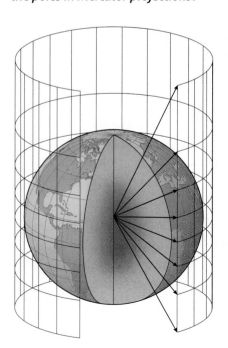

Map Projections

Maps—road maps, world maps, maps that show physical features such as mountains and valleys, and even treasure maps—help you determine where you are and where you are going. They are models of Earth's surface. Scientists use maps to locate various places and to show the distribution of various features or types of material. For example, an Earth scientist might use a map to plot the distribution of a certain type of rock or soil. Other scientists could draw ocean currents on a map.

✔ **Reading Check** *What are possible uses a scientist would have for maps?*

Many maps are made as projections. A map projection is made when points and lines on a globe's surface are transferred onto paper, as shown in **Figure 12.** Map projections can be made in several different ways, but all types of projections distort the shapes of landmasses or their areas. Antarctica, for instance, might look smaller or larger than it is as a result of the projection that is used for a particular map.

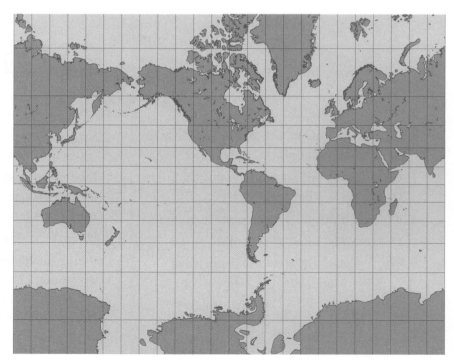

Figure 13
Robinson projections show little distortion in continent shapes and sizes.

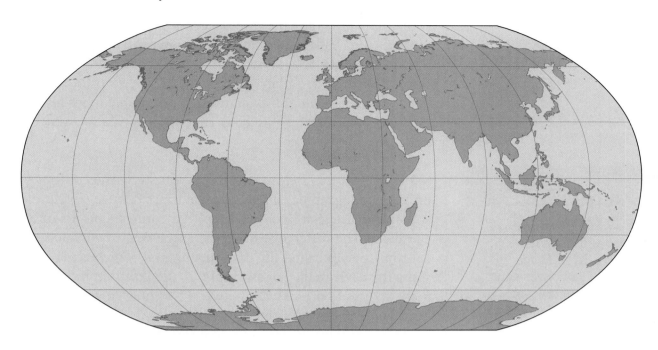

Mercator Projection Mercator (mer KAY ter) projections are used mainly on ships. They project correct shapes of continents, but the areas are distorted. Lines of longitude are projected onto the map parallel to each other. As you learned earlier, only latitude lines are parallel. Longitude lines meet at the poles. When longitude lines are projected as parallel, areas near the poles appear bigger than they are. Greenland, in the Mercator projection in **Figure 12,** appears to be larger than South America, but Greenland is actually smaller.

Robinson Projection A Robinson projection shows accurate continent shapes and more accurate land areas. As shown in **Figure 13,** lines of latitude remain parallel, and lines of longitude are curved as they are on a globe. This results in less distortion near the poles.

Conic Projection When you look at a road map or a weather map, you are using a conic (KAH nihk) projection. Conic projections, like the one shown in **Figure 14,** often are used to produce maps of small areas. These maps are well suited for middle latitude regions but are not as useful for mapping polar or equatorial regions. **Conic projections** are made by projecting points and lines from a globe onto a cone.

✔ Reading Check *How are conic projections made?*

Figure 14
Small areas are mapped accurately using conic projections.

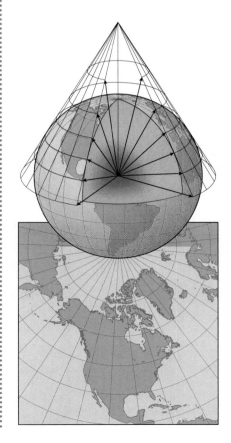

Topographic Maps

For nature hiking, a conic map projection can be helpful by directing you to the location where you will start your hike. On your hike, however, you would need a detailed map identifying the hills and valleys of that specific area. A **topographic map,** shown in **Figure 15,** models the changes in elevation of Earth's surface. With such a map, you can determine your location relative to identifiable natural features. Topographic maps also indicate cultural features such as roads, cities, dams, and other structures built by people.

Contour Lines Before your hike, you study the contour lines on your topographic map to see the trail's changes in elevation. A **contour line** is a line on a map that connects points of equal elevation. The difference in elevation between two side-by-side contour lines is called the contour interval, which remains constant for each map. For example, if the contour interval on a map is 10 m and you walk between two lines anywhere on that map, you will have walked up or down 10 m.

In mountainous areas, the contour lines are close together. This situation models a steep slope. However, if the change in elevation is slight, the contour lines will be far apart. Often large contour intervals are used for mountainous terrain, and small contour intervals are used for fairly flat areas. Why? **Table 1** gives additional tips for examining contour lines.

Index Contours Some contour lines, called index contours, are marked with their elevation. If the contour interval is 5 m, you can determine the elevation of other lines around the index contour by adding or subtracting 5 m from the elevation shown on the index contour.

Table 1 Contour Rules

1. **Contour lines close around hills and basins.** To decide whether you're looking at a hill or basin, you can read the elevation numbers or look for hachures (ha SHOORZ). These are short lines drawn at right angles to the contour line. They show depressions by pointing toward lower elevations.

2. **Contour lines never cross.** If they did, it would mean that the spot where they cross would have two different elevations.

3. **Contour lines form Vs that point upstream when they cross streams.** This is because streams flow in depressions that are beneath the elevation of the surrounding land surface. When the contour lines cross the depression, they appear as Vs pointing upstream on the map.

Figure 15

Planning a hike? A topographic map will show you changes in elevation. With such a map, you can see at a glance how steep a mountain trail is, as well as its location relative to rivers, lakes, roads, and cities nearby. The steps in creating a topographic map are shown here.

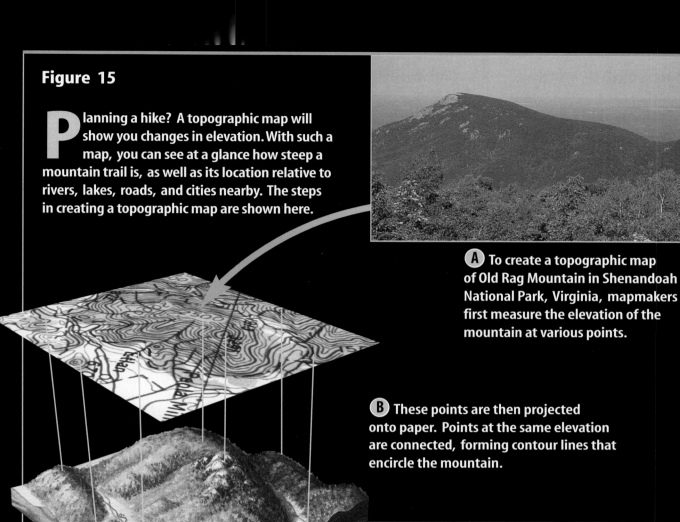

A To create a topographic map of Old Rag Mountain in Shenandoah National Park, Virginia, mapmakers first measure the elevation of the mountain at various points.

B These points are then projected onto paper. Points at the same elevation are connected, forming contour lines that encircle the mountain.

C Where contour lines on a topographic map are close together, elevation is changing rapidly—and the trail is very steep!

Map Scale When planning your hike, you'll want to determine the distance to your destination before you leave. Because maps are small models of Earth's surface, distances and sizes of things shown on a map are proportional to the real thing on Earth. Therefore, real distances can be found by using a scale.

The **map scale** is the relationship between the distances on the map and distances on Earth's surface. Scale often is represented as a ratio. For example, a topographic map of the Grand Canyon might have a scale that reads 1:80,000. This means that one unit on the map represents 80,000 units on land. If the unit you wanted to use was a centimeter, then 1 cm on the map would equal 80,000 cm on land. The unit of distance could be feet or millimeters or any other measure of distance. However, the units of measure on each side of the ratio must always be the same. A map scale also can be shown in the form of a small bar that is divided into sections and scaled down to match real distances on Earth.

Map Legend Topographic maps and most other maps have a legend. A **map legend** explains what the symbols used on the map mean. Some frequently used symbols for topographic maps are shown in the appendix at the back of the book.

Map Series Topographic maps are made to cover different amounts of Earth's surface. A map series includes maps that have the same dimensions of latitude and longitude. For example, one map series includes maps that are 7.5 minutes of latitude by 7.5 minutes of longitude. Other map series include maps covering larger areas of Earth's surface.

Geologic Maps

One of the more important tools to Earth scientists is the geologic map. Geologic maps show the arrangement of rocks at Earth's surface. Using geologic maps and data collected from rock exposures, a geologist can infer how rock layers might look below Earth's surface. The block diagram in **Figure 16** is a 3-D model that illustrates a solid section of Earth. The top surface of the block is the geologic map. Side views of the block are called cross sections, which are derived from the surface map. Developing block diagrams and cross sections is extremely important for the exploration and extraction of natural resources. What can a scientist do to determine whether a cross section accurately represents the underground features?

Figure 16
Geologists use block diagrams to understand Earth's subsurface. The different colors represent different rock layers.

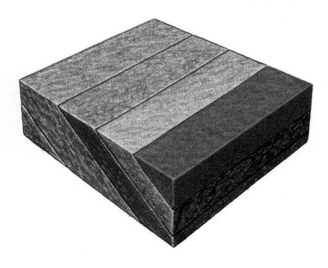

Three-Dimensional Maps Topographic maps and geologic maps are two-dimensional models that are used to study features of Earth's surface. To visualize Earth three dimensionally, scientists often rely on computers. Using computers, information is digitized to create a three-dimensional view of features such as rock layers or river systems. Digitizing is a process by which points are plotted on a coordinate grid.

Map Uses As you have learned, Earth can be viewed in many different ways. Maps are chosen depending upon the situation. If you wanted to determine New Zealand's location relative to Canada and you didn't have a globe, you probably would examine a Mercator projection. In your search, you would use lines of latitude and longitude, and a map scale. If you wanted to travel across the country, you would rely on a road map, or conic projection. You also would use a map legend to help locate features along the way. To scale the highest peak in your region, you would take along a topographic map.

Problem-Solving Activity

How can you create a cross section from a geologic map?

Earth scientists are interested in knowing the types of rocks and their configurations underground. To help them visualize this, they use geologic maps. Geologic maps offer a two-dimensional view of the three-dimensional situation found under Earth's surface. You don't have to be a professional geologist to understand a geologic map. Use your ability to create graphs to interpret this geologic map.

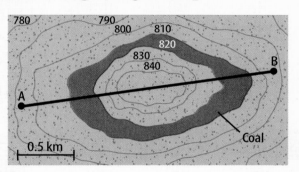

Identifying the Problem

At the right is a simple geologic map showing where a coal seam is found on Earth's surface. Place a straight edge of paper along the line marked A–B and mark the points where it meets a contour. Make a different color mark where it meets the exposure of coal. Make a graph on which the various elevations are marked on the *y*-axis. Lay your marked edge of paper along the *x*-axis and transfer the points directly above onto the proper elevation line. Now connect the dots to draw in the land's surface and connect the marks you made for the coal seam separately.

Solving the Problem

1. What type of topography does the map represent?
2. At what elevation is the coal seam?
3. Does this seam tilt, or is it horizontal? Explain how you know.

Figure 17
Sensors on *Landsat 7* detect light reflected off landforms on Earth.

Remote Sensing

Scientists use remote-sensing techniques to collect much of the data used for making maps. Remote sensing is a way of collecting information about Earth from a distance, often using satellites.

Landsat One way that Earth's surface has been studied is with data collected from Landsat satellites, as shown in **Figure 17.** These satellites take pictures of Earth's surface using different wavelengths of light. The images can be used to make maps of snow cover over the United States or to evaluate the impact of forest fires, such as those that occurred in the western United States during the summer of 2000. The newest Landsat satellite is *Landsat 7,* which was launched in April of 1999. It can acquire the most detailed Landsat images yet.

Global Positioning System The Global Positioning System, or GPS, is a satellite-based, radio-navigation system that allows users to determine their exact position anywhere on Earth. Twenty-four satellites orbit 20,200 km above the planet. Each satellite sends a position signal and a time signal. The satellites are arranged in their orbits so that signals from at least six can be picked up at any given moment by someone using a GPS receiver. By processing the signals, the receiver calculates the user's exact location. GPS technology is used to navigate, to create detailed maps, and to track wildlife.

Section Assessment

1. How do Mercator, Robinson, and conic projections differ?
2. Why does Greenland appear to be larger on a Mercator projection than it does on a Robinson projection?
3. Why can't contour lines ever cross?
4. What is a geologic map?
5. **Think Critically** Would a map that covers a large area have the same map scale as a map that covers a small region? How would the scales differ?

Skill Builder Activities

6. **Making Models** Architects make detailed maps called scale drawings to help them plan their work. Make a scale drawing of your classroom. **For more help, refer to the** Science Skill Handbook.
7. **Communicating** Draw a map in your Science Journal that your friends could use to get from school to your home. Include a map legend and a map scale. **For more help, refer to the** Science Skill Handbook.

Activity

Making a Topographic Map

Have you ever wondered how topographic maps are made? Today, radar and remote-sensing devices aboard satellites collect data, and computers and graphic systems make the maps. In the past, surveyors and aerial photographers collected data. Then, maps were hand drawn by cartographers, or mapmakers. In this activity, you can practice cartography.

Materials
plastic model of a landform
water tinted with food coloring
transparency
clear, plastic storage box with lid
beaker
metric ruler
tape
transparency marker

What You'll Investigate
How is a topographic map made?

Goals
- **Draw** a topographic map.
- **Compare and contrast** contour intervals.

Procedure

1. Using the ruler and the transparency marker, make marks up the side of the storage box that are 2 cm apart.
2. Secure the transparency to the outside of the box lid with tape.
3. Place the plastic model in the box. The bottom of the box will be zero elevation.
4. Using the beaker, pour water into the box to a height of 2 cm. Place the lid on the box.
5. Use the transparency marker to trace the top of the water line on the transparency.

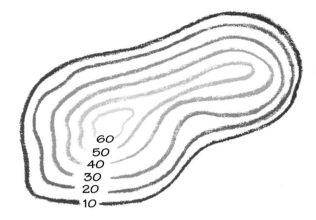

6. Using the scale 2 cm = 10 m, mark the elevation on the line.
7. Remove the lid and add water until a depth of 4 cm is reached.
8. Map this level on the storage box lid and record the elevation.
9. Repeat the process of adding 2 cm of water and tracing until the landform is mapped.
10. Transfer the tracing of the landform onto a sheet of white paper.

Conclude and Apply

1. What is the contour interval of this topographic map?
2. How does the distance between contour lines on the map show the steepness of the slope on the landform model?
3. **Determine** the total elevation of the landform you have selected.
4. How was elevation represented on your map?
5. How are elevations shown on topographic maps?
6. Must all topographic maps have a contour line that represents 0 m of elevation? Explain.

Constructing Landforms

Most maps perform well in helping you get from place to place. A road map, for example, will allow you to choose the shortest route from one place to another. If you are hiking, though, distance might not be so important. You might want to choose a route that avoids steep terrain. In this case you need a map that shows the highs and lows of Earth's surface, called relief. Topographic maps use contour lines to show the landscape in three dimensions. Among their many uses, such maps allow hikers to choose routes that maximize the scenery and minimize the physical exertion.

Recognize the Problem

What does a landscape depicted on a two-dimensional topographic map look like in three dimensions?

Thinking Critically

How can you model a landscape?

Goals

- **Research** how contour lines show relief on a topographic map.
- **Determine** what scale you can best use to model a landscape of your choice.

- Working cooperatively with your classmates, model a landscape in three dimensions from the information given on a topographic map.

Possible Materials

U.S. Geological Survey 7.5 minute quadrangle maps
sandbox sand
rolls of brown paper towels
spray bottle filled with water
ruler

Data Source

SCIENCE*Online* Go to the Glencoe Science Web site at **science.glencoe.com** for more information about topographic maps.

Planning the Model

1. **Choose** a topographic map showing a landscape easily modeled using sand. Check to see what contour interval is used on the map. Use the index contours to find the difference between the lowest and the highest elevations shown on the landscape. Check the distance scale to determine how much area the landscape covers.

2. **Determine** the scale you will use to convert the elevations shown on your map to heights on your model. Make sure the scale is proportional to the distances on your map.

3. **Plan** a model of the landscape in sand by sketching the main features and their scaled heights onto paper. Note the degree of steepness found on all sides of the features.

Check the Model Plans

1. **Prepare** a document that shows the scale you plan to use for your model and the calculations you used to derive that scale. Remember to use the same scale for distance as you use for height. If your landscape is fairly flat, you can exaggerate the vertical scale by a factor of two or three. Be sure your paper is neat, is easy to follow, and includes all units. Present the document to your teacher for approval.

2. **Research** how the U.S. Geological Survey creates topographic maps and find out how it decides upon a contour interval for each map. This information can be obtained from the Glencoe Science Web site.

Making the Model

1. Using the sand, spray bottle, and ruler, create a scale model of your landscape on the brown paper towels.

2. **Check** your topographic map to be sure your model includes the landscape features at their proper heights and proper degrees of steepness.

Analyzing and Applying Results

1. Did your model accurately represent the landscape depicted on your topographic map? Discuss the strengths and weaknesses of your model.

2. Why was it important to use the same scale for height and distance? If you exaggerated the height, why was it important to indicate the exaggeration on your model?

3. Why did the mapmakers choose the contour interval used on your topographic map?

4. **Predict** the contour intervals mapmakers might choose for topographic maps of the world's tallest mountains—the Himalayas, and for topographic maps of Kansas, which is fairly flat.

LOCATION,

New York Harbor in 1849

Rich Midwest farmland

Georgia peaches

Why is New York City at the mouth of the Hudson River and not 300 km inland? Why are there more farms in Iowa than in Alaska? What's the reason for growing lots of peaches in Georgia but not in California's Death Valley? It's all about location. The landforms, climate, soil, and resources in an area determine where cities and farms grow and what people connected with them do.

Landforms Are Key

When many American cities were founded hundreds of years ago, waterways were the best means of transportation. Old cities such as New York City and Boston are located on deep harbors where ships could land with people and goods. Rivers also were major highways centuries ago. They still are. A city such as New Orleans, located at the mouth of the Mississippi River, receives goods from the entire river valley.

It then ships the goods from its port to places far away.

Topography and soil also play a role in where activities such as farming take root. States such as Iowa and Illinois have many farms because they have lots of flat land and fertile soil. Growing crops is more difficult in mountainous areas or where soil is stony and poor.

Climate and Soil

Climate limits the locations of cities and farms, as well. The fertile soil and warm, moist climate of Georgia make it a perfect place to grow peaches. California's Death Valley can't support such crops because it's a hot desert. Deserts are too dry to grow much of anything without irrigation. Deserts also don't have large population centers unless water is brought in from far away. Los Angeles and Las Vegas are both desert cities that are huge only because they pipe in water from hundreds of miles away.

Resources Rule

The location of an important natural resource can change the rules. A gold deposit or an oil field can cause a town to grow in a place where the topography, soil, and climate are not favorable. For example, thousands of people now live in parts of Alaska only because of the great supply of oil there. People settled in rugged areas of the Rocky Mountains to mine gold and silver. Maine has a harsh climate and poor soil. But people settled along its coast because they could catch lobsters and fish in the nearby North Atlantic.

LOCATION

Alaska pipeline

Maine fishing and lobster industry

The rules that govern where towns grow and where people live are a bit different now than they used to be. Often information, not goods, moves from place to place on computers that can be anywhere. But as long as people farm, use minerals, and transport goods from place to place, the natural environment and natural resources will always help determine where people are and what they do.

Cities, farms, and industries grow in logical places

CONNECTIONS Research Why was your community built where it is? Research its history. What types of economic activity were important when it was founded? Did topography, climate, or resources determine its location? Are they important today? Report to the class.

Chapter ① Study Guide

Reviewing Main Ideas

Section 1 Landforms

1. The three main types of landforms are plains, plateaus, and mountains.

2. Plains are large, flat areas. Plateaus are relatively flat, raised areas of land made up of nearly horizontal rocks that have been uplifted. Mountains rise high above the surrounding land. *Which type of landform is shown in the photograph below?*

Section 2 Viewpoints

1. Latitude and longitude form an imaginary grid system that enables points on Earth to be located exactly.

2. Latitude is the distance in degrees north or south of the equator. Longitude is the distance in degrees east or west of the prime meridian.

3. Reference lines have been established for measuring latitude and longitude. Latitude is measured from Earth's equator, an imaginary line halfway between Earth's poles. Longitude is measured from the prime meridian. The prime meridian runs from pole to pole through Greenwich, England.

4. Earth is divided into 24 time zones. Each time zone represents a 1-h difference. The International Date Line separates different calendar days. *How many time zones are in the United States?*

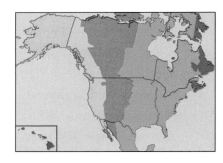

Section 3 Maps

1. Mercator, Robinson, and conic projections are made by transferring points and lines on a globe's surface onto paper.

2. Topographic maps show the elevation of Earth's surface. Geologic maps show the types of rocks that make up Earth's surface. *What type of map is shown here?*

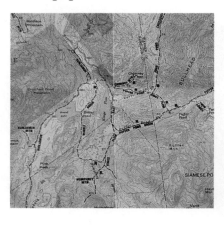

3. Remote sensing is a way of collecting information about Earth from a distance. Satellites are important remote-sensing devices.

FOLDABLES
Reading & Study Skills

After You Read

To help you review the three main landform types, use the Foldable you made at the beginning of this chapter.

Visualizing Main Ideas

Complete the following concept map on landforms.

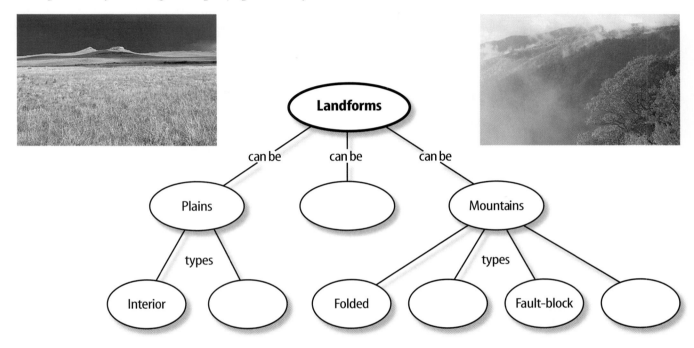

Landforms

can be / can be / can be

Plains / ( ) / Mountains

Plains — types — Interior / ( )

Mountains — types — Folded / ( ) / Fault-block / ( )

Vocabulary Review

Vocabulary Words

a. conic projection
b. contour line
c. equator
d. fault-block mountain
e. folded mountain
f. latitude
g. longitude
h. map legend
i. map scale
j. plain
k. plateau
l. prime meridian
m. topographic map
n. upwarped mountain
o. volcanic mountain

THE PRINCETON REVIEW **Study Tip**

Make a plan! Before you start your homework, write a checklist of what you need to do for each subject. As you finish each item, check it off.

Using Vocabulary

For each set of terms below, choose the one term that does not belong and explain why it does not belong.

1. upwarped mountain, equator, volcanic mountain

2. plain, plateau, prime meridian

3. topographic map, contour line, volcanic mountain

4. prime meridian, equator, folded mountain

5. fault-block mountain, upwarped mountain, plateau

6. prime meridian, map scale, contour line

Checking Concepts

Choose the word or phrase that best answers the question.

1. What makes up about 50 percent of all land areas in the United States?
   A) plateaus
   B) plains
   C) mountains
   D) volcanoes

2. Where is the north pole located?
   A) 0°N
   B) 180°N
   C) 50°N
   D) 90°N

3. What kind of mountains are the Hawaiian Islands?
   A) fault-block
   B) volcanic
   C) upwarped
   D) folded

4. What are lines that are parallel to the equator called?
   A) lines of latitude
   B) prime meridians
   C) lines of longitude
   D) contour lines

5. How many degrees apart are the 24 time zones?
   A) 10
   B) 34
   C) 15
   D) 25

6. Which type of map is distorted at the poles?
   A) conic
   B) topographic
   C) Robinson
   D) Mercator

7. Which type of map shows changes in elevation at Earth's surface?
   A) conic
   B) topographic
   C) Robinson
   D) Mercator

8. What is measured with respect to sea level?
   A) contour interval
   B) elevation
   C) conic projection
   D) sonar

9. What kind of map shows rock types making up Earth's surface?
   A) topographic
   B) Robinson
   C) geologic
   D) Mercator

10. Which major U.S. landform includes the Grand Canyon?
    A) Great Plains
    B) Colorado Plateau
    C) Gulf Coastal Plain
    D) Appalachian Mountains

Thinking Critically

11. How would a topographic map of the Atlantic Coastal Plain differ from a topographic map of the Rocky Mountains?

12. If you left Korea early Wednesday morning and flew to Hawaii, on what day of the week would you arrive?

13. If you were flying directly south from the north pole and reached 70° north latitude, how many more degrees of latitude would you pass over before reaching the south pole?

14. Using a map, arrange these cities in order from the city with the earliest time to the one with the latest time on a given day: Anchorage, Alaska; San Francisco, California; Bangor, Maine; Denver, Colorado; Houston, Texas.

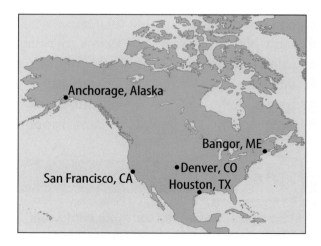

15. How is a map with a scale of 1:50,000 different from a map with a scale of 1:24,000?

Developing Skills

16. Comparing and Contrasting Compare and contrast Mercator, Robinson, and conic map projections.

17. Forming Hypotheses You are visiting a mountain in the northwest part of the United States. The mountain has steep sides and is not part of a mountain range. A crater can be seen at the top of the mountain. Hypothesize about what type of mountain you are visiting.

18. Concept Mapping Complete the following concept map about parts of a topographic map.

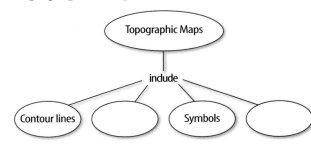

Performance Assessment

19. Poem Create a poem about the different types of landforms. Include characteristics of each landform in your poem. Display your poem with those of your classmates.

20. Poster Create a poster showing how satellites can be used for remote sensing.

TECHNOLOGY

Go to the Glencoe Science Web site at **science.glencoe.com** or use the **Glencoe Science CD-ROM** for additional chapter assessment.

THE PRINCETON REVIEW Test Practice

Alicia was looking at a map of the United States because her science teacher suggested that she learn about the landform regions in the United States.

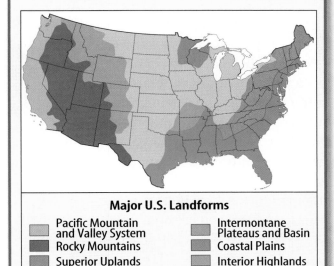

Major U.S. Landforms

- Pacific Mountain and Valley System
- Rocky Mountains
- Superior Uplands
- Appalachian Highlands
- Intermontane Plateaus and Basin
- Coastal Plains
- Interior Highlands
- Interior Plains

Study the diagram and answer the following questions.

1. Which technological development would have had the greatest impact on the accuracy of Alicia's map?
  A) radio communications
  B) measurement with lasers
  C) computer-assisted design
  D) satellite imaging

2. Which of the following landform regions would contain high, rugged mountains?
  F) Coastal Plains
  G) Interior Plains
  H) Appalachian Highlands
  J) Rocky Mountains

Weathering and Soil

Can you imagine how these balanced rocks were formed? For millions of years, nature has been working on them, wearing away softer materials and leaving behind more resistant rock. In this chapter, you'll read about how rocks are weathered into small fragments such as sand and clay. You also will learn how soil forms, how it erodes, and how to prevent soil erosion.

What do you think?

Science Journal Examine the picture below with a classmate. Discuss what you think this might be or what is happening. Here's a hint: *It's a strange place to grow.* Write your answer or best guess in your Science Journal.

 **EXPLORE ACTIVITY**

Weathering breaks apart rock by exposing it to natural elements such as water and ice. Do you think you can simulate weathering on Earth's surface?

Model weathering

1. Form groups of four or five students as instructed by your teacher.
2. Fill a coffee can one third of the way full with small cobbles and pebbles obtained from your school yard.
3. Observe the cobbles and pebbles that you collected. Sketch their shapes in your Science Journal.
4. Put the lid on the coffee can and take turns shaking the can vigorously from side to side for several minutes.
5. Remove the lid and examine the rocks.

Observe

Describe in your Science Journal what happened to the rocks. How is this similar to weathering?

Before You Read

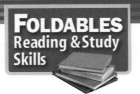 **FOLDABLES**
Reading & Study Skills

Making a Vocabulary Study Fold To help you study this chapter, make the following vocabulary Foldable. Knowing the definition of vocabulary words in a chapter is a good way to ensure you have understood the content.

1. Place a sheet of notebook paper in front of you so the short side is at the top and the holes are on the right side. Fold the paper in half from the left side to the right side.
2. Through the top thickness of paper, cut along every third line from the outside edge to the center fold, forming tabs as shown.
3. On the front of each tab, write a vocabulary word listed on the first page of each section in this chapter. On the back of each tab, define the word.
4. As you read the chapter, write a sentence using the vocabulary words.

1 Weathering

What **You'll Learn**

- **Describe** the difference between mechanical weathering and chemical weathering.
- **Explain** the effects of climate on weathering.

Vocabulary

weathering
mechanical weathering
ice wedging
chemical weathering
oxidation
climate

Why **It's Important**

Weathering causes rocks to crumble and shapes many landforms.

Weathering and Its Effects

Can you believe that tiny moss plants, a burrowing vole shrew, and even oxygen in the air can affect solid rock? These things and many more weaken and break apart rock at Earth's surface. Together, surface processes that work to break down rock are called **weathering.**

Weathering breaks rock into smaller and smaller pieces, such as sand, silt, and clay. These smaller, loose pieces are called sediment. The terms sand, silt, and clay are used to describe specific sizes of sediment. Sediment then changes gradually into soil. The formation of soil depends upon the amount of weathering that occurs in a specific place.

Over millions of years, weathering has changed Earth's surface. The process continues today. Weathering wears mountains down to hills as shown in **Figure 1.** Rocks at the top of mountains are broken down by weathering and then carried downhill by gravity, water, and ice. Weathering also produces strange rock formations like those shown at the beginning of this chapter. Two different types of weathering—mechanical weathering and chemical weathering—work together to shape Earth's surface.

Figure 1
Over long periods of time, weathering wears mountains down to rolling hills.

Figure 2
Growing tree roots can be agents of mechanical weathering.

A Tree roots can grow beneath a sidewalk, cracking the concrete and pushing it up.

B Tree roots also can grow into cracks in rock, breaking it apart.

Mechanical Weathering

Mechanical weathering occurs when rocks are broken apart by physical processes. This means that the chemical makeup of the rock stays the same. Each fragment keeps the same characteristics as the original rock. Growing plants, burrowing animals, and expanding ice are some of the things that can mechanically weather rock. These physical processes produce enough force to break rocks into smaller pieces.

Reading Check *What can cause mechanical weathering?*

Figure 3
Small animals mechanically weather rock when they burrow by breaking apart sediment and moving it to the surface.

Plants and Animals Water and nutrients that collect in the cracks of rocks result in conditions in which plants can grow. As the roots grow, they wedge rock apart. You've seen this kind of mechanical weathering if you've ever tripped on a crack in a sidewalk near a tree, as shown in **Figure 2A.** Sometimes the roots will wedge rock apart, as shown in **Figure 2B.**

Burrowing animals also cause mechanical weathering as shown in **Figure 3.** As these animals burrow, they loosen sediments and push them to the surface. Once the sediments are brought to the surface, other weathering processes can act on them.

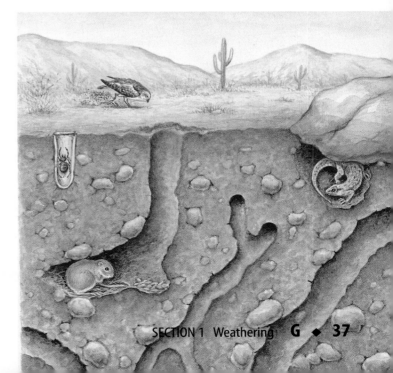

Figure 4
When water enters cracks in rock and freezes, it expands, causing the cracks to enlarge and the rock to break apart.

Figure 5
As rock is broken apart by mechanical weathering, the amount of rock surface exposed to air and water increases. The background squares show the total number of surfaces exposed.

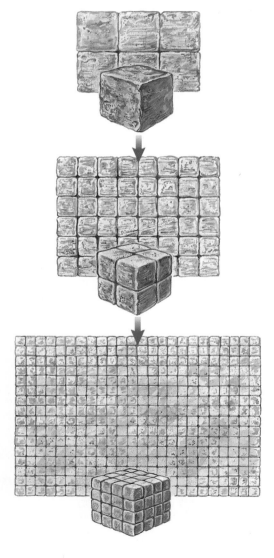

Ice Wedging The mechanical weathering process known as ice wedging is illustrated in **Figure 4. Ice wedging** occurs in temperate and cold climates where water enters cracks in rocks and freezes. Because water expands when it turns to ice, pressure builds up in the cracks. This pressure can extend the cracks and break apart rock. The ice then melts, allowing more water to enter the crack, where it freezes and breaks the rock even more. Ice wedging is most noticeable in the mountains, where warm days and cold nights are common. It is one process that wears down mountain peaks. This cycle of freezing and thawing not only breaks up rocks, but also can break up roads and highways. When water enters cracks in road pavement and freezes, it forces the pavement apart. This causes potholes to form in roads.

Surface Area Mechanical weathering by plants, animals, and ice wedging reduces rocks to smaller pieces. These small pieces have more surface area than the original rock body, as shown in **Figure 5.** As the amount of surface area increases, more rock is exposed to water and oxygen. This results in a different type of weathering called chemical weathering.

Chemical Weathering

The second type of weathering, **chemical weathering,** occurs when chemical reactions dissolve the minerals in rocks or change them into different minerals. This type of weathering changes the chemical composition of the rock, which can weaken the rock. Next, you will see how chemical weathering happens.

Natural Acids Naturally formed acids can weather rocks chemically. When water mixes with carbon dioxide gas in the air or soil, a weak acid, called carbonic acid, forms. This is the same weak acid that makes soft drinks fizzy, especially when shaken. Carbonic acid reacts with minerals such as calcite, which is the main mineral that makes up limestone. This reaction causes the calcite to dissolve. Over many thousands of years, carbonic acid has weathered so much limestone that caves, such as the one shown in **Figure 6,** have formed.

Chemical weathering also occurs when naturally formed acids come in contact with other rocks. Over a long period of time, the mineral feldspar, which is found in granite, some types of sandstone, and other rocks, is broken down into a clay mineral called kaolinite (KAY uh luh nite). Kaolinite clay is common in some soils. Clay is an end product of weathering.

✔ **Reading Check** *How does kaolinite clay form?*

Research Visit the Glencoe Science Web site at **science.glencoe.com** for more information about chemical weathering. Communicate to your class what you learn.

Figure 6
Caves form when slightly acidic groundwater dissolves large amounts of limestone.

Carbon dioxide + Water = Carbonic acid
Carbonic acid dissolves limestone.

Observing the Formation of Rust

Procedure 🥽 🧤
1. Place some **steel wool** in a **glass petri dish** with 1 cm of **water**.
2. Observe for several days.

Analysis
1. What changes occurred?
2. What caused the changes?
3. How are these changes related to weathering?

Plant Acids Some roots and decaying plants give off acids that also can dissolve minerals in rock. When these minerals are dissolved, the rock is weakened. Eventually, the rock will break into smaller pieces. Do you know how a plant can benefit by being able to dissolve rock?

Oxygen Oxygen helps cause chemical weathering. You've seen rusty swing sets, nails, and cars. Rust is caused by oxidation. **Oxidation** (ahk sih DAY shun) occurs when metallic materials are exposed to oxygen and water over prolonged periods of time. For example, when minerals containing iron are exposed to water and the oxygen in air, the iron in the mineral can form a new mineral that resembles rust. One common example of this type of weathering is alteration of the iron-bearing mineral magnetite to a rustlike mineral called limonite, as shown in **Figure 7.** Can you think of an example of a mineral, other than magnetite, that is weathered by oxidation?

Effects of Climate

Mechanical and chemical weathering occur everywhere. However, climate can affect the rate of weathering in different parts of the world. **Climate** is the pattern of weather that occurs in a particular area over many years. In cold climates, where freezing and thawing are frequent, mechanical weathering rapidly breaks down rocks through the process of ice wedging. Chemical weathering is more rapid in warm, wet climates. Thus, chemical weathering occurs quickly in tropical areas such as the Amazon River region of South America. Lack of moisture in deserts and low temperatures in polar regions slow down chemical weathering. Which type of weathering do you think is most rapid in the area where you live?

Figure 7
Iron-containing minerals like the magnetite shown here can weather to form a rustlike mineral called limonite. *How is this similar to rust forming on your bicycle chain?*

A

B

Figure 8
Different types of rock weather at different rates. **A** In humid climates, marble statues weather rapidly and become discolored. **B** Granite statues weather more slowly.

Effects of Rock Type Rock type also can affect the rate of weathering in a particular climate. In wet climates, for example, marble weathers more rapidly than granite, as shown in **Figure 8.**

Now you can understand how weathering affects rocks, caves, mountains, and even buildings and streets. Weathering is an important part of the rock cycle. When weathering breaks down rocks, it produces sediment that can form sedimentary rocks. Weathering also begins the process of forming soil from rock and sediment. This is discussed in the next section.

Section Assessment

1. What is the difference between mechanical and chemical weathering?
2. Explain how tree roots can weather rock. How can prairie dogs weather rock?
3. What effect does carbonic acid have on limestone?
4. How does climate affect the rate of chemical weathering?
5. **Think Critically** Why does limestone often form cliffs in dry climates but not in wet climates?

Skill Builder Activities

6. **Concept Mapping** Make a network tree concept map about mechanical weathering. **For more help, refer to the** Science Skill Handbook.
7. **Using an Electronic Spreadsheet** Create a spreadsheet that identifies examples of weathering that you see around your neighborhood and school. Classify each example as the result of mechanical weathering, chemical weathering, or both. **For more help, refer to the** Technology Skill Handbook.

The Nature of Soil

As You Read

What You'll Learn

- **Explain** how soil develops from rock.
- **Describe** soil by comparing soil horizons.
- **Describe** factors that affect the development of soils.

Vocabulary

soil
humus
horizon
soil profile
litter
leaching

Why It's Important

Much of the food you eat is grown in soil. The quality of food you eat reflects the quality of the soil it grows in.

Formation of Soil

How often have you been told "Take off those dirty shoes before you come into this house"? Ever since you were a child, you've had experience with soil. Soil is found in many places—backyards, empty city lots, farm fields, gardens, and forests.

What is soil and where does it come from? A layer of rock and mineral fragments produced by weathering covers the surface of Earth. As you learned in Section 1, weathering gradually breaks rocks into smaller and smaller fragments. However, these fragments do not become soil until plants and animals live in them. Plants and animals add organic matter, the remains of once-living organisms, to the rock fragments. Organic matter can include leaves, twigs, roots, and dead worms and insects. After organic matter has been added, soil as you know it begins to develop. **Soil** is a mixture of weathered rock, decayed organic matter, mineral fragments, water, and air.

Soil can take thousands of years to form and ranges from 60 m thick in some areas to just a few centimeters thick in others. Climate, slope, types of rock, types of vegetation, and length of time that rock has been weathering all affect the formation of soil, as shown in **Figure 9.** For example, different kinds of soils develop in tropical regions than in polar regions. Soils that develop on steep slopes are different from soils that develop on flat land. **Figure 10** illustrates how soil develops from rock.

Figure 9
Five different factors affect soil formation. *How does time influence the development of soils?*

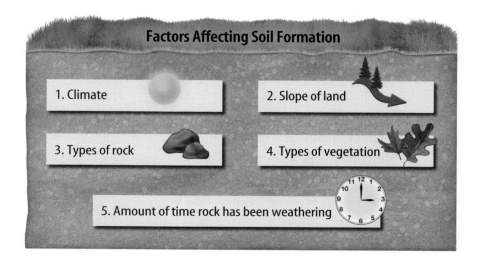

Factors Affecting Soil Formation

1. Climate
2. Slope of land
3. Types of rock
4. Types of vegetation
5. Amount of time rock has been weathering

Figure 10

I t may take hundreds of years to form, but soil is constantly evolving from solid rock, as this series of illustrations shows. Soil is a mixture of weathered rock,
mineral fragments, and organic material—the remains
of dead plants and animals—along with water and air.

A Natural acids in rainwater
weather the surface of exposed bedrock. Water can
also freeze in cracks, causing rocks to fracture and
break apart. The inset photo shows weathered rock
in the Tien Shan Mountains of Central Asia.

B Plants take root in the cracks and among
bits of weathered rock—shown in the inset
photo above. As they grow, plants, along with
other natural forces, continue the process of
breaking down rocks, and a thin layer of soil
begins to form.

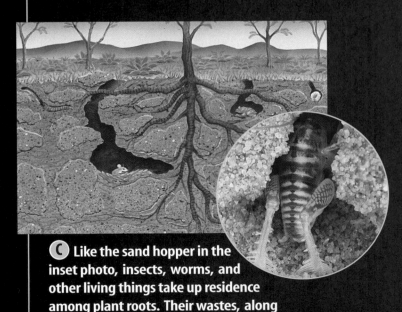

C Like the sand hopper in the
inset photo, insects, worms, and
other living things take up residence
among plant roots. Their wastes, along
with dead plant material, add organic

D As organic matter increases and underlying
bedrock continues to break down, the soil layer
thickens. Rich topsoil supports trees and other
plants with large root systems.

Composition of Soil

As you have seen already, soil is made up of rock and mineral fragments, organic matter, air, and water. The rock and mineral fragments found in soils come from rocks that have been weathered. Most of these fragments are small particles of sediment such as clay, silt, and sand. However, some larger pieces of rock also might be present.

Most organic matter in soil comes from plants. Plant leaves, stems, and roots all contribute organic matter to soil. Animals and microorganisms provide additional organic matter when they die. After plant and animal material gets into soil, fungi and bacteria cause it to decay. The decayed organic matter turns into a dark-colored material called **humus** (HYEW mus). Humus serves as a source of nutrients for plants. As worms, insects, and rodents burrow throughout soil, they mix the humus with the fragments of rock. Good-quality surface soil has about as much humus as weathered rock material.

Reading Check *What does humus do for soil?*

Soil has many small spaces between individual soil particles that are filled with air or water. In swampy areas, water may fill the spaces year-round. In other areas, the spaces in soil are filled mostly with air.

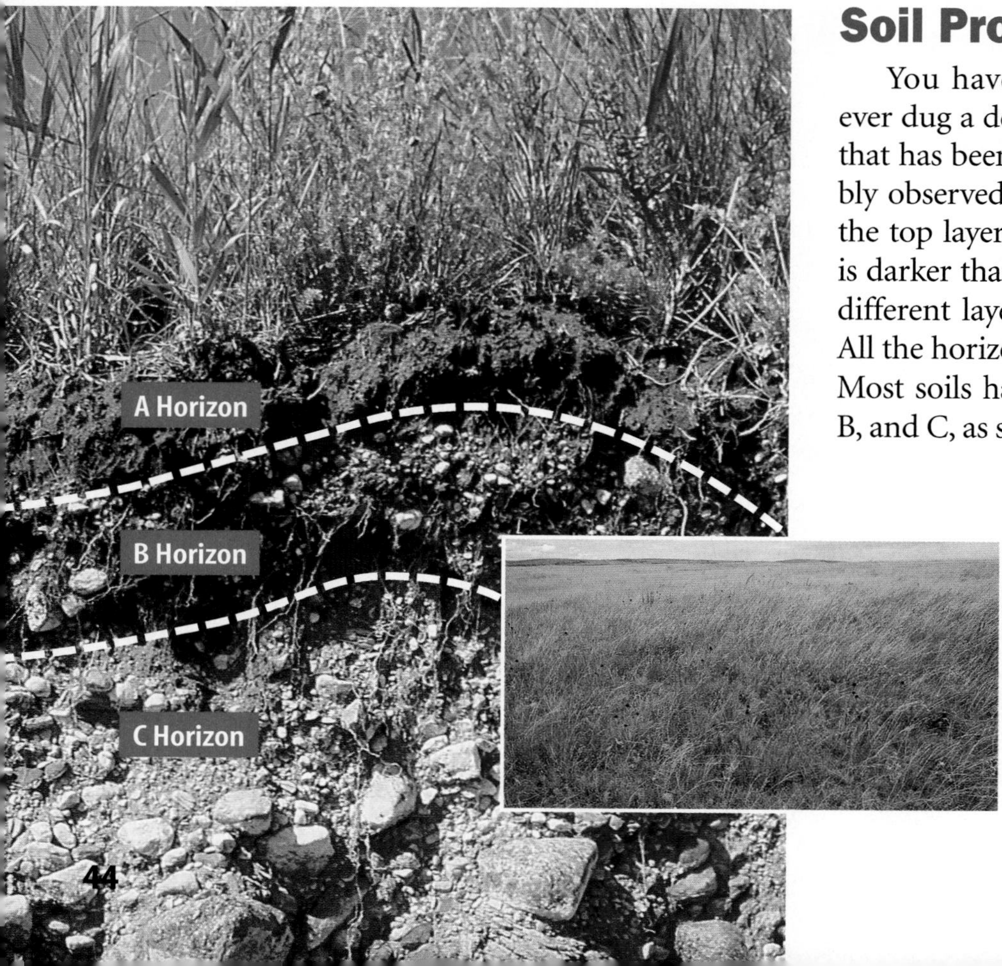

Soil Profile

You have seen layers of soil if you've ever dug a deep hole or driven along a road that has been cut into a hillside. You probably observed that most plant roots grow in the top layer of soil. The top layer typically is darker than the soil layers below it. These different layers of soil are called **horizons**. All the horizons of a soil form a **soil profile**. Most soils have three horizons—labeled A, B, and C, as shown in **Figure 11.**

A Horizon

B Horizon

C Horizon

Figure 11
This soil, which developed beneath a grassy prairie, has three main horizons. *How is the A horizon different from the other two horizons?*

44

Horizon A The A horizon is the top layer of soil. In a forest or unplowed area, the A horizon might be covered with litter. **Litter** consists of leaves, twigs, and other organic material that eventually can be changed to humus by decomposing organisms. Litter helps prevent erosion and holds water. The A horizon also is known as topsoil. Topsoil has more humus and fewer rock and mineral particles than the other layers in a soil profile. The A horizon generally is dark and fertile. The dark color of soil is caused by organic material, which provides nutrients for plant growth and development.

Horizon B The layer below the A horizon is the B horizon. Because litter does not add organic matter to this horizon, it is lighter in color than the A horizon and contains less humus. As a result, the B horizon is less fertile. The B horizon contains material moved down from the A horizon by the process of leaching.

Leaching is the removal of minerals that have been dissolved in water. The process of leaching resembles making coffee in a drip coffeemaker. In a coffeemaker, water drips through ground coffee. In soil, water seeps through the A horizon. In a coffeemaker, water absorbs the flavor and color from the coffee and flows into a coffeepot below. In soil, water reacts with humus and carbon dioxide to form acid. The acid dissolves some of the minerals in the A horizon and carries the material into the B horizon, as shown in **Figure 12.**

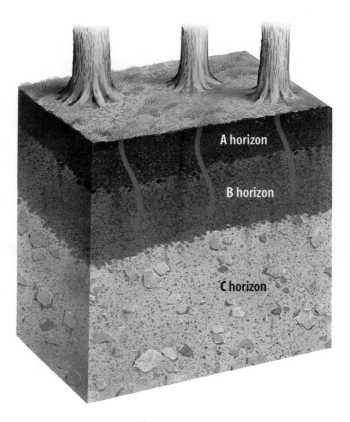

Figure 12
Leaching removes material from the upper layer of soil. Much of this material then is deposited in the B horizon.

Reading Check *How does leaching transport material from the A horizon to the B horizon?*

Horizon C The C horizon consists of partially weathered rock and is the bottom horizon in a soil profile. It is often the thickest soil horizon. This horizon does not contain much organic matter and is not strongly affected by leaching. It usually is composed of coarser sediment than the soil horizons above it. What would you find if you dug to the bottom of the C horizon? As you might have guessed, you would find rock—the rock that gave rise to the soil horizons above it. This rock is called the parent material of the soil. The C horizon is the soil layer that is most like the parent material.

Life Science
INTEGRATION

Earthworms in the A horizon swallow sediment to obtain food. These worms then excrete waste into the soil. This material is fertile and helps produce high-quality soil. Do research to find out how other animals affect soil development.

Glacial Deposits At many places on Earth, the land is covered by material that was deposited by glaciers. This unsorted mass of clay, silt, sand, and boulders covers much of the United States, creating, for example, the flat landscapes of the Midwest. The soils that developed on this glacial material are extremely fertile and are an important part of the Midwest's agricultural industry. How does this soil profile differ from the one described earlier? If you were to dig through the C horizon, you would find bedrock as before, but it would not be the rock the soil formed from. What material did this soil develop from?

Math Skills Activity

Calculating Percentages of Soil Particles

The properties of soil, such as the ability to hold water, are determined by the abundances of different types of particles. Therefore, it is important to determine particle percentages in soils.

Sample Problem

The circle graph represents a soil sample containing particles of clay, silt, and sand. Determine what percentage of the sample is clay.

20 g
Sand particles

15 g
Clay particles

15 g
Silt particles

1. *This is what you know:*

   sand weight: 20 g
   clay weight: 15 g
   silt weight: 15 g

2. *This is what you need to find:*

   total weight of the sample
   percentage of clay particles

3. *These are the equations you need to use:*

   sand weight + clay weight + silt weight = total weight
   decimal equivalent of percentage = clay weight/total weight
   decimal equivalent of percentage × 100 = percentage of clay

4. *Solve for the total weight:*   20 g + 15 g + 15 g = 50 g

5. *Solve for the decimal equivalent of percentage:*   15 g/50 g = 0.3

6. *Solve for the percentage of particle type:*   0.3 × 100 = 30% clay particles

---

Practice Problem

A second soil sample is taken that contains 30 g of sand, 30 g of clay, and 15 g of silt. What percentage of the entire soil sample is silt? Draw a circle graph for this sample.

For more help, refer to the Math Skill Handbook.

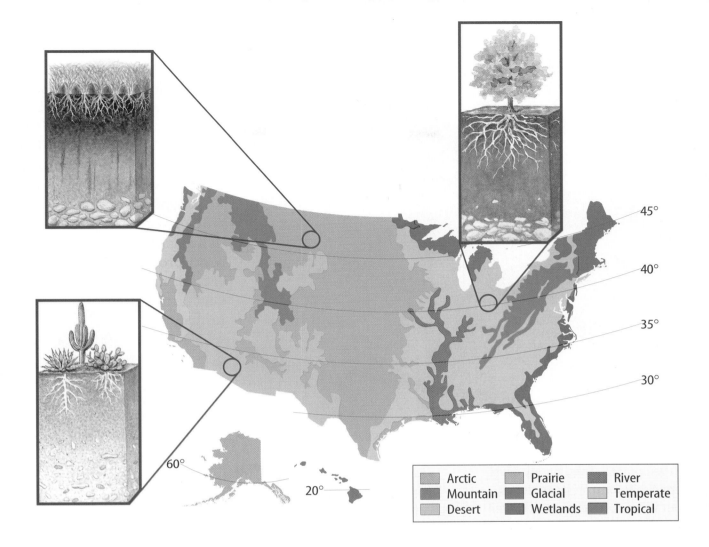

Arctic		Prairie		River	
Mountain		Glacial		Temperate	
Desert		Wetlands		Tropical	

Soil Types

If you travel across the country and look at soils, you will notice that they are not all the same. Some soils are thick and red, some are brown with hard, rounded rock nodules, and some have thick, black A horizons. Many different types of soils exist, as shown in **Figure 13.**

Soil Types Reflect Climate Different regions on Earth have different climates. Deserts are dry, prairies are semidry, and temperate forests are mild and moist. These places also have different types of soils. Soils in deserts contain little organic material and also are thinner than soil horizons in wetter climates. Prairie soils have thick, dark A horizons because the grasses that grow there contribute lots of organic matter. Temperate forest soils have thinner A horizons and B horizons that have been enriched in many elements because of leaching. The abundant rainfall in forests promotes leaching. Other regions such as tundra and tropical areas also have distinct soils.

Figure 13
The United States has nine different soil types. They vary in color, depth, texture, and fertility.

Other Factors Parent rock has a strong effect on the soils that develop from it. Clay soils often develop on rocks like basalt, because minerals in the rock weather to clay. What type of soil do you think might develop on sandstone? Rock type also can affect the type of vegetation that grows in a region, because different rocks provide different nutrients for plant growth. Type of vegetation then affects soil formation.

Time also affects soil development. If weathering has been occurring for only a short time, the parent rock determines the soil characteristics. As weathering continues, the soil resembles the parent rock less and less.

Figure 14
The slope of the land affects soil development. Thin, poorly developed soils form on steep slopes, but valleys often have thick, well-developed soils. *Why is this so?*

Slope also is a factor affecting soil profiles as shown in **Figure 14.** On steep slopes, soil horizons often are poorly developed, because material moves downhill before it can be weathered much. In bottomlands, sediments and water are plentiful. Bottomland soils are often thick, dark, and full of organic material.

Section Assessment

1. List five factors that affect soil development.

2. Why do soil profiles contain layers or horizons?

3. How do organisms help soils develop dark A horizons?

4. How does horizon B differ from horizon A and horizon C?

5. **Think Critically** Why is the soil profile in a tropical rain forest different from one in a desert?

Skill Builder Activities

6. **Concept Mapping** Make an events chain concept map that explains how soil develops. **For more help, refer to the Science Skill Handbook.**

7. **Using Statistics** A farmer collected five soil samples from a field and tested their acidity or pH. His data were the following: 7.5, 8.2, 7.7, 8.1, and 8.0. Calculate the mean of these data. Also, determine the range and median. **For more help, refer to the Math Skill Handbook.**

Activity

Soil Characteristics

Y ou've probably noticed a number of different types of soils. Collect samples of soil to compare from around your neighborhood and from designated areas of your school grounds.

What You'll Investigate
What are the characteristics of soils?

Materials

soil sample	water
cheesecloth squares	250-mL beakers (3)
sand	watch
100-mL graduated cylinder	large polystyrene or plastic cups (3)
gravel	pie pans
plastic coffee-can lids (3)	hand lens
clay	scissors
rubber bands (3)	thumbtack

Goals
■ **Analyze** permeability of different soils.

Safety Precautions

WARNING: *Use care when punching holes in the bottom of the cups with the thumbtack.*

Procedure

1. Spread the soil sample in a pie pan.
2. **Describe** the color of the soil and examine the soil with a hand lens. Describe the different particles.
3. Rub a small amount of soil between your fingers. Describe how it feels. Also, press the soil sample together. Does it stick together? Wet the sample and try this again. Record all your observations.

4. **Test** soil to see how water moves through it. Label the three cups A, B, and C. Using a thumbtack, punch ten holes in and around the bottom of each cup.
5. Cover the area of holes with a square of cheesecloth and secure with a rubber band.
6. To hold the cups over the beakers, cut the three coffee-can lids so that the cups will just fit inside the hole (see photo). Place a cup and lid over each beaker.
7. Fill cup A halfway with dry sand and cup B halfway with clay. Fill cup C halfway with a mixture of equal parts of sand, gravel, and clay.
8. Use the graduated cylinder to pour 100 mL of water into each cup. Record the time when the water is first poured into each cup and when the water first drips from each cup.
9. Allow the water to drip for 25 min, then measure and record the amount of water in each beaker.

Conclude and Apply

1. How does the addition of gravel and sand affect the permeability of clay?
2. **Describe** three characteristics of soil. Which characteristics affect permeability?

Soil Erosion

As You Read

What You'll Learn

- **Explain** why soil is important.
- **Identify** human activities that lead to soil loss.
- **Describe** ways to reduce soil loss.

Vocabulary
terracing

Why It's Important

If topsoil is eroded, soil becomes much less fertile.

Figure 15
Removing vegetation can lead to severe soil erosion. **A** Trees protect the soil from erosion in this forested region. **B** When forest is removed, soil erodes rapidly.

Soil—An Important Resource

While picnicking at a local park, a flash of lightning and a clap of thunder tell you that a storm is upon you. Watching the pounding rain from the park shelter, you notice that the water flowing off of the ball diamond is muddy, not clear. The flowing water is carrying away some of the soil that used to be on the field. This process is called soil erosion. Soil erosion is harmful because plants do not grow as well when topsoil has been lost.

Causes and Effects of Soil Erosion

Soil is eroded when it is moved from the place where it formed. Erosion occurs when water flows along Earth's surface or when wind picks up and transports sediments. Generally, erosion is more common on steep slopes than on gentle slopes. It's also more common in areas where there is little vegetation. Under normal conditions, a balance between soil production and soil erosion often is maintained. This means that soil forms at about the same rate as it is eroded. However, when vegetation is removed or slopes are steepened, soil erodes much faster than it can be produced. Many human activities result in the removal of vegetation and the steepening of slopes, as shown in **Figure 15.** Some of these activities are described in this section.

Figure 16
Tropical rain forests often are
cleared by burning. *How can
this increase soil erosion?*

Physics
INTEGRATION

Rain falling on farm fields
can be an important agent
of erosion. The erosive
force of rain depends on
how much rain falls and on
how hard the rain falls.
What type of rains do you
think would have the most
energy to erode soil?

Agricultural Cultivation Did you know that the population
of Earth increases by nearly 95 million people every year? More
people means that more food is needed. This has led to increased
use of farmable land and to rapid soil erosion in many places.
Plowing mechanically turns and loosens the soil, improving it for
crops. However, this practice also removes the plant cover that
holds soil particles in place, leaving soils vulnerable to wind and
water erosion. Over time, this practice can reduce soil quality.

Forest Harvesting When forests are removed, soil is
exposed and erosion increases. This creates severe problems in
many parts of the world, but tropical regions are especially at
risk. Each year, thousands of square kilometers of tropical rain
forest are cleared for lumber, farming, and grazing, as shown in
Figure 16. Soils in tropical rain forests appear rich in nutrients
but are almost infertile below the first few centimeters. The soil
is useful to farmers for only a few years before the nutrients are
gone. Farmers then clear new land, repeating the process and
increasing the damage to the soil.

Overgrazing In most places, land can be grazed with little
damage to soil. However, overgrazing can increase soil erosion.
In some arid regions of the world, sheep and cattle raised for
food are grazed on grasses until almost no ground cover
remains to protect the soil. When natural vegetation is removed
from land that receives little rain, plants are slow to grow back.
Without protection, soil is carried away by wind, and the moisture in the soil evaporates.

Research Visit the
Glencoe Science Web site at
science.glencoe.com
for information on soil erosion
research and how this research
can benefit the environment.
Communicate to your class
what you learn.

 **Reading Check** *How does overgrazing affect soil?*

Urban Construction Each year in the United States, about 6,100 km² of land are developed for roadways and other structures. You've probably noticed that when construction takes place, land is cleared of vegetation and soil is moved. During the construction process, water and wind erode soils. Areas that have been strip mined also are susceptible to soil erosion. Eroded soil can enter streams, causing them to fill up with sediment, as shown in **Figure 17.**

Figure 17
Erosion from exposed land can cause streams to fill with excessive amounts of sediment. *How could this damage streams?*

Figure 18
No-till farming helps prevent soil erosion because fields are not plowed before planting.

Preventing Soil Erosion

Each year more than 4 billion metric tons of soil are eroded in the United States. Soil is a resource that must be managed and protected. People can do several things to conserve soil.

Manage Crops All over the world, farmers work to slow down soil erosion. They plant shelter belts of trees to break the force of the wind and cover bare soils with decaying plants to hold soil particles in place. In dry areas, instead of plowing under vegetation, many farmers graze animals on the vegetation. Proper grazing management can maintain vegetation and reduce soil erosion.

In recent years, many farmers have begun to practice no-till farming. Normally, farmers till or plow their fields one or more times each year. In no-till farming, seen in **Figure 18,** plant stalks are left in the field over the winter months. At the next planting, farmers seed crops without destroying these stalks and without plowing the soil. No-till farming provides cover for the soil year-round, which reduces water runoff and slows soil erosion. The left-over stalks also keep weeds from growing in the fields.

☑ **Reading Check** *How can farmers reduce soil erosion?*

Reduce Erosion on Slopes On gentle slopes, planting along the natural contours of the land, as in **Figure 19,** helps reduce soil erosion. This practice, called contour farming, slows the flow of water down the slope and helps prevent the formation of gullies.

Where slopes are steep, terracing often is used. **Terracing** (TER uh sing) is a method in which steep-sided, level topped areas are built onto the sides of steep hills and mountains so that crops can be grown. These terraces reduce runoff by creating flat areas and shorter sections of slope. In the Philippines, Japan, China, and Peru, terraces have been used for centuries.

Reduce Erosion at Construction Sites A variety of methods are used at construction sites to help reduce erosion. During the construction process, exposed ground sometimes is covered with mulch, mats, or plastic coverings. Water is sprayed onto bare soil to prevent erosion by wind. When construction is complete, topsoil is added in areas where it was removed and trees are planted. Some areas are sodded, but if an area is to be seeded, soil is reinforced using netting and straw. Netting and straw make the surface layer more stable, which allows plant seeds to germinate quickly and vegetation to uniformly cover any slopes. Along steeper slopes, retaining walls made of concrete, stones, or wood keep soil and rocks from sliding downhill.

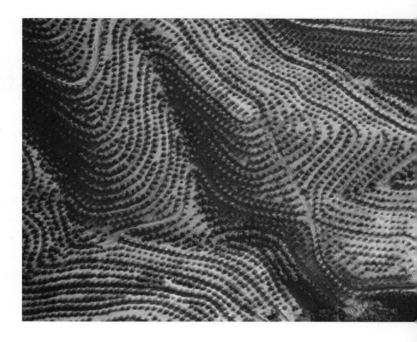

Figure 19
This orchard was planted along the natural contours of the land. *Why was this done?*

Section ③ Assessment

1. Why is soil important?
2. Why does soil erosion increase when soil is plowed?
3. How can urban construction cause soil erosion?
4. What are two ways erosion can be reduced at construction sites?
5. **Think Critically** How can contour farming help water soak into the ground?

Skill Builder Activities

6. **Recognizing Cause and Effect** Explain how soil erosion contributes to pollution of streams and lakes. **For more help, refer to the** Science Skill Handbook.

7. **Communicating** In your Science Journal, write a poem about the causes and effects of soil erosion. **For more help, refer to the** Science Skill Handbook.

Weathering Chalk

Chalk is a type of limestone made of the shells of microscopic organisms. The famous White Cliffs of Dover, England, are made up of chalk. This experiment will help you understand how chalk can be chemically weathered.

Recognize the Problem

How can you simulate chemical weathering of chalk? What variables affect the rate of chemical weathering?

Form a Hypothesis

How do you think acidity, surface area, and temperature affect the rate of chemical weathering of chalk? What happens to chalk in water or acid (vinegar)? How will the size of the chalk pieces affect the rate of weathering? What will happen if you heat the acid? Make hypotheses to support your ideas.

Possible Materials

equal-sized pieces of chalk (6)
small beakers or clear plastic cups (2)
metric ruler
water
white vinegar (100 mL)
hot plate
250-mL graduated cylinder
computer probe for temperature

Goals

- **Design** experiments to compare the effects of acidity, surface area, and temperature on the rate of chemical weathering of chalk.
- **Describe** factors that affect chemical weathering.
- **Explain** how the chemical weathering of chalk is similar to the chemical weathering of rocks.
- **Describe** how the factors used in this experiment apply to different parts of the world.

Safety Precautions

Wear safety goggles when pouring acids. Be careful when using a hot plate and heated solutions.
WARNING: *If mixing liquids, always add acid to water.*

Test Your Hypothesis

Plan

1. **Develop** hypotheses about the effects of acidity, surface area, and temperature on the rate of chemical weathering.

2. **Decide** how to test your first hypothesis. List the steps needed to test the hypothesis.

3. Repeat step 2 for your other two hypotheses.

4. **Design** data tables in your Science Journal. Make one for acidity, one for surface area, and one for temperature.

5. **Identify** what remains constant in your experiment and what varies. Each test should have only one variable being tested. Determine the control for each experiment.

6. **Summarize** your data in a graph. Decide from reading the **Science Skill Handbook** which type of graph to use.

Do

1. Make sure your teacher approves your plan before you start.

2. Carry out the three experiments as planned.

3. While you are conducting the experiments, record your observations and complete the data tables in your Science Journal.

4. Graph your data to show how each variable affected the rate of weathering.

Analyze Your Data

1. **Analyze** your graph to find out which substance—water or acid—weathered the chalk more quickly. Was your hypothesis supported by your data?

2. **Infer** from your data whether the amount of surface area makes a difference in the rate of chemical weathering. Explain.

Draw Conclusions

1. **Explain** how the chalk was chemically weathered.

2. How does heat affect the rate of chemical weathering?

3. What does this imply about weathering in the tropics and in polar regions?

Communicating
Your Data

Compare your results with those of your classmates. How were your data similar? How were they different? **For more help, refer to the** Science Skill Handbook.

Landscape, History, and the Pueblo Imagination
by Leslie Marmon Silko

In this excerpt, Leslie Marmon Silko, a woman of Pueblo, Hispanic, and American heritage, explains what ancient Pueblo people believed about the circle of life on Earth.

You see that after a thing is dead, it dries up. It might take weeks or years, but eventually if you touch the thing, it crumbles under your fingers. It goes back to dust. The soul of the thing has long since departed. With the plants and wild game the soul may have already been borne back into bones and blood or thick green stalk and leaves. Nothing is wasted. What cannot be eaten by people or in some way used must then be left where other living creatures may benefit. What domestic animals or wild scavengers can't eat will be fed to the plants. The plants feed on the dust of these few remains.

. . . Corn cobs and husks, the rinds and stalks and animal bones were not regarded by the ancient people as filth or garbage. The remains were merely resting at a midpoint in their journey back to dust. . . .

The dead become dust . . . . The ancient Pueblo people called the earth the Mother Creator of all things in this world. Her sister, the Corn mother, occasionally merges with her because all . . . green life rises out of the depths of the earth.

Rocks and clay . . . become what they once were. Dust.

A rock shares this fate with us and with animals and plants as well.

Understanding Literature

Repetition Many authors use repetition as a literary tool. Repetition is the recurrence of sounds, words, or phrases in a piece of writing. Poets often use repetition to give their poems a particular rhythm. In Silko's passage above, she repeatedly uses the word *dust*. This repetition reminds the reader of the common link between rocks, clay, plants, and animals. Also, it gives this passage a storytelling quality that makes the reader feel like he or she is reading a myth or legend instead of a work of nonfiction.

Science Connection In this chapter, you learned how weathered rocks and mineral fragments combine with organic matter to make soil. Silko's writing explains how the ancient Pueblo people understood that all living matter returns to the earth, or becomes dust. Lines such as "green life rises out of the depths of the earth," show that the Pueblo people understood that the earth, or rocks and mineral fragments, must combine with living matter in order to make soil and support plant life. Are there other ways in which your scientific understanding of the formation of soil is similar to the ancient Pueblo beliefs outlined in Silko's writing?

Linking Science and Writing

Using Repetition Write a one-page, how-to paper for your classmates on a type of soil conservation practice. For instance, the subject can be no-till agriculture, strip-cropping, or contour plowing. Use repetition as a tool to remind your readers of important steps in the process.

Career Connection

Soil Scientist

Elvia Niebla works for the U.S. Environmental Protection Agency (EPA) studying soil and soil pollution. Soil scientists explain how people can use soil effectively. They develop plans that keep people from contaminating soil and that keep soil from eroding. Niebla's research has even helped keep hamburger safe to eat. How? In a report for the EPA, she explained how meat could be contaminated when cows graze on contaminated soil. She is now the National Coordinator of the Global Change Research Program.

SCIENCE *Online* To learn more about careers in soil science, visit the Glencoe Science Web site at **science.glencoe.com**.

Chapter **2** Study Guide

Reviewing Main Ideas

Section 1 Weathering

1. Mechanical weathering breaks apart rock without changing its chemical composition. Plants, animals, and ice wedging are important agents of mechanical weathering. *How can this prairie dog weather rock?*

2. Chemical weathering changes the composition of rocks. Acidic water can dissolve rock or certain minerals within a rock. Some plants cause chemical weathering by secreting acids. Exposure to oxygen causes some rocks to weather, forming rustlike minerals.

Section 2 The Nature of Soil

1. Soil is a mixture of rock and mineral fragments, organic matter, air, and water.

2. Soil develops as rock is weathered and organic matter is added by organisms. Soil has horizons that differ in their color and composition. *How could the plants in the photo help soil develop?*

3. Climate, parent rock, slope of the land, type of vegetation, and the time that rock has been weathering affect the development of soil and cause different soils to have different characteristics.

Section 3 Soil Erosion

1. Soil is eroded when it is transported by wind and water. Erosion is more common on steep slopes and in areas where there is no ground cover.

2. Human activities like plowing, harvesting forests, overgrazing animals, and construction can increase soil erosion. *How does this netting help reduce soil erosion?*

3. Windbreaks, no-till farming, contour planting, and terracing help reduce soil erosion in farm fields. The best way to reduce soil erosion at construction sites is to replace vegetation quickly.

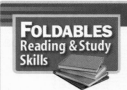

FOLDABLES
Reading & Study Skills

After You Read

To help you review the vocabulary words, use the Foldable you made at the beginning of the chapter.

Visualizing Main Ideas

Complete the following concept map on weathering.

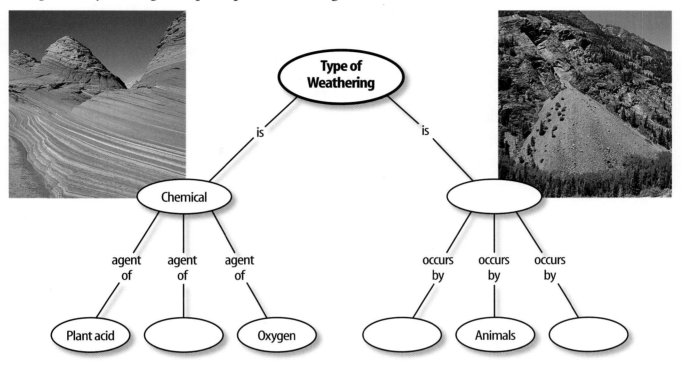

Vocabulary Review

Vocabulary Words

a. chemical weathering
b. climate
c. horizon
d. humus
e. ice wedging
f. leaching
g. litter
h. mechanical weathering
i. oxidation
j. soil
k. soil profile
l. terracing
m. weathering

THE PRINCETON REVIEW **Study Tip**

Make flashcards for new vocabulary words. Put the word on one side and the definition on the other. Use them to quiz yourself.

Using Vocabulary

The sentences below include vocabulary words that have been used incorrectly. Change the incorrect vocabulary words so that the sentence reads correctly. Underline your change.

1. Mechanical weathering causes a change in a rock's composition.

2. Leaching forms from organic matter such as leaves and roots.

3. The A, B, and C layers of a soil make up the soil horizon.

4. Ice wedging transports materials to the B horizon.

5. Litter occurs when many materials containing iron are exposed to oxygen and water.

Chapter 2 Assessment

Checking Concepts

Choose the word or phrase that best answers the question.

1. Which of the following is caused by acids produced by plants?
   A) soil erosion
   B) overgrazing
   C) mechanical weathering
   D) chemical weathering

2. What occurs when roots force rocks apart?
   A) mechanical weathering
   B) leaching
   C) ice wedging
   D) chemical weathering

3. What reacts with iron to form rust?
   A) oxygen
   C) feldspar
   B) carbon dioxide
   D) paint

4. Which of the following is an agent of mechanical weathering?
   A) ice wedging
   C) leaching
   B) oxidation
   D) desert formation

5. In which region is chemical weathering most rapid?
   A) cold, dry
   C) warm, moist
   B) cold, moist
   D) warm, dry

6. What is a mixture of weathered rock, organic matter, air, and water called?
   A) soil
   C) carbon dioxide
   B) limestone
   D) clay

7. What is decayed organic matter called?
   A) leaching
   C) soil
   B) humus
   D) sediment

8. Where is most humus found?
   A) A horizon
   C) C horizon
   B) B horizon
   D) D horizon

9. What does no-till farming help prevent?
   A) leaching
   C) overgrazing
   B) crop rotation
   D) soil erosion

10. What is done to reduce erosion on steep slopes?
    A) weathering
    C) terracing
    B) overgrazing
    D) forest harvesting

Thinking Critically

11. Which type of weathering, mechanical or chemical, would you expect to have more effect in a polar region? Explain.

12. Explain how off-road vehicles affect soil erosion.

13. How does increasing human population affect soil erosion?

14. Why is it difficult to replace lost topsoil?

15. Describe how chemical weathering can form a cave.

Developing Skills

16. **Using Variables, Constants, and Controls** Juan wanted to know if planting grass on a slope would prevent soil from being washed away. To find out, he put the same amount and kind of soil in two identical pans. In one of the pans, he planted sod. To create equal slopes for his test, he placed identical wooden wedges under one end of each pan. He carefully poured the same amount of water at the same rate over the soil in the two pans. What is Juan's control? What factors in his activity are constants? What variable is he testing?

17. Classifying Classify the following as examples of either chemical or mechanical weathering: rocks oxidize to form rustlike minerals, freezing and thawing of water causes a cliff face to break apart, acids from mosses discolor rocks, tree roots break rocks apart, and water seeping through cracks in limestone dissolves away some of the rock.

18. Concept Mapping Complete the events chain concept map that shows two ways in which acids can cause chemical weathering.

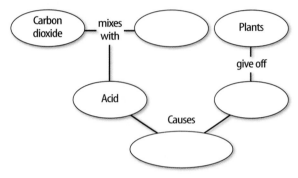

19. Forming a Hypothesis Over time, crop yields on a farm field diminish in spite of repeated applications of fertilizer. What hypothesis could be tested to explain this? How could an explanation benefit the farm owner?

Performance Assessment

20. Design a Landscape Find a slope in your area that might benefit from erosion maintenance. Design a landscape map showing the types of plants you would introduce and where you would put them.

TECHNOLOGY

Go to the Glencoe Science Web site at **science.glencoe.com** or use the **Glencoe Science CD-ROM** for additional chapter assessment.

Test Practice

Scientists in North Dakota have recently analyzed a sample of soil for sand, silt, and clay. They placed their results in the following table.

Horizon	Percent		
	Sand	**Silt**	**Clay**
A	16.2	54.4	29.4
B	10.5	50.2	39.3
C	31.4	48.4	20.2
R (Bedrock)	31.7	50.1	18.2

Study the table and answer the following questions.

1. According to this information, which soil horizon has the lowest percentage of sand?
A) horizon A
B) horizon B
C) horizon C
D) horizon R

2. According to the table, horizon R refers to _____ .
F) topsoil
G) bedrock
H) humus
J) gravel

3. According to the information in the table, the best description of the soil in the table above would be _____ .
A) sandy
B) silty
C) clayey
D) organic

Erosional Forces

Loosened by years of wind, water, and ice, these displaced rocks came crashing down on the Karakoram Highway. Blocked by the boulders, travelers observe the aftermath of a powerful erosion force. As you can see, transport of rocks and sediment downslope can impact the lives of humans. In this chapter, you'll learn about some of the forces that cause erosion. You'll see how gravity, glaciers, and wind erode and deposit Earth materials—constantly changing landscapes.

What do you think?

Science Journal Look at the picture below with a classmate. Discuss what you think this might be or what is happening. Here's a hint: *Someone used to live here.* Write your answer or best guess in your Science Journal.

Can you think of ways to move something without touching it? In nature, sediment is moved from one location to another by a variety of forces. What are some of these forces? In this activity, you will investigate to find out.

Demonstrate sediment movement

WARNING: *Do not pour sand or gravel down the drain.*

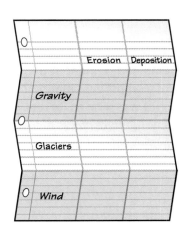

1. Place a small pile of a sand and gravel mixture in one end of a large shoe box lid.

2. Move the sediment pile to the other end of the lid without touching the particles with your hands. You may touch and manipulate the box lid.

3. Try to move the mixture in a number of different ways.

Observe

In your Science Journal, describe the methods you used to move the sediment. Which method was most effctive? Explain how your methods compare with forces of nature that move sediment.

Before You Read

FOLDABLES
Reading & Study Skills

Making an Organizational Study Fold
Make the following Foldable to help you organize your thoughts about erosion and deposition.

1. Place a sheet of paper in front of you so the short side is at the top.

2. Fold the paper in half from the top to bottom. Then fold it in half again. Unfold all the folds.

3. Trace over all the fold lines. Label the columns *Erosion* and *Deposition.* Label the rows *Gravity, Glaciers,* and *Wind* as shown.

4. As you read the chapter, record information including specific examples of erosion and deposition in the rows of your Foldable.

Erosion by Gravity

As You Read

What You'll Learn

- **Explain** the differences between erosion and deposition.
- **Compare and contrast** slumps, creep, rockfalls, rock slides, and mudflows.
- **Explain** why building on steep slopes might not be wise.

Vocabulary

erosion   slump
deposition   creep
mass movement

Why It's Important

Many natural features throughout the world were shaped by erosion.

Erosion and Deposition

Do you live in an area where landslides occur? As **Figure 1** shows, large piles of sediment and rock can move downhill with devastating results. Such events often are triggered by heavy rainfall. The muddy debris at the lower end of the slide comes from material that once was further up the hillside. The displaced soil and rock debris is a product of erosion (ih ROH zhun). **Erosion** is a process that wears away surface materials and moves them from one place to another.

What wears away sediments? How were you able to move the pile of sediments in the Explore Activity? If you happened to tilt the box lid, you took advantage of an important erosional force—gravity. Gravity is the force of attraction that moves all objects toward Earth's center. Other causes of erosion, also called agents of erosion, are water, wind, and glaciers.

Water and wind erode materials only when they have enough energy of motion to do work. For example, air can't move much sediment on a calm day, but a strong wind can move dust and even larger particles. Glacial erosion works differently by slowly moving sediment that is trapped in solid ice. As the ice melts, sediment is deposited, or dropped. Sometimes sediment is carried farther by moving meltwater.

Figure 1
The jumbled sediment at the base of a landslide is material that once was located farther uphill. *What force moves materials toward the center of Earth?*

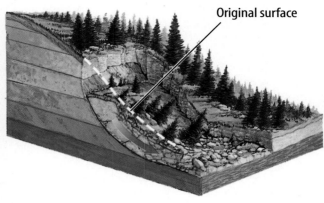

Original surface

Dropping Sediments Agents of erosion drop the sediments they are carrying as they lose energy. This is called **deposition.** When sediments are eroded, they are not lost from Earth—they are just relocated.

Mass Movement

The greater an object's mass is, the greater its gravitational force is. Earth has such a great mass that gravity is a major force of erosion and deposition. Rocks and other materials, especially on steep slopes, are pulled toward the center of Earth by gravity.

A **mass movement** is any type of erosion that happens as gravity moves materials downslope. Some mass movements are so slow that you hardly notice they're happening. Others happen quickly—possibly causing catastrophes. Common types of mass movement include slump, creep, rockfalls, rock slides, and mudflows. Landslides are mass movements that can be one of these types or a combination of these types of mass movement.

✔ **Reading Check** *What is a mass movement?*

Slump When a mass of material slips down along a curved surface, the mass movement is called **slump.** Often, when a slope becomes too steep, the base material no longer can support the rock and sediment above it. The soil and rock slips downslope as one large mass or breaks into several sections.

Sometimes a slump happens when water moves to the base of a slipping mass of sediment. This water weakens the slipping mass and can cause movement of material downhill. Or, if a strong rock layer lies on top of a weaker layer—commonly clay—the clay can weaken further under the weight of the rock. The clay no longer can support the strong rock on the hillside. As shown in **Figure 2,** a curved scar is left where the slumped materials originally rested.

Figure 2
Slump occurs when material slips downslope as one large mass.
What might have caused this slump to happen?

Modeling Slump
Procedure 🥽 👔 ⊘
WARNING: *Do not pour lab materials down the drain.*
1. Place one end of a **baking pan** on **two bricks** and position the other end over a sink with a sealed drain.
2. Fill the bottom half of the pan with **gelatin powder,** and the top half of the pan with **aquarium gravel.** Place a large, **flat rock** on the gravel.
3. Using a **watering can,** sprinkle water on the materials in the pan for several minutes. Record your observations in your **Science Journal.**

Analysis
1. What happened to the different sediments in the pan?
2. Explain how your experiment models slump.

Figure 3
Over time, creep has deformed these railroad tracks.

Figure 4
Rockfalls and rockslides move solid materials rapidly downslope.

A Rockfalls, such as this one, occur as material free falls through the air.

Creep The next time you travel, look along the roadway or trail for slopes where trees and fence posts lean downhill. Leaning trees and human-built structures show another mass movement called creep. **Creep** occurs when sediments slowly shift their positions downhill, as **Figure 3** illustrates. Creep is common in areas of freezing and thawing.

Rockfalls and Rock Slides Signs along mountainous roadways warn of another type of mass movement called rockfalls. Rockfalls happen when blocks of rock break loose from a steep slope and tumble through the air. As they fall, these rocks crash into other rocks and knock them loose. More and more rocks break loose and tumble to the bottom. The fall of a single, large rock down a steep slope can cause serious damage to structures at the bottom. During the winter, when ice freezes in the cracks of rocks, the cracks expand and extend. In the spring, the pieces of rock break loose and fall down the mountainside, as shown in **Figure 4A.**

Rock slides occur when layers of rock—usually steep layers—slip downslope suddenly. Rock slides, like rockfalls, are fast and can be destructive in populated areas. They commonly occur in mountainous areas or in areas with steep cliffs, as shown in **Figure 4B.** Rock slides happen most often after heavy rains or during earthquakes, but they can happen on any rocky slope at any time without warning.

B Rock slides are common in regions where layers of rock are steep.

Original position of mass

Moving mass

Mudflows What would happen if you took a long trip and forgot to turn off the sprinkler in your hillside garden before you left? If the soil is usually dry, the sprinkler water could change your yard into a muddy mass of material much like chocolate pudding. Part of your garden might slide downhill. You would have made a mudflow, a thick mixture of sediments and water flowing down a slope. The mudflow in **Figure 5** caused a lot of destruction.

Mudflows usually occur in areas that have thick layers of loose sediments. They often happen after vegetation has been removed by fire. When heavy rains fall on these areas, water mixes with sediment, causing it to become thick and pasty. Gravity causes this mass to flow downhill. When a mudflow finally reaches the bottom of a slope, it loses its energy of motion and deposits all the sediment and everything else it has been carrying. These deposits often form a mass that spreads out in a fan shape. Why might mudflows cause more damage than floodwaters?

Figure 5
Mudflows, such as these in the town of Sarno, Italy, have enough energy to move almost anything in their paths. *How do mudflows differ from slumps, creep, and rock slides?*

> ✓ **Reading Check** *What conditions are favorable for triggering mudflows?*

Mudflows, rock slides, rockfalls, creep, and slump are similar in some ways. They all are most likely to occur on steep slopes, and they all depend on gravity to make them happen. Also, all types of mass movement occur more often after a heavy rain. The water adds mass and creates fluid pressure between grains and layers of sediment. This makes the sediment expand—possibly weakening it.

Consequences of Erosion

People like to have a great view and live in scenic areas away from noise and traffic. To live this way, they might build or move into houses and apartments on the sides of hills and mountains. When you consider gravity as an agent of erosion, do you think steep slopes are safe places to live?

Building on Steep Slopes When people build homes on steep slopes, they constantly must battle naturally occurring erosion. Sometimes builders or residents make a slope steeper or remove vegetation. This speeds up the erosion process and creates additional problems. Some steep slopes are prone to slumps because of weak sediment layers underneath.

Making Steep Slopes Safe Plants can be beautiful or weedlike—but they all have root structures that hold soil in place. One of the best ways to reduce erosion is to plant vegetation. The deeper the roots go, the more valuable the plant is for erosion control. Plants also absorb large amounts of water. Drainage pipes or tiles inserted into slopes, as shown in **Figure 6,** can prevent water from building up, too. These materials help increase the stability of a slope by allowing excess water to flow out of a hillside more easily.

Walls made of concrete or railroad ties also can reduce erosion by holding soil and rocks in place. However, preventing mass movements on a slope is difficult because rain or earthquakes can weaken all types of Earth materials, eventually causing them to move downhill.

 Reading Check *What can be done to slow erosion on steep slopes?*

Figure 6
Some slopes are stabilized by inserting tile that helps drain water from them.

People who live in areas with erosion problems spend a lot of time and money trying to preserve their land. Sometimes they're successful in slowing down erosion, but they never can eliminate erosion and the danger of mass movement. Eventually, gravity wins. Sediment moves from place to place, constantly reducing elevation and changing the shape of the land.

Section ① Assessment

1. Define the term *erosion* and name the forces that cause it.

2. Explain how deposition changes the surface of Earth.

3. What characteristics do all types of mass movements have in common?

4. Describe ways to help slow erosion on steep slopes.

5. **Think Critically** When people build houses and roads, they often pile up dirt or cut into the sides of hills. Predict how this might affect sediment on a slope. Explain how to control the effects of such activities.

Skill Builder Activities

6. **Comparing and Contrasting** Compare and contrast rockfalls and rock slides. **For more help, refer to the** Science Skill Handbook.

7. **Using an Electronic Spreadsheet** Pretend that you live along a beach where the water is 500 m from your front door. Each year, slumping causes about 1.5 m of your beach to cave into the water. Design a spreadsheet that will predict how much property will be left each year for ten years. Type a formula that will compute the amount of land left the second year. **For more help, refer to the** Technology Skill Handbook.

2 Glaciers

How Glaciers Form and Move

If you've ever gone sledding, snowboarding, or skiing, you might have noticed that after awhile, the snow starts to pack down under your weight. A snowy hillside can become icy if it is well traveled. In much the same way, glaciers form in regions where snow accumulates. Some areas of the world, as shown in **Figure 7,** are so cold that snow remains on the ground year-round. When snow doesn't melt, it piles up. As it accumulates slowly, the increasing weight of the snow becomes great enough to compress the lower layers into ice. Eventually, there can be enough pressure on the ice so that it becomes plasticlike. The mass slowly begins to bend and flow in a thick plasticlike lower layer, and the glacier glides downhill. A large mass of ice and snow moving on land under its own weight is a **glacier.**

Ice Eroding Rock

Glaciers are agents of erosion. As glaciers pass over land, they erode it, changing features on the surface. Glaciers then carry eroded material along and deposit it somewhere else. Glacial erosion and deposition change large areas of Earth's surface. How is it possible that something as fragile as snow or ice can push aside trees, drag rocks along , and change the surface of Earth?

As You Read

What You'll Learn

- **Explain** how glaciers move.
- **Describe** evidence of glacial erosion and deposition.
- **Compare and contrast** till and outwash.

Vocabulary

glacier   moraine
plucking   outwash
till

Why It's Important

Glacial erosion and deposition create many landforms on Earth.

Figure 7
The white regions on this map show areas that are glaciated today.

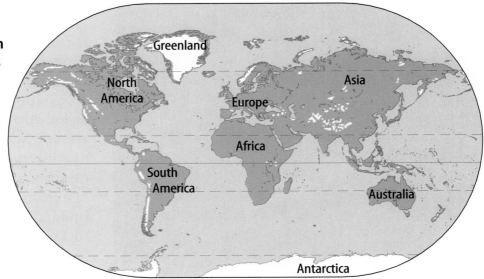

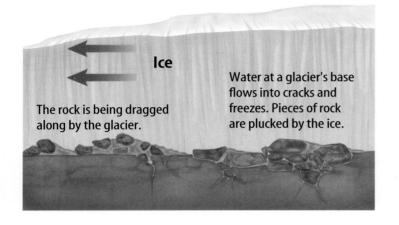

Ice

The rock is being dragged along by the glacier.

Water at a glacier's base flows into cracks and freezes. Pieces of rock are plucked by the ice.

Plucking Glaciers weather and erode solid rock. When glacial ice melts, water flows into cracks in rocks. Later, the water refreezes in these cracks, expands, and fractures the rock. Pieces of rock then are lifted out by the ice, as shown in **Figure 8.** This process, called **plucking,** results in boulders, gravel, and sand being added to the bottom and sides of a glacier.

✓ **Reading Check** *What is plucking?*

Figure 8
Plucking is a process that picks up loosened rock particles over which a glacier is moving.

Transporting and Scouring As it moves forward over land, a glacier can transport huge volumes of sediment and rock. Plucked rock fragments and sand at its base scour and scrape the soil and bedrock like sandpaper against wood, eroding the ground below even more. When bedrock is gouged deeply by rock fragments being dragged along, marks such as those in **Figure 9** are left behind. These marks, called grooves, are deep, long, parallel scars on rocks. Shallower marks are called striations (stri AY shuns). Grooves and striations indicate the direction in which the glacier moved.

Ice Depositing Sediment

When glaciers begin to melt, they are unable to carry much sediment. The sediment drops, or is deposited, on the land. When a glacier melts and begins to shrink back, it is said to retreat. As it retreats, a jumble of boulders, sand, clay, and silt is left behind. This mixture of different-sized sediments is called

Figure 9
When glaciers melt, striations or grooves can be found on the rocks beneath. These glacial grooves on Kelley's Island, Ohio give evidence of past glacial erosion and movement.

till. Till deposits can cover huge areas of land. Thousands of years ago, huge ice sheets in the northern United States left enough till behind to fill valleys completely and make these areas appear flat. Till areas include the wide swath of what are now wheat farms running northwestward from Iowa to northern Montana. Some farmland in parts of Ohio, Indiana, and Illinois, and the rocky pastures of New England are also regions that contain till deposits.

Moraine Deposits Till also is deposited at the end of a glacier when it stops moving forward, as shown in **Figure 10.** Unlike the till that is left behind as a sheet of sediment over the land, this type of deposit doesn't cover such a wide area. Rocks and soil are moved to the end of the glacier, much like items on a grocery store conveyor belt. Because of this, a big ridge of material piles up that looks as though it has been pushed along by a bulldozer. Such a ridge is called a **moraine.** Moraines deposited along the sides of a glacier are shown in **Figure 10.**

Outwash Deposits When glacial ice starts to melt, the meltwater can deposit sediment that is different from till. Material deposited by the meltwater from a glacier, most often beyond the end of the glacier, is called **outwash.** Meltwater carries sediments and deposits them in layers. Heavier sediments drop first, so bigger pieces of rock are deposited closer to the glacier. The outwash from a glacier also can form into a fan-shaped deposit when the stream of meltwater deposits sand and gravel in front of the glacier.

✔ Reading Check *What is outwash?*

Eskers Another type of outwash deposit looks like a long, winding ridge. This deposit forms in a melting glacier when meltwater forms a river within the ice, as shown in **Figure 11A.** This river carries sand and gravel and deposits them within its channel. When the glacier melts, a winding ridge of sand and gravel, called an esker (ES kur), is left behind. An esker is shown in **Figure 11B.**

Figure 10
Till is being deposited by this glacier.

Figure 11
Eskers are glacial deposits formed by meltwater.

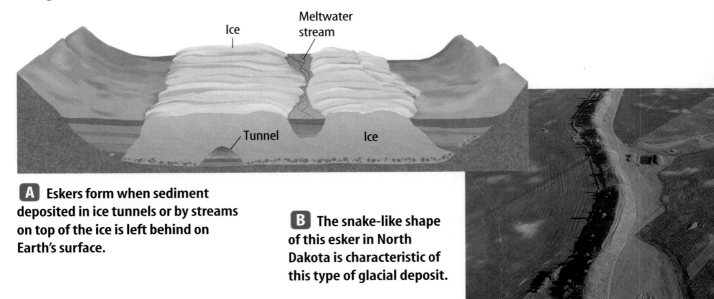

Ice

Meltwater stream

Tunnel   Ice

A Eskers form when sediment deposited in ice tunnels or by streams on top of the ice is left behind on Earth's surface.

B The snake-like shape of this esker in North Dakota is characteristic of this type of glacial deposit.

Continental Glaciers

The two types of glaciers are continental glaciers and valley glaciers. Today, continental glaciers like the one in **Figure 12** cover only ten percent of Earth, mostly near the poles in Antarctica and Greenland. These continental glaciers are huge masses of ice and snow. Continental glaciers are thicker than some mountain ranges. Glaciers make it impossible to see most of the land features in Antarctica and Greenland.

✓ Reading Check *In what regions on Earth would you expect to find continental glaciers?*

Figure 12
Continental glaciers and valley glaciers are agents of erosion and deposition. This continental glacier covers a large area in Antarctica.

Climate Changes In the past, continental glaciers covered as much as 28 percent of Earth. **Figure 13** shows how much of North America was covered by glaciers during the most recent ice advance. These periods of widespread glaciation are known as ice ages. Extensive glaciers have covered large portions of Earth many times over the last 2 million to 3 million years. During this time, glaciers advanced and retreated many times over much of North America. The average air temperature on Earth was about 5°C lower during these ice ages than it is today. The last major advance of ice reached its maximum extent about 18,000 years ago. After this last advance of glaciers, the ends of the ice sheets began to recede, or move back, by melting.

Figure 13
This map shows how far the continental glaciers spread in North America until about 18,000 years ago. *Was your location covered? If so, what evidence of glaciers does your area show?*

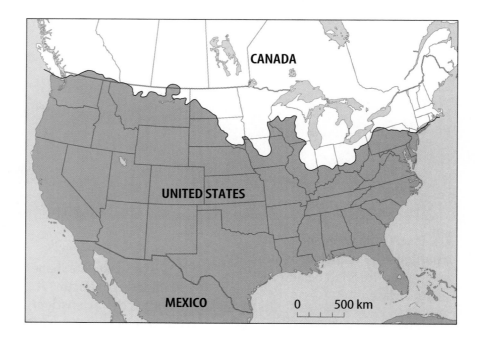

Valley Glaciers

Valley glaciers occur even in today's warmer global climate. In the high mountains where the average temperature is low enough to prevent snow from melting during the summer, valley glaciers grow and creep along. **Figure 14** shows a valley glacier in Africa.

Evidence of Valley Glaciers If you visit the mountains, you can tell whether valley glaciers ever existed there. You might look for striations, then search for evidence of plucking. Glacial plucking often occurs near the top of a mountain where a glacier is mainly in contact with solid rock. Valley glaciers erode bowl-shaped basins, called cirques (SURKS), into the sides of mountains. If two valley glaciers side by side erode a mountain peak, a long ridge called an arête (ah RAYT) forms between them. If valley glaciers erode a mountain from several directions, a sharpened peak called a horn might form. **Figure 15A** shows some features formed by valley glaciers.

Valley glaciers flow down mountain slopes and along valleys, eroding as they go. Valleys that have been eroded by glaciers have a different shape from those eroded by streams. Stream-eroded valleys are normally V-shaped. Glacially eroded valleys are U-shaped because a glacier plucks and scrapes soil and rock from the sides as well as from the bottom. A U-shaped valley is illustrated in **Figure 15B.**

Figure 14
Valley glaciers, like these on Mount Kilimanjaro in north Tanzania, Africa, form between mountain peaks that lie above the snow line, where snow lasts all year.

Figure 15
Valley glaciers transform the mountains over which they pass.

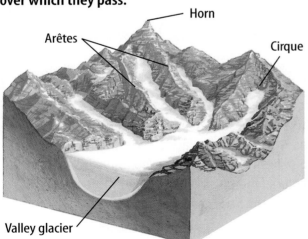

A Bowl-shaped basins called cirques form by erosion at the start of a valley glacier. Arêtes form where two adjacent valley glaciers meet and erode a long, sharp ridge. Horns are sharpened peaks formed by glacial action in three or more cirques.

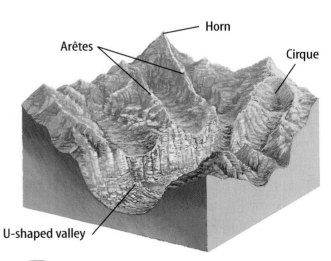

B U-shaped valleys result when valley glaciers move through regions once occupied by streams.

Figure 16
Sand and gravel deposits left by glaciers are important starting materials for the construction of roadways and buildings.

Collect Data Visit the Glencoe Science Web site at **science.glencoe.com** for data about uses of glacial deposits. Communicate to your class what you learn.

Importance of Glaciers

Glaciers have had a profound effect on Earth's surface. They have eroded mountaintops and transformed valleys. Vast areas of the continents have sediments that were deposited by great ice sheets. Today, glaciers in polar regions and in mountains continue to change the surface features of Earth.

In addition to changing the appearance of Earth's surface, glaciers leave behind sediments that are economically important, as illustrated in **Figure 16.** The sand and gravel deposits from glacial outwash and eskers are important resources. These deposits are excellent starting materials for the construction of roads and buildings.

Section Assessment

1. How do glaciers move?
2. Describe two ways in which a glacier can cause erosion.
3. Till and outwash are glacial deposits. Explain how till and outwash are different.
4. How do moraines form? What are moraines made of?
5. **Think Critically** Rivers and lakes that receive water from glacial meltwater often appear milky blue in color. What do you think might cause the milky appearance of these waters?

Skill Builder Activities

6. **Recognizing Cause and Effect** Since 1900, the Alps have lost 50 percent of their ice caps, and New Zealand's glaciers have shrunk by 26 percent. Describe what you think the effects of glacial melting have been. **For more help, refer to the Science** Skill Handbook.

7. **Researching Information** The term *erratic* comes from the Latin word *errare,* meaning "to wander." Research how glaciers move erratics. Write a poem about the "life" of an erratic. **For more help, refer to the** Science Skill Handbook.

Activity

Glacial Grooving

Throughout the world's mountainous regions, 200,000 valley glaciers are moving in response to gravity.

What You'll Investigate
How is the land affected when a valley glacier moves downslope?

Materials

sand
large plastic or
   metal tray
*stream table
ice block
books (2 or 3)

*wood block
metric ruler
overhead light source
   with reflector
*Alternate materials

Safety Precautions

WARNINGS: *Do not pour sand down the drain. Make sure source is plugged into a GFI electrical outlet. Do not touch light source—it may be hot.*

Goals
■ **Compare** stream and glacial valleys.

Procedure

1. Set up the large tray of sand as shown. Place books under one end of the tray to make a slope.
2. Cut a narrow channel, like a river, through the sand. Measure and record its width and depth. Draw a sketch that includes these measurements.
3. Position the overhead light source to shine on the channel as shown.
4. Force the ice block into the channel at the upper end of the tray.

5. Gently push the ice along the channel until it's halfway between the top and bottom of the tray, and directly under the light.
6. Turn on the light and allow the ice to melt. Record what happens.
7. **Record** the width and depth of the ice channel. Make a scale drawing.

Conclude and Apply

1. **Explain** how you can determine the direction that a glacier traveled from the location of deposits.
2. **Explain** how you can determine the direction of glacial movement from sediments deposited by meltwater.
3. How do valley glaciers affect the surface over which they move?

Glacier Data			
Sample Data	Width (cm)	Depth (cm)	Observations
Original Channel	1–2	3	Stream channel looked V-shaped
Glacier Channel			
Meltwater Channel			

③ Wind

What You'll Learn

- **Explain** how wind causes deflation and abrasion.
- **Recognize** how loess and dunes form.

Vocabulary

deflation   loess
abrasion   dune

Why It's Important

Wind erosion and deposition change landscapes, especially in dry climates.

Figure 17
The odd shape of this boulder was produced by wind abrasion.

Wind Erosion

When air moves, it picks up loose material and transports it to other places. Air differs from other erosional forces because it usually cannot pick up heavy sediments. Unlike rivers that move in confined places like channels and valleys, wind carries and deposits sediments over large areas. For example, wind is capable of picking up and carrying dust particles from fields or volcanic ash high into the atmosphere and depositing them thousands of kilometers away.

Deflation Wind erodes Earth's surface by deflation (dih FLAY shun) and abrasion (uh BRAY zhun). When wind erodes by **deflation,** it blows across loose sediment, removing small particles such as silt and sand. The heavier, coarser material is left behind.

Abrasion When windblown sediments strike rock, the surface of the rock gets scraped and worn away by a process called abrasion. **Abrasion** shown in **Figure 17** is similar to sandblasting. Workers use machines that spray a mixture of sand and water under high pressure against a building. The friction wears away dirt from stone, concrete, or brick walls. It also polishes the walls of buildings by breaking away small pieces and leaving an even, smooth finish. Wind acts like a sandblasting machine, rolling and blowing sand grains along. These sand grains strike against rocks and break off small fragments. The rocks become pitted and are worn down.

✔ **Reading Check**   *How is wind abrasion similar to sandblasting?*

Deflation and abrasion happen to all land surfaces but occur mostly in deserts, beaches, and plowed fields. These areas have fewer plants to hold the sediments in place. When winds blow over them, there is little to hold them down.

Sandstorms Even when the wind blows strongly, it seldom carries sand grains higher than 0.5 m from the ground. However, sandstorms do occur. When the wind blows forcefully in the sandy parts of deserts, sand grains bounce along and hit other sand grains, causing more and more grains to rise into the air. These windblown sand grains form a low cloud just above the ground. Most sandstorms occur in deserts, but they can occur in other arid regions as shown in **Figure 18.**

Dust Storms When soil is moist, it stays packed on the ground, but when it dries out, it can be eroded by wind. Soil is composed largely of silt- and clay-sized particles. Because these small particles weigh less than sand-sized particles of the same material, wind can move them high into the air.

Silt and clay particles are small and closely packed. A faster wind is needed to lift these fine particles of soil than is needed to lift grains of sand. However, after they are airborne, the wind can carry them long distances. Where the land is dry, dust storms can cover hundreds of kilometers. These storms blow topsoil from open fields, overgrazed areas, and places where vegetation has disappeared. In the 1930s, silt and dust picked up in Kansas fell in New England and in the North Atlantic Ocean. Dust blown from the Sahara has been traced as far away as the West Indies—a distance of at least 6000 km.

Figure 18
Sandstorms can obscure visibility over large regions.

Problem-Solving Activity

Factors Affecting Wind Erosion

There are many factors that compound the effects of wind erosion. But is there anything that can be done to minimize erosion?

Identifying the Problem

Wind velocity and duration, the size of sediment particles, the size of the area subjected to the wind, and the amount of vegetation present all affect how much soil is eroded by wind. The table shows different combinations of these factors. It also includes an erosion rating that depends upon what factors pertain to an area.

Factors Affecting Wind Erosion					
Factor	**Descriptions of Factors**				
Wind velocity	high	high	low	low	low
Duration of wind	long	long	short	long	long
Particle size	coarse	fine	coarse	coarse	fine
Surface area	large	large	small	small	large
Amount of vegetation	high	low	high	high	high
Erosion rating	some	a lot	a little	some	?

Solving the Problem

1. Looking at the table, can you figure out which factors increase and which factors decrease the amount of erosion?
2. From what you've discovered , can you estimate the missing erosion rating?

Reducing Wind Erosion

Life Science INTEGRATION

As you've learned, wind erosion is most common where there are no plants to protect the soil. Therefore, one of the best ways to slow or stop wind erosion is to plant vegetation. This practice helps conserve many natural reserves and farmland.

Windbreaks People in many countries plant vegetation to reduce wind erosion. For centuries, farmers have planted trees along their fields to act as windbreaks that prevent soil erosion. As the wind hits the trees, its energy of motion is reduced. It no longer is able to lift particles.

In one study, a thin belt of cottonwood trees reduced the effect of a 25-km/h wind to about 66 percent of its normal speed, or to about 16.5 km/h. Tree belts also trap snow and hold it on land. This increases the moisture level of the soil, which helps prevent further erosion.

Roots Along many seacoasts and deserts, vegetation is planted to reduce erosion. Plants with fibrous root systems, such as grasses, work best at stopping wind erosion. Grass roots are shallow and slender with many fibers. They twist and turn between particles in the soil and hold it in place.

Planting vegetation is a good way to reduce the effects of deflation and abrasion. Even so, if the wind is strong and the soil is dry, nothing can stop erosion completely. **Figure 19** shows a project designed to decrease wind erosion.

Figure 19
Rows of grasses and rocks were installed on these dunes in Qinghai, China to reduce wind erosion.

Deposition by Wind

Sediments blown away by wind eventually are deposited. Over time, these windblown deposits develop into landforms, such as accumulations of loess and dunes.

Loess Some examples of large deposits of windblown sediments are found near the Mississippi and Missouri Rivers. These wind deposits of fine-grained sediments known as **loess** (LOOS) are shown in **Figure 20.** Strong winds that blew across glacial outwash areas carried the sediments and deposited them. The sediments settled on hilltops and in valleys. Once there, the particles packed together, creating a thick, unlayered, yellowish-brown-colored deposit. Loess is as fine as talcum powder. Many farmlands of the midwestern United States have fertile soils that developed from loess deposits.

Dunes Do you notice what happens when wind blows sediments against an obstacle such as a rock or a clump of vegetation? The wind sweeps around or over the obstacle. Like a river, air drops sediment when its energy decreases. Sediment starts to build up behind the obstacle. The sediment itself then becomes an obstacle, trapping even more material. If the wind blows long enough, the mound will become a dune, as shown in **Figure 21.** A **dune** (DOON) is a mound of sediments drifted by the wind.

✓ Reading Check *What is a dune?*

Dunes are common in desert regions. You also can see sand dunes along the shores of oceans, seas, or lakes. If dry sediments exist in an area where prevailing winds or sea breezes blow daily, dunes build up. Sand or other sediment will continue to build up and form a dune until the sand runs out or the obstruction is removed. Some desert sand dunes can grow to 100 m high, but most are much shorter.

Moving Dunes A sand dune has two sides. The side facing the wind has a gentler slope. The side away from the wind is steeper. Examining the shape of a dune tells you the direction from which the wind usually blows.

Unless sand dunes are planted with grasses, most dunes move, or migrate away from the direction of the wind. This process is shown in **Figure 22.** Some dunes are known as traveling dunes because they move rapidly across desert areas. As they lose sand on one side, they build it up on the other.

Figure 20
This sediment deposit is composed partially of wind-blown loess.

Figure 21
Loose sediment of any type can form a dune if enough of it is present and an obstacle lies in the path of the wind.

Figure 22

Sand blown loose from dry desert soil often builds up into dunes. A dune may begin to form when windblown sand is deposited in the sheltered area behind an obstacle, such as a rock outcrop. The sand pile grows as more grains accumulate. As shown in the diagram at right, dunes are mobile, gradually moved along by wind.

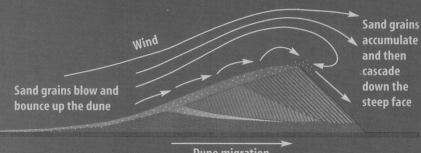

Wind

Sand grains blow and bounce up the dune

Sand grains accumulate and then cascade down the steep face

Dune migration

▲ A dune migrates as sand blows up its sloping side and then cascades down the steeper side. Gradually, a dune moves forward—in the same direction that the wind is blowing—as sand, lost from one side, piles up on the other side.

▲ Dunes are made of sediments eroded from local materials. Although many dunes are composed of quartz and feldspar, the brillant white dunes in White Sands National Park, New Mexico, are made of gypsum.

▲ Deserts may expand when humans move into the transition zone between habitable land and desert. Here, villagers in Mauritania in northwestern Africa shovel the sand that encroaches on their schoolhouse daily.

◀ The dunes at left are coastal dunes from the Laguna Madre region of South Texas on the Gulf of Mexico. Note the vegetation in the photo, which has served as an obstacle to trap sand.

Dune Shape The shape of a dune depends on the amount of sand or other sediment available, the wind speed and direction, and the amount of vegetation present. One common dune shape is a crescent-shaped dune known as a barchan (BAR kun) dune. The open side of a barchan dune faces the direction that the wind is blowing. When viewed from above, the points of the crescent are directed downwind. This type of dune forms on hard surfaces where the sand supply is limited.

Another common type of dune, called a transverse dune, forms where sand is abundant. Transverse dunes are so named because the long directions of these dunes are perpendicular to the general wind direction. In regions where the wind direction changes, star dunes, shown in **Figure 23,** form pointed structures. Other dune forms also exist, some of which show a combination of features.

Shifting Sediments When dunes and loess form, the landscape changes. Wind, like gravity, running water, and glaciers, shapes the land. New landforms created by these agents of erosion are themselves being eroded. Erosion and deposition are part of a cycle of change that constantly shapes and reshapes the land.

Figure 23
Star dunes form in areas where the wind blows from several different directions.

Section 3 Assessment

1. Compare and contrast abrasion and deflation. Describe how they affect the surface of Earth.

2. Explain the differences between dust storms and sandstorms. Describe how the energy of motion affects the deposition of sand and dust by these storms.

3. Explain what loess is made of and how a loess deposit forms.

4. Why do farmers plant trees along the edges of their fields?

5. **Think Critically** You notice that sand is piling up behind a fence outside your apartment building. Explain why this occurs.

Skill Builder Activities

6. **Predicting** Predict the sequence of the following events about dune formation. **For more help, refer to the** Science Skill Handbook.
   a. Grains collect to form a mound.
   b. Wind blows sand grains around an obstacle.
   c. Wind blows over an area and causes deflation.
   d. Vegetation grows on the dune.

7. **Solving One-Step Equations** Between 1972 and 1992, the Sahara Desert increased by nearly 700 km^2 in Mali and the Sudan. Calculate the average number of square kilometers the desert increased each year between 1972 and 1992. **For more help, refer to the** Math Skill Handbook.

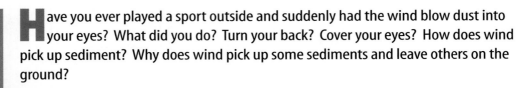

Blowing in the Wind

Have you ever played a sport outside and suddenly had the wind blow dust into your eyes? What did you do? Turn your back? Cover your eyes? How does wind pick up sediment? Why does wind pick up some sediments and leave others on the ground?

Recognize the Problem

What factors affect wind erosion?

Form a Hypothesis

How does moisture in sediment affect the ability of wind to erode sediments? Does the speed of the wind limit the size of sediments it can transport? Form a hypothesis about how sediment moisture affects wind erosion. Form another hypothesis about how wind speed affects the size of the sediment the wind can transport.

Goals
■ **Observe** the effects of soil moisture and wind speed on wind erosion.
■ **Design** and carry out experiments that test the effects of soil moisture and wind speed on wind erosion.

Possible Materials
flat pans (4)
fine sand (400 mL)
gravel (400 mL)
hairdryer
sprinkling can
water
28-cm × 35-cm cardboard sheets (4)
tape
mixing bowl
metric ruler
wind speed indicator

Safety Precautions

Wear your safety goggles at all times when using the hairdryer on sediments. Make sure the dryer is plugged into a GFI electrical outlet.

Test Your Hypothesis

Plan

1. As a group, agree upon and write your hypothesis statements.

2. **List** the steps needed to test your first hypothesis. Plan specific steps and vary only one factor at a time. Then, list the steps needed to test your second hypothesis. Test only one factor at a time.

3. Mix the sediments in the pans. Plan how you will fold cardboard sheets and attach them to the pans to keep sediments contained.

4. **Design** data tables in your Science Journal. Use them as your group collects data.

5. **Identify** all constants, variables, and controls of the experiment. One example of a control is a pan of sediment not subjected to any wind.

Do

1. Make sure your teacher approves your plan before you start.

2. Carry out the experiments as planned.

3. While doing the experiments, write any observations that you or other members of your group make. Summarize your data in the data tables you designed in your Science Journal.

Sediment Movement		
Sediment	**Wind Speed**	**Sediment Moved**
Fine Sand (dry)	low	
	high	
Fine Sand (wet)	low	
	high	
Gravel (dry)	low	
	high	
Gravel (wet)	low	
	high	
Fine Sand and Gravel (dry)	low	
	high	
Fine Sand and Gravel (wet)	low	
	high	

Analyze Your Data

1. **Compare** your results with those of other groups. Explain what might have caused any differences among the groups.

2. **Explain** the relationship that exists between the speed of the wind and the size of the sediments it transports.

Draw Conclusions

1. How does energy of motion of the wind influence sediment transport? What is the general relationship between wind speed and erosion?

2. **Explain** the relationship between the sediment moisture and the amount of sediment moved by the wind.

Communicating Your Data

Design a table on poster board or construction paper that summarizes the results of your experiment. Use your table to explain your interpretations to others in the class. **For more help, refer to the** Science Skill Handbook.

Losing Against Erosion

Did you know...

...Some sand dunes migrate as much as 30 m per year. In a coastal region of France, traveling dunes have buried forests, farms, and villages. The dunes were halted by anti-erosion practices, such as planting grass in the sand and growing a barrier of trees between the dunes and farmland.

...Wind erosion never stops. Wind erosion robs rural areas in the United States of as much as 5,590 kg of soil per hectare per year. One hectare is equivalent to 10,000 m^2. This amounts to removing one small truckload of soil from an area about the size of a football field each year.

...Erosion can move mountains. Between 1982 and 1983, El Niño caused rockfalls along Highway 1 in California. The falling rock from the mountain alongside the road forced a section to close. The rocks stranded the residents of Half Moon Bay until the road was cleared.

...In 1959, an earthquake triggered a mass movement in Madison River Canyon, Montana. About 21 million km³ of rock and soil slid down the canyon at an estimated 160 km/h. This type of mass movement of earth is called a rock slide.

Homes in Danger from Shoreline Erosion by the Year 2060

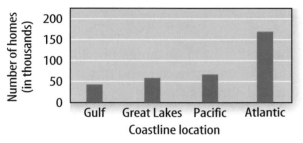

...Glaciers, one of nature's most powerful erosional forces, can move more than 30 m per day. In one week, a fast-moving glacier can travel the length of almost two football fields. Glaciers such as these are unusual—most move less than 30 cm per day.

Do the Math

1. If you could devise a method to slow soil loss due to wind erosion by 25 percent, how much soil would be saved each year in the United States?
2. If erosion destroys 300 m of shoreline every 100 years, how long would it take to destroy 1 km of shoreline?
3. If a sand dune is traveling at 30 m per year, how many meters does it travel in one month?

Go Further

Go to **science.glencoe.com** to learn about landslides. When is a landslide called a mud slide? In which U.S. states are mud slides most likely to occur?

Reviewing Main Ideas

Section 1 Erosion by Gravity

1. Erosion is the process that wears down and transports sediment.

2. Deposition occurs when an agent of erosion loses its energy and can no longer carry its load of sediment.

3. Slump, creep, rock slides, and mudflows are all mass movements caused by gravity. *Explain the differences between rock slides and mudflows.*

Section 2 Glaciers

1. Glaciers are powerful agents of erosion. As water freezes and thaws in cracks, it breaks off pieces of surrounding rock. These pieces then are incorporated into glacial ice by plucking.

2. As sediment embedded in the base of a glacier moves across the land, grooves and striations form. Glaciers deposit two kinds of material—till and outwash. *Which of these two sediments describes a jumbled pile of rocks and sediment?*

Section 3 Wind

1. Deflation occurs when wind erodes only fine-grained sediments, leaving coarse sediments behind. *Why doesn't wind normally pick up large-grained sediments?*

2. The pitting and polishing of rocks and grains of sediment by windblown sediment is called abrasion.

3. Wind deposits include loess and dunes. Loess consists of fine-grained particles that are tightly packed. Dunes form when windblown sediments accumulate behind an obstacle.

4. Dunes are common landforms in desert regions. The shapes and orientations of dunes can provide clues about the prevailing wind directions in an area.

FOLDABLES
Reading & Study Skills

After You Read

Use the Foldable you made at the beginning of the chapter to compare and contrast the forces causing erosion and deposition.

Visualizing Main Ideas

Complete the following concept map on erosional forces. Use the following terms and phrases: abrasion, striations, leaning trees and structures, curved scar on slope, deflation, rockslides and rockfalls, *and* mudflows.

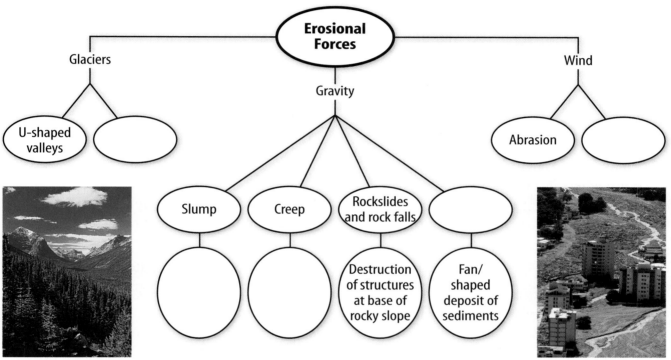

Vocabulary Review

Vocabulary Words

a. abrasion
b. creep
c. deflation
d. deposition
e. dune

f. erosion
g. glacier
h. loess
i. mass movement

j. moraine
k. outwash
l. plucking
m. slump
n. till

Study Tip

Make sure to read your class notes after each lesson. Reading them will help you better understand what you've learned, as well as prepare you for the next day's lesson.

Using Vocabulary

Each phrase below describes a vocabulary word from the list. In your Science Journal, write the term that matches each description.

1. loess, dunes, and moraines are examples
2. slowest mass movement
3. freeze-thaw action at the base of a glacier
4. much like sandblasting
5. gravity transport of material downslope
6. sand and gravel deposited by meltwater
7. glacial deposit composed of sediment with many sizes and shapes

Chapter ③ Assessment

Checking Concepts

Choose the word or phrase that best answers the question.

1. Which of the following is suggested by leaning trees on a hillside?
   A) abrasion
   B) creep
   C) slump
   D) mudflow

2. The best plants for reducing wind erosion have what type of root system?
   A) taproot
   B) striated
   C) fibrous
   D) sheet

3. What does a valley glacier create at the point where it starts?
   A) esker
   B) moraine
   C) till
   D) cirque

4. Which is caused by glacial erosion?
   A) eskers
   B) arêtes
   C) moraines
   D) warmer climate

5. What term describes a mass of snow and ice in motion?
   A) loess deposit
   B) glacier
   C) outwash
   D) abrasion

6. What shape do glacier-created valleys have?
   A) V-shaped
   B) L-shaped
   C) U-shaped
   D) S-shaped

7. Which term is an example of a feature created by deposition?
   A) cirque
   B) abrasion
   C) striation
   D) dune

8. Which characteristic is common to all agents of erosion?
   A) They carry sediments when they have enough energy of motion.
   B) They are most likely to erode when sediments are moist.
   C) They create deposits called dunes.
   D) They erode large sediments before they erode small ones.

9. What type of wind erosion leaves pebbles and boulders behind?
   A) deflation
   B) loess
   C) abrasion
   D) sandblasting

10. What is a ridge formed by deposition of till called?
   A) striation
   B) esker
   C) cirque
   D) moraine

Thinking Critically

11. How can striations give information about the direction that a glacier moved?

12. How effective would a retaining wall made of fine wire mesh be against erosion?

13. Sand dunes often migrate. What can be done to prevent the migration of beach dunes?

14. A researcher finds evidence of movement of ice within a glacier. Explain how this could occur.

15. The end of a valley glacier is at a lower elevation than its point of origin is. How does this help explain melting at its end while snow and ice still are accumulating where it originated?

Developing Skills

16. **Making and Using Tables** Make a table to contrast continental and valley glaciers.

17. **Testing a Hypothesis** Explain how to test the effect of glacial thickness on a glacier's ability to erode.

18. **Forming Hypotheses** Hypothesize why silt in loess deposits is transported farther than sand in dune deposits.

19. Concept Mapping Copy and complete the events chain concept map below to show how a sand dune forms. Use the terms and phrases: *sand accumulates, dune, dry sand,* and *obstruction traps.*

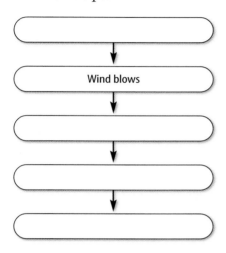

```
┌──────────────────────┐
│                      │
└──────────────────────┘
           │
           ▼
┌──────────────────────┐
│      Wind blows      │
└──────────────────────┘
           │
           ▼
┌──────────────────────┐
│                      │
└──────────────────────┘
           │
           ▼
┌──────────────────────┐
│                      │
└──────────────────────┘
           │
           ▼
┌──────────────────────┐
│                      │
└──────────────────────┘
```

20. Classifying Classify the following as erosional or depositional features: loess, cirque, U-shaped valley, sand dune, abraded rock, striation, and moraine.

Performance Assessment

21. Poster Make a poster with magazine photos showing glacial features in North America. Add a map to locate each feature.

22. Design an Experiment Design an experiment to see how the amount of moisture added to sediments affects mass movement. Keep all variables constant except the amount of moisture in the sediment. Try your experiment.

TECHNOLOGY

Go to the Glencoe Science Web site at **science.glencoe.com** or use the **Glencoe Science CD-ROM** for additional chapter assessment.

THE PRINCETON REVIEW — **Test Practice**

Ms. Lee was reviewing examples of erosion caused by gravity for her science class.

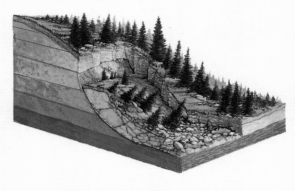

Examine the diagram above and answer the following questions.

1. This diagram shows the shape, in cross section, of one example of erosion by gravity. Which of the following choices best matches this type of erosion?
A) slump   **C)** rock slide
B) creep   **D)** mudflow

2. Select the most likely cause of this type of mass wasting from the choices below.
F) Pieces of rock became loosened and fell freely through the air.
G) Heavy rains caused a fluid mass of mud to form and flow rapidly downhill.
H) After a heavy rain, the underlying sediment was weakened and could no longer support the sediment and rock above it.
J) Sediments slowly shifted their positions downhill.

Water Erosion and Deposition

Bryce Canyon National Park in Utah is home to the Hoodoo Formations. What carved these canyons and helped create these magnificent sculptures? They were made by one of the most powerful forces on Earth—water. Water, in the form of light rain or a great river, causes erosion. In this chapter, you will learn how rainwater runoff forms streams. You also will learn how water carries sediment and deposits it far from its source.

What do you think?

Science Journal Look at the picture below with a classmate. Discuss what you think this might be. Here's a hint: *It's something out of this world.* Write your answer in your Science Journal.

EXPLORE ACTIVITY

Moving water has great energy. Sometimes rainwater falls softly and soaks slowly into soil. Other times it rushes down a slope with tremendous force and carries away valuable topsoil. What determines whether rain soaks into the ground or runs off and wears away the surface?

Model how erosion works

1. Place an aluminum pie pan on your desktop.

2. Put a pile of dry soil about 7 cm high into the pan.

3. Slowly drip water from a dropper onto the pile and observe what happens next.

4. Drip the water faster and continue to observe what happens.

5. Repeat steps 1 through 4, but this time change the slope of the hill. Start again with dry soil.

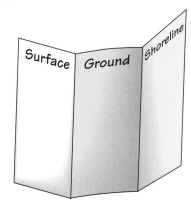

Observe

Record in your Science Journal what effect the water had on the different slopes.

Before You Read

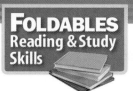

FOLDABLES
Reading & Study Skills

Making a Main Ideas Study Fold A main idea consists of the major concepts or topics talked about in a chapter. Before you read the chapter, make the following Foldable to help you identify the main ideas of this chapter.

1. Place a sheet of paper in front of you so the long side is at the top. Fold the left side and right side of the paper in to divide the paper into equal thirds.

2. Open the paper and label the three rows *Surface, Ground,* and *Shoreline,* as shown.

3. As you read the chapter, list characteristics of each type of water. Then, across the bottom of each fold, draw a picture of surface water, groundwater, and a shoreline.

Surface Water

As You Read

***What* You'll Learn**

- **Identify** the causes of runoff.
- **Compare** rill, gully, sheet, and stream erosion.
- **Identify** three different stages of stream development.
- **Explain** how alluvial fans and deltas form.

Vocabulary

runoff   drainage basin
channel   meander
sheet erosion

***Why* It's Important**

Runoff and streams shape Earth's surface.

Figure 1

A In areas with gentle slopes and vegetation, little runoff and erosion take place. **B** Lack of vegetation has led to severe soil erosion in some areas.

Runoff

Picture this. You pour a glass of milk, and it overflows, spilling onto the table. You grab a towel to clean up the mess, but the milk is already running through a crack in the table, over the edge, and onto the floor. This is similar to what happens to rainwater when it falls to Earth. Some rainwater soaks into the ground and some evaporates, turning into a gas. The rainwater that doesn't soak into the ground or evaporate runs over the ground. Eventually, it enters streams, lakes, or the ocean. Water that doesn't soak into the ground or evaporate but instead flows across Earth's surface is called **runoff.** If you've ever spilled milk while pouring it, you've experienced something similar to runoff.

Factors Affecting Runoff What determines whether rain soaks into the ground or runs off? The amount of rain and the length of time it falls are two factors that affect runoff. Light rain falling over several hours probably will have time to soak into the ground. Heavy rain falling in less than an hour or so will run off because it cannot soak in fast enough, or it can't soak in because the ground cannot hold any more water.

Other Factors Another factor that affects the amount of runoff is the steepness, or slope, of the land. Gravity, the attractive force between all objects, causes water to move down slopes. Water moves rapidly down steep slopes so it has little chance to soak into the ground. Water moves more slowly down gentle slopes and across flat areas. Slower movement allows water more time to soak into the ground.

Vegetation, such as grass and trees, also affects the amount of runoff. Just like milk running off the table, water will run off smooth surfaces that have little or no vegetation. Imagine a tablecloth on the table. What would happen to the milk then? Runoff slows down when it flows around plants. Slower-moving water has a greater chance to sink into the ground. By slowing down runoff, plants and their roots help prevent soil from being carried away. Large amounts of soil may be carried away in areas that lack vegetation, as shown in **Figure 1.**

Effects of Gravity When you lie on the ground and feel as if you are being held in place, you are experiencing the effects of gravity. Gravity is the attracting force all objects have for one another. The greater the mass of an object is, the greater its force of gravity is. Because Earth has a much greater mass than any of the objects on it, Earth's gravitational force pulls objects toward its center. Water runs downhill because of Earth's gravitational pull. When water begins to run down a slope, it picks up speed. As its speed increases, so does its energy. Fast-moving water, shown in **Figure 2,** carries more soil than slow-moving water does.

The force that drives most types of erosion is gravity. Gravity gives water its potential, or stored, energy. When this energy is changed into kinetic energy, or energy of motion, water becomes a powerful force strong enough to move mountains. Find out how water has shaped the region in which you live.

Figure 2
During floods, the high volume of fast-moving water erodes large amounts of soil.

Figure 3
Heavy rains can remove large amounts of sediment, forming deep gullies in the side of a slope.

Figure 4
When water accumulates, it can flow in sheets like the water seen flowing over the hood of this car.

Water Erosion

Suppose you and several friends walk the same way to school each day through a field or an empty lot. You always walk in the same footsteps as you did the day before. After a few weeks, you've worn a path through the field. When water travels down the same slope time after time, it also wears a path. The wearing away of soil and rock is called erosion.

Rill and Gully Erosion You may have noticed a groove or small ditch on the side of a slope that was left behind by running water. This is evidence of rill erosion. Rill erosion begins when a small stream forms during a heavy rain. As this stream flows along, it has enough energy to erode and carry away soil. Water moving down the same path creates a groove, called a **channel,** on the slope where the water eroded the soil. If water frequently flows in the same channel, rill erosion may change over time into another type of erosion called gully erosion.

During gully erosion, a rill channel becomes broader and deeper. **Figure 3** shows gullies that were formed when water carried away large amounts of soil.

Sheet Erosion Water often erodes without being in a channel. Rainwater that begins to run off during a rainstorm often flows as thin, broad sheets before forming rills and streams. For example, when it rains over an area, the rainwater accumulates until it eventually begins moving down a slope as a sheet, like the water flowing off the hood of the car in **Figure 4.** Water also can flow as sheets if it breaks out of its channel.

Floodwaters spilling out of a river can flow as sheets over the surrounding flatlands. Streams flowing out of mountains fan out and may flow as sheets away from the foot of the mountain. **Sheet erosion** occurs when water that is flowing as sheets picks up and carries away sediments.

Stream Erosion Sometimes water continues to flow along a low place it has formed. As the water in a stream moves along, it picks up sediments from the bottom and sides of its channel. By this process, a stream channel becomes deeper and wider.

The sediment that a stream carries is called its load. Water picks up and carries some of the lightweight sediments, called the suspended load. Larger, heavy particles called the bed load just roll along the bottom of the stream channel, as shown in **Figure 5.** Water can even dissolve some rocks and carry them away in solution. The different-sized sediments scrape against the bottom and sides of the channel like a piece of sandpaper. Gradually, these sediments can wear away the rock by a process called abrasion.

Figure 5
This cross section of a stream channel shows the location of the suspended load and the bed load. *How does the stream carry dissolved material?*

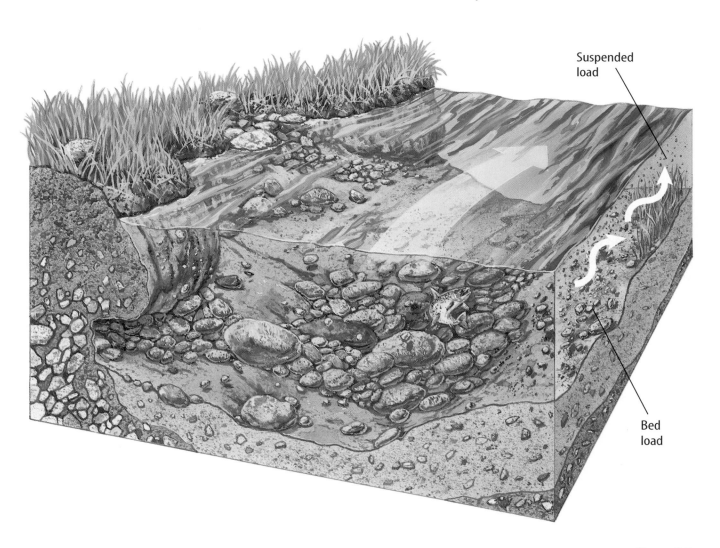

Suspended load

Bed load

River System Development

Have you spent time near a river or stream in your community? Each day, probably millions of liters of water flow through that stream. Where does all the water come from? Where is it flowing to?

River Systems Streams are parts of river systems. The water comes from rills, gullies, and smaller streams located upstream. Just as the tree in **Figure 6A** is a system containing twigs, branches, and a trunk, a river system also has many parts. Runoff enters small streams, which join together to form larger streams. Larger streams come together to form rivers. Rivers grow and carry more water as more streams join.

Drainage Basins A **drainage basin** is the area of land from which a stream or river collects runoff. Compare a drainage basin to a bathtub. Water that collects in a bathtub flows toward one location—the drain. Likewise, all of the water in a river system eventually flows to one location—the main river, or trunk. The largest drainage basin in the United States is the Mississippi River drainage basin shown in **Figure 6B.**

✔ **Reading Check** *What is a drainage basin?*

SCIENCE *Online*

Research Visit the Glencoe Science Web site at **science.glencoe.com** to learn more about drainage basins in your region. Make a poster that summarizes your findings, and share it with your class.

Figure 6
River systems can be compared with the structure of a tree.

A The system of twigs, branches, and the trunk that make up a tree is similar to the system of streams and rivers that make up a river system.

B A large number of the streams and rivers in the United States are part of the Mississippi River drainage basin, or watershed. *What river represents the trunk of this system?*

Stages of Stream Development

Streams come in a variety of forms. Some are narrow and swift moving, and others are wide and slow moving. Streams differ because they are in different stages of development. These stages depend on the slope of the ground over which the stream flows. Streams are classified as young, mature, or old. **Figure 8** shows how the stages come together to form a river system.

The names of the stages of development aren't always related to the actual age of a river. The New River in West Virginia is one of the oldest rivers in North America. However, it has a steep valley and flows swiftly. As a result, it is classified as a young stream.

Young Streams A stream that flows swiftly through a steep valley is a young stream. A young stream may have whitewater rapids and waterfalls. Water flowing through a narrow channel with a rough bottom has a high level of energy and erodes the stream bottom faster than its sides.

Mature Streams The next stage in the development of a stream is the mature stage. A mature stream flows more smoothly through its valley. Over time, most of the rocks in the streambed that cause waterfalls and rapids are eroded by running water and the sediments it carries.

Erosion is no longer concentrated on the bottom in a mature stream. A mature stream starts to erode more along its sides, and curves develop. These curves form because the speed of the water changes throughout the width of the channel.

Water in a shallow area of a stream moves slower because it drags along the bottom. In the deeper part of the channel, the water flows faster. If the deep part of the channel is next to one side of the river, water will erode that side and form a slight curve. Over time, the curve grows to become a broad arc called a **meander** (mee AN dur), as shown in **Figure 7.**

The broad, flat valley floor formed by a meandering stream is called a floodplain. When a stream floods, it often will cover part or all of the floodplain.

Figure 7
A meander is a broad bend in a river or stream. As time passes, erosion of the outer bank increases the bend.

Figure 8

Although no two streams are exactly alike, all go through three main stages—young, mature, and old—as they flow from higher to lower ground. A young stream, below, surging over steep terrain, moves rapidly. In a less steep landscape, right, a mature stream flows more smoothly. On nearly level ground, the stream—considered old—winds leisurely through its valley. The various stages of a stream's development are illustrated here.

Waterfall

Rapids

A A young stream begins at a source—here, a melting mountain glacier. From its source, the stream flows swiftly downhill, cutting a narrow valley.

B A mature stream flows smoothly through its valley. Mature streams often develop broad curves called meanders.

C Old streams flow through broad, flat floodplains. Near its mouth, the stream gradually drops its load of silt. This sediment forms a delta, an area of flat, fertile land extending into the ocean.

Oxbow lake

Research Visit the Glencoe Science Web site at **science.glencoe.com** to find out about major rivers in the United States. Classify two of these streams as young, mature, or old.

Old Streams The last stage in the development of a stream is the old stage. An old stream flows smoothly through a broad, flat floodplain that it has deposited. South of St. Louis, Missouri, the lower Mississippi River is in the old stage.

Major river systems, such as the Mississippi River, usually contain streams in all stages of development. In the upstream portion of a river system, you find whitewater streams moving swiftly down mountains and hills. At the bottom of mountains and hills, you find streams that start to meander and are in the mature stage of development. These streams meet at the trunk of the drainage basin and form a major river.

✔ **Reading Check** *How do old streams differ from young streams?*

Too Much Water

Sometimes heavy rains or a sudden melting of snow can cause large amounts of water to enter a river system. What happens when a river system has too much water in it? The water needs to go somewhere, and out and over the banks is the only choice. A river that overflows its banks can bring disaster by flooding homes or washing away bridges or crops.

Dams and levees are built in an attempt to prevent this type of flooding. A dam is built to control the water flow downstream. It may be built of soil, sand, or steel and concrete. Levees are mounds of earth that are built along the sides of a river. Dams and levees are built to prevent rivers from overflowing their banks. Unfortunately, they do not stop the water when flooding is great. This was the case in 1993 when heavy rains caused the Mississippi River to flood parts of nine midwestern states. Flooding resulted in billions of dollars in property damage. **Figure 9** shows some of the damage caused by this flood.

As you have seen, floods can cause great amounts of damage. But at certain times in Earth's past, great floods have completely changed the surface of Earth in a large region. Such floods are called catastrophic floods.

Figure 9
Flooding causes problems for people who live along major rivers. Floodwater broke through a levee during the Mississippi River flooding in 1993.

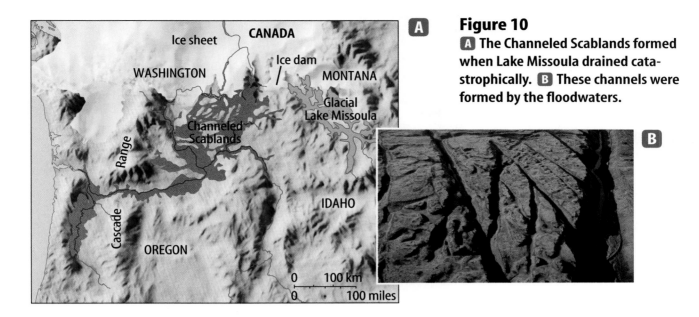

Figure 10

A The Channeled Scablands formed when Lake Missoula drained catastrophically. **B** These channels were formed by the floodwaters.

Catastrophic Floods During Earth's long history, many catastrophic floods have dramatically changed the face of the surrounding area. One catastrophic flood formed the Channeled Scablands in eastern Washington State, shown here in **Figure 10.** A vast lake named Lake Missoula covered much of western Montana. A natural dam of ice formed this lake. As the dam melted or was eroded away, tremendous amounts of water suddenly escaped through what is now the state of Idaho into Washington. In a short period of time, the floodwater removed overlying soil and carved channels into the underlying rock, some as deep as 50 m. Flooding occurred several more times as the lake refilled with water and the dam broke loose again. Scientists say the last such flood occurred about 13,000 years ago.

Deposition by Surface Water

You know how hard it is to carry a heavy object for a long time without putting it down. As water moves throughout a river system, it loses some of its energy of motion. The water can no longer carry some of its sediment. As a result, it drops, or is deposited, to the bottom of the stream.

Some stream sediment is carried only a short distance. In fact, sediment often is deposited within the stream channel itself. Other stream sediment is carried great distances before being deposited. Sediment picked up when rill and gully erosion occur are examples of this. Water usually has a lot of energy as it moves down a steep slope. When water begins flowing on a level surface, it slows, loses energy, and deposits its sediment. Water also loses energy and deposits sediment when it empties into an ocean or lake.

Mini LAB

Observing Runoff Collection

Procedure
1. Put a plastic **rain gauge** into a narrow **drinking glass** and place the glass in the sink.
2. Fill a plastic **sprinkling can** with **water.**
3. Hold the sprinkling can one-half meter above the sink for 30 s.
4. Record the amount of water in the rain gauge.
5. After emptying the rain gauge, place a **plastic funnel** into the rain gauge and sprinkle again for 30 s.
6. Record the amount of water in the gauge.

Analysis
Explain how a small amount of rain falling on a drainage basin can have a big effect on a river or stream.

Figure 11

A This satellite image of the Nile River Delta in Egypt shows the typical triangular shape. The green color shows areas of vegetation. **B** Agriculture is important on the Nile Delta.

Deltas and Fans Sediment that is deposited as water empties into an ocean or lake forms a triangular, or fan-shaped, deposit called a delta, shown in **Figure 11.** When the river waters empty from a mountain valley onto an open plain, the deposit is called an alluvial (uh LEW vee ul) fan. The Mississippi River is an example of the topics presented in this section. Runoff causes rill and gully erosion. Sediment is picked up and carried into the larger streams that flow into the Mississippi River. As the Mississippi River flows, it cuts into its banks and picks up more sediment. Where the land is flat, the river deposits some of its sediment in its own channel. As the Mississippi enters the Gulf of Mexico, it slows, dropping much of its sediment and forming the Mississippi River delta.

Section 1 Assessment

1. How does the slope of an area affect runoff?
2. Compare rill and gully erosion.
3. Describe the three stages of stream development.
4. What is a delta?
5. **Think Critically** How is a stream's rate of flow related to the amount of erosion it causes? How is it related to the size of the sediments it deposits?

Skill Builder Activities

6. **Comparing and Contrasting** Compare and contrast the characteristics of rill, gully, sheet, and stream erosion. **For more help,** refer to the Science Skill Handbook.

7. **Using an Electronic Spreadsheet** Design a table to compare and contrast sheet, rill, gully, and stream erosion. **For more help,** refer to the Technology Skill Handbook.

Groundwater

Groundwater Systems

What would have happened if the spilled milk in Section 1 ran off the table onto a carpeted floor? It probably would have quickly soaked into the carpet. Water that falls on Earth can soak into the ground just like the milk into the carpet.

Water that soaks into the ground becomes part of a system, just as water that stays above ground becomes part of a river system. Soil is made up of many small rock and mineral fragments. These fragments are all touching one another, as shown in **Figure 12,** but some empty space remains between them. Holes, cracks, and crevices exist in the rock underlying the soil. Water that soaks into the ground collects in these pores and empty spaces and becomes part of what is called **groundwater.**

How much of Earth's water do you think is held in the small openings in rock? Scientists estimate that 14 percent of all freshwater on Earth exists as groundwater. This is almost 30 times more water than is contained in all of Earth's lakes and rivers.

As You Read

What **You'll Learn**

- **Recognize** the importance of groundwater.
- **Describe** the effect that soil and rock permeability have on groundwater movement.
- **Explain** how groundwater dissolves and deposits minerals.

Vocabulary

groundwater	water table
permeable	spring
impermeable	geyser
aquifer	cave

Why **It's Important**

The groundwater system is an important source of your drinking water.

Figure 12
Soils have many small, connected pores through which water can move.

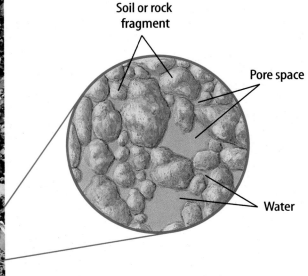

Soil or rock fragment

Pore space

Water

Measuring Pore Space

Procedure

1. Use two identical, **clear-plastic containers.**
2. Put 3 cm of **sand** in one container and 3 cm of **gravel** in the other.
3. Pour **water** slowly into the containers and stop when the water just covers the top of the sediment.
4. Record the volume of water used in each.

Analysis

Which substance has more pore space—sand or gravel?

Figure 13
A stream's surface level is the water table. Below that is the zone of saturation.

Permeability A groundwater system is similar to a river system. However, instead of having channels that connect different parts of the drainage basin, the groundwater system has connecting pores. Soil and rock are **permeable** (PUR mee uh bul) if the pore spaces are connected and water can pass through them. Sandstone is an example of a permeable rock.

Soil or rock that has many large, connected pores is permeable. Water can pass through it easily. However, if a rock or sediment has few pore spaces or they are not well connected, then the flow of groundwater is blocked. These materials are **impermeable,** which means that water cannot pass through them. Granite has few or no pore spaces at all. Clay has many small pore spaces, but the spaces are not well connected.

✔ **Reading Check** *How does water move through permeable rock?*

Groundwater Movement How deep into Earth's crust does groundwater go? **Figure 13** shows a model of a groundwater system. Groundwater keeps going deeper until it reaches a layer of impermeable rock. When this happens, the water stops moving down. As a result, water begins filling up the pores in the rocks above. A layer of permeable rock that lets water move freely is an **aquifer** (AK wuh fur). The area where all of the pores in the rock are filled with water is the zone of saturation. The upper surface of this zone is the **water table.**

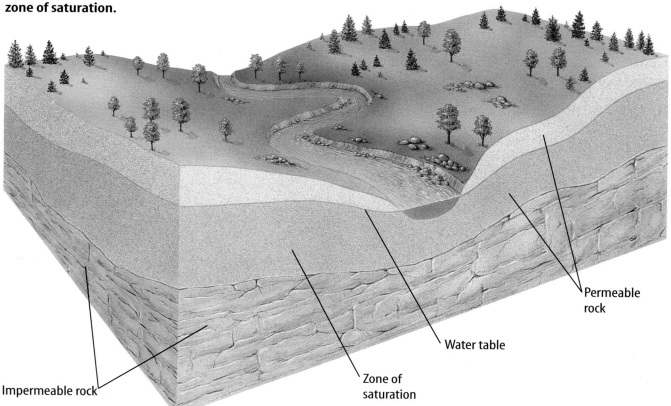

Permeable rock

Water table

Zone of saturation

Impermeable rock

Water Table

Why are the zone of saturation and the water table so important? An average United States resident uses about 626 L of water per day. That's enough to fill nearly two thousand soft drink cans. Many people get their water from groundwater through wells that have been drilled into the zone of saturation. However, the supply of groundwater is limited. During a drought, the water table drops. This is why you should conserve water.

Math Skills Activity

Calculating the Rate of Groundwater Flow

You and your family are hiking and the temperature is hot. You feel as if you can't walk one step farther. Luckily, relief is in sight. On the side of a nearby hill you see a stream, and you rush to splash some water on your face. Although you probably feel that it's taking you forever to reach the stream, your pace is quick when compared to how long it takes groundwater to flow through the aquifer that feeds the stream. The following problem will give you some idea of just how slowly groundwater flows through an aquifer.

Example Problem

You've run 200 m to get some water from a stream. How long does it take the groundwater in the aquifer to travel the same distance? The groundwater flows at a rate of 0.6 m/day.

Solution

1 *This is what you know:*
the distance that the groundwater has to travel: $d = 200$ m
the rate that groundwater flows through the aquifer: $r = 0.6$ m/day

2 *This is what you want to find:* time $= t$

3 *This is the equation you use:* $r \times t = d$ (rate $\times$ time $=$ distance)

4 *Solve the equation for* t *and then substitute known values:* $t = \dfrac{d}{r} = \dfrac{(200 \text{ m})}{(0.6 \text{ m/day})} = 333.33$ days

> #### Practice Problem
>
> The groundwater in an aquifer flows at a rate of 0.5 m/day. How far does the groundwater move in a year?

For more help, refer to the Math Skill Handbook.

Figure 14
The years on the pole show how much the ground level dropped in the San Joaquin Valley, California, between 1925 and 1977.

Figure 15
The pressure of water in a sloping aquifer keeps an artesian well flowing. *What limits how high water can flow in an artesian well?*

Wells A good well extends deep into the zone of saturation, past the top of the water table. Groundwater flows into the well, and a pump brings it to the surface. Because the water table sometimes drops during very dry seasons, even a good well can go dry. Then time is needed for the water table to rise, either from rainfall or through groundwater flowing from other areas of the aquifer.

Where groundwater is the main source of drinking water, the number of wells and how much water is pumped out is important. If a large factory were built in such a town, the demand on the groundwater supply would be even greater. Even in times of normal rainfall, the wells could go dry if water were taken out at a rate greater than the rate at which it can be replaced.

In areas where too much water is pumped out, the land level can sink from the weight of the sediments above the now-empty pore spaces. **Figure 14** shows what occurred when too much groundwater was removed in a region of California.

One type of well doesn't need a pump to bring water to the surface. An artesian well is a well in which water rises to the surface under pressure. Artesian wells are less common than other types of wells because of the special conditions they require.

As shown in **Figure 15,** the aquifer for an artesian well needs to be located between two impermeable layers that are sloping. Water enters at the high part of the sloping aquifer. The weight of the water in the higher part of the aquifer puts pressure on the water in the lower part. If a well is drilled into the lower part of the aquifer, the pressurized water will flow to the surface. Sometimes, the pressure is great enough to force the water into the air, forming a fountain.

✔ **Reading Check**   *Why does water flow from an artesian well?*

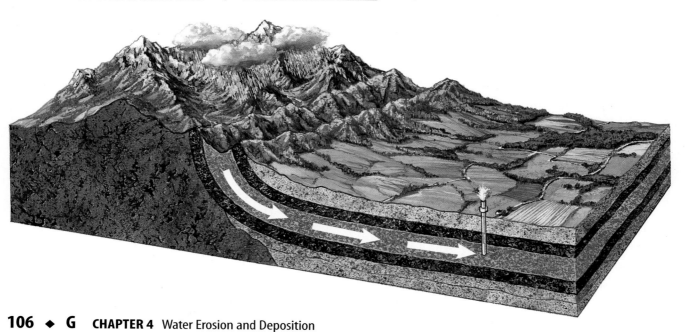

Springs In some places, the water table is so close to Earth's surface that water flows out and forms a **spring.** Springs are found on hillsides or other places where the water table meets a sloping surface. Springs often are used as a source of freshwater.

The water from most springs is a constant, cool temperature because soil and rock are good insulators and protect the groundwater from changes in temperature on Earth's surface. However, in some places, magma rises to within a few kilometers of Earth's surface and heats the surrounding rock. Groundwater that comes in contact with these hot rocks is heated and can come to the surface as a hot spring.

Geysers When water is put into a teakettle to boil, it heats slowly at first. Then some steam starts to come out of the cap on the spout, and suddenly the water starts boiling. The teakettle starts whistling as steam is forced through the cap. A similar process can occur with groundwater. One of the places where groundwater is heated is in Yellowstone National Park in Wyoming. Yellowstone has hot springs and geysers. A **geyser** is a hot spring that erupts periodically, shooting water and steam into the air. Groundwater is heated to high temperatures, causing it to expand underground. This expansion forces some of the water out of the ground, taking the pressure off of the remaining water. The remaining water boils quickly, with much of it turning to steam. The steam shoots out of the opening like steam out of a teakettle, forcing the remaining water out with it. Yellowstone's famous geyser, Old Faithful, pictured in **Figure 16,** shoots between 14,000 and 32,000 L of water and steam into the air about once every 80 min.

The Work of Groundwater

Although water is the most powerful agent of erosion on Earth's surface, it also can have a great effect underground. Water mixes with carbon dioxide gas to form a weak acid called carbonic acid. Some of this carbon dioxide is absorbed from the air by rainwater or surface water. Most carbon dioxide is absorbed by groundwater moving through soil. One type of rock that is dissolved easily by this acid is limestone. Acidic groundwater moves through natural cracks and pores in limestone, dissolving the rock. Gradually, the cracks in the limestone enlarge until an underground opening called a **cave** is formed.

Chemistry
INTEGRATION

Acid rain occurs when gases released by burning oil and coal mix with water in the air. Infer what effect acid rain can have on a statue made of limestone.

Figure 16
Yellowstone's famous geyser, Old Faithful, used to erupt once about every 76 min. An earthquake on January 9, 1998, slowed Old Faithful's "clock" by 4 min to an average of one eruption about every 80 min. The average height of the geyser's water is 40.5 m.

Cave Formation You've probably seen a picture of the inside of a cave, like the one shown in **Figure 17,** or perhaps you've visited one. Groundwater not only dissolves limestone to make caves, but it also can make deposits on the insides of caves.

Water often drips slowly from cracks in the cave walls and ceilings. This water contains calcium ions dissolved from the limestone. If the water evaporates while hanging from the ceiling of a cave, a deposit of calcium carbonate is left behind. Stalactites form when this happens over and over. Where drops of water fall to the floor of the cave, a stalagmite forms. The words *stalactite* and *stalagmite* come from Greek words that mean "to drip."

Sinkholes If underground rock is dissolved near the surface, a sinkhole may form. A sinkhole is a depression on the surface of the ground that forms when the roof of a cave collapses or when material near the surface dissolves. Sinkholes are common features in places like Florida and Kentucky that have lots of limestone and enough rainfall to keep the groundwater system supplied with water. Sinkholes can cause property damage if they form in a populated area.

In summary, when rain falls and becomes groundwater, it might dissolve limestone and form a cave, erupt from a geyser, or be pumped from a well to be used at your home.

Figure 17
Water dissolves rock to form caves and also deposits material to form spectacular formations, such as these in Carlsbad Caverns in New Mexico.

Section Assessment

1. Describe how water enters the groundwater system.
2. How does the permeability of soil and rocks affect the flow of groundwater?
3. Describe why a well might go dry.
4. Explain how caves form.
5. **Think Critically** Would you expect water in wells, geysers, and hot springs to contain dissolved materials? Why or why not?

Skill Builder Activities

6. **Comparing and Contrasting** Compare and contrast wells, geysers, and hot springs. **For more help, refer to the** Science Skill Handbook.
7. **Drawing Conclusions** Read an article about geothermal energy and draw a diagram in your Science Journal explaining how it works. Also, list the limitations of this energy source. **For more help, refer to the** Science Skill Handbook.

3 Ocean Shoreline

The Shore

Picture yourself sitting on a beautiful, white-sand beach like the one shown in **Figure 18.** Nearby, palm trees sway in the breeze. Children play in the quiet waves lapping at the water's edge. It's hard to imagine a place more peaceful. Now, picture yourself sitting along another shore. You're on a high cliff watching waves crash onto boulders far below. Both of these places are shorelines. An ocean shoreline is where land meets the ocean.

The two shorelines just described are different even though both experience surface waves, tides, and currents. These actions cause shorelines to change constantly. Sometimes you can see these changes from hour to hour. Why are shorelines so different? You'll understand why they look different when you learn about the forces that shape shorelines.

As You Read

What You'll Learn
- **Identify** the different causes of shoreline erosion.
- **Compare and contrast** different types of shorelines.
- **Describe** some origins of sand.

Vocabulary
longshore current
beach

Why It's Important
Constantly changing shorelines impact the people who live and work by them.

Figure 18
A Waves, tides, and currents cause shorelines to change constantly. **B** Waves approaching the shoreline at an angle create a longshore current.

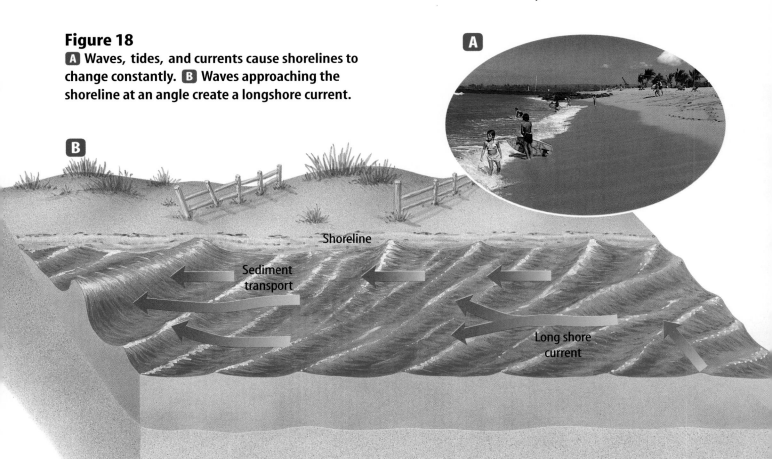

Shoreline

Sediment transport

Long shore current

Shoreline Forces When waves constantly pound against the shore, they break rocks into ever-smaller pieces. Currents move many metric tons of sediment along the shoreline. The sediment grains grind against each other like sandpaper. The tide goes out carrying sediment to deeper water. When the tide returns, it brings new sediment with it. These forces are always at work, slowly changing the shape of the shoreline. Water is always in motion along the shore.

The three major forces at work on the shoreline are waves, currents, and tides. Winds blowing across the water make waves. Waves, crashing against a shoreline, are a powerful force. They can erode and move large amounts of material in a short time. Waves usually collide with a shore at slight angles. This creates a **longshore current** of water that runs parallel to the shoreline. Longshore currents, shown in **Figure 18B,** carry many metric tons of loose sediments and act like rivers of sand in the ocean.

✔ **Reading Check** *How does a longshore current form?*

Tides create currents that move at right angles to the shore. These are called tidal currents. Outgoing tides carry sediments away from the shore, and incoming tides bring new sediments toward the shore. Tides work with waves to shape shorelines. You've seen the forces that affect all shorelines. Now you will see the differences that make one shore a flat, sandy beach and another shore a steep, rocky cliff.

Figure 19
Along a rocky shoreline, the force of pounding waves breaks rock fragments loose, then grinds them into smaller and smaller pieces.

Rocky Shorelines

Rocks and cliffs are the most common features along rocky shorelines like the one in **Figure 19.** Waves crash against the rocks and cliffs. Sediments in the water grind against the cliffs, slowly wearing the rock away. Then rock fragments broken from the cliffs are ground up by the endless motion of waves. They are transported as sediment by longshore currents.

Softer rocks become eroded before harder rocks do, leaving islands of harder rocks. This takes thousands of years, but remember that the ocean never stops. In a single day, about 14,000 waves crash onto shore.

Sandy Beaches

Smooth, gently sloping shorelines are different from steep, rocky shorelines. Beaches are the main feature here. **Beaches** are deposits of sediment that are parallel to the shore.

Beaches are made up of different materials. Some are made of rock fragments from the shoreline. Many sands are made of grains of quartz, and others are made of seashell fragments. These fragments range in size from stones larger than your hand to fine sand. Sand grains range from 0.06 mm to 2 mm in diameter. Why do many beaches have particles of this size? Waves break rocks and seashells down to sand-sized particles like those shown in **Figure 20.** The constant wave motion bumps sand grains together. This bumping not only breaks particles into smaller pieces but also smooths off their jagged corners making them more rounded.

Reading Check *How do waves affect beach particles?*

Sand in some places is made of other things. For example, Hawaii's black sands are made of basalt, and its green sands are made of the mineral olivine. Jamaica's white sands are made of coral and shell fragments.

Figure 20
Beach sand varies in size, color, and composition. **A** This quartz sand from a Texas beach is clear and glassy. **B** Some Hawaiian beaches are composed of black basalt sand.

Figure 21
Shorelines change constantly. Human development is often at risk from shoreline erosion.

Sand Erosion and Deposition

Longshore currents carry sand along beaches to form features such as barrier islands, spits, and sandbars. Storms and wind also move sand. Thus, beaches are fragile, short-term land features that are damaged easily by storms and human activities such as some types of construction. Communities in widely separated places such as Long Island, New York; Malibu, California; and Padre Island, Texas, have problems because of beach erosion.

Barrier Islands Barrier islands are sand deposits that lie parallel to the shore but are separated from the mainland. These islands start as underwater sand ridges formed by breaking waves. Hurricanes and storms add sediment to them, raising some to sea level. When a barrier island becomes large enough, the wind blows the loose sand into dunes, keeping the new island above sea level. As with all seashore features, barrier islands are short term, lasting from a few years to a few centuries.

The forces that build barrier islands also can erode them. Storms and waves carry sediments away. Beachfront development, as in **Figure 21,** can be affected by shoreline erosion.

Section Assessment

1. What major forces cause shoreline erosion?
2. Contrast the features you would find along a steep, rocky shoreline with the features you would find along a gently sloping, sandy shoreline.
3. How could the type of shoreline affect the types of sediments you might find there?
4. List several materials that beach sand might be composed of. Where do these materials come from?
5. **Think Critically** How would erosion and deposition of sediment along a shoreline be affected if the longshore current was blocked by a wall built out into the water?

Skill Builder Activities

6. **Concept Mapping** Make an events chain concept map that shows how the sand from a barrier island can become a new barrier island 100 years from now. Use these terms: *barrier island, breaking waves, wind, longshore currents,* and *new barrier island.* **For more help, refer to the** Science Skill Handbook.

7. **Solving One-Step Equations** If 14,000 waves crash onto a shore daily, how many waves crash onto it in a year? Calculate how many have crashed onto it since you were born. Explain how you found your answer. **For more help, refer to the** Math Skill Handbook.

Activity

Classifying Types of Sand

You know that sand is made of many different kinds of grains, but did you realize that the slope of a beach is related to the size of its grains? The coarser the grain size is, the steeper the beach is. The composition of sand also is important. Many sands are mined because they have economic value.

What You'll Investigate
What characteristics can be used to classify different types of beach sand?

Materials
samples of different sands (3)
magnifying glass
*stereomicroscope
magnet
*Alternate materials

Goals
- ■ **Observe** differences in sand.
- ■ **Identify** characteristics of beach sand.
- ■ **Infer** sediment sources.

Procedure

1. **Design** a data table in which to record your data when you compare the three sand samples. You will need five columns in your table. One column will be for the samples and the others for the characteristics you will be examining.

Angular   Sub-Angular   Sub-Rounded   Rounded

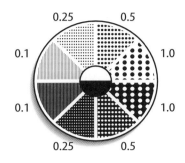

Sand gauge
(measurements in mm)

2. Use the diagram to determine the average roundness of each sample.

3. **Identify** the grain size of your samples by using the sand gauge above. To determine the grain size, place sand grains in the middle of the circle of the sand gauge. Use the upper half of the circle for dark-colored particles and the bottom half for light-colored particles.

4. Decide on two other characteristics to examine that will help you classify your samples.

Conclude and Apply

1. **Compare and contrast** some characteristics of beach sand.

2. Why are there variations in the characteristics of different sand samples?

3. What do your observations tell you about the sources of the three samples?

Communicating Your Data

Compare your results with those of other students. **For more help, refer to the Science Skill Handbook.**

Activity

Water Speed and Erosion

What would it be like to make a raft and use it to float on a river? Would it be easy? Would you feel like Tom Sawyer? Probably not. You'd be at the mercy of the current. Strong currents create fast rivers. But does fast moving water affect more than just floating rafts and other objects? How does the speed of a stream or river affect its ability to erode?

What You'll Investigate

How does the speed of water affect its ability to erode?

Materials
paint roller pan
sand
1-L beaker
rubber tubing (20 cm)
metric ruler
water
stopwatch
screen
wood block
disposable wallpaper trays

Goals
- ■ Assemble an apparatus for measuring the effect of water speed on erosion.
- ■ **Observe and measure** the ability of water traveling at different speeds to erode sand.

Safety Precautions

Wash your hands after you handle the sand. Immediately clean up any water that spills on the floor.

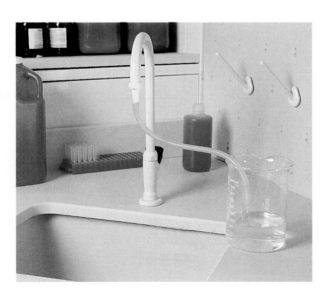

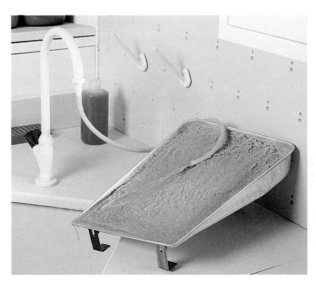

Procedure

1. Copy the data table below.

2. Place the screen in the sink. Pour moist sand into your pan and smooth out the sand. Set one end of the pan on the wood block and hang the other end over the screen in the sink. Excess water will flow onto the screen in the sink.

3. Attach one end of the hose to the faucet and place the other end in the beaker. Turn on the water so that it trickles into the beaker. Time how long it takes for the trickle of water to fill the beaker to the 1-L mark. Divide 1 L by your time in seconds to calculate the water speed. Record the speed in your data table.

4. Without altering the water speed, hold the hose over the end of the pan that is resting on the wood block. Allow the water to flow into the sand for 2 min. At the end of 2 min, turn off the water.

5. **Measure** the depth and length of the eroded channel formed by the water. Count the number of branches formed on the channel. Record your measurements and observations in your data table.

6. Empty the excess water from the tray and smooth out the sand. Repeat steps 3 through 5 two more times increasing your water speed each time.

Water Speed and Erosion			
Water Speed (Liters per Second)	Depth of Channel	Length of Channel	Number of Channel Branches

Conclude and Apply

1. **Identify** the constants and variables in your experiment.

2. Which water speed created the deepest and longest channel?

3. Which water speed created the greatest number of branches?

4. **Infer** the effect that water speed has on erosion.

5. **Predict** how your results would have differed if one end of the pan had been raised higher.

6. **Infer** how streams and rivers can shape Earth's surface.

𝒞ommunicating
Your Data

Write a pamphlet for people buying homes near rivers or streams that outlines the different effects that water erosion could have on their property.

Is there hope for America's coastlines or is beach erosion a "shore" thing?

Sands

Water levels are rising along the coastline of the United States. Serious storms and the building of homes and businesses along the shore are leading to the eroding of anywhere from 70 percent to 90 percent of the U.S. coastline. A report from the Federal Emergency Management Agency (FEMA) confirms this. The report says that one meter of United States beaches will be eaten away each year for the next 60 years. Since 1965, the federal government has spent millions of dollars replenishing more than 1,300 eroding sandy shores around the country. And still the tide continues to turn.

One meter of United States' beaches erode each year.

The slowly eroding beaches are upsetting to residents and officials of many communities who depend on their shore to earn money from visitors. Some city and state governments are turning to beach nourishment—a process in which sand is taken from the seafloor and dumped on beaches. The process is expensive, however. The state of Delaware, for example, is spending 7,000,000 dollars to bring in sand for its beaches.

Some geologists believe that beach nourishment does not work. They explain that the grains of the new sand are often smaller and finer than the original beach sand, so it erodes faster, carried back out to sea by waves.

Dredged sand is pumped on to an eroded beach in Long Beach, North Carolina.

This beach house will collapse as its underpinnings are eroded.

in Time

Despite the odds, some people think beach nourishment is still the way to go even if it isn't a permanent solution. One person in favor of nourishing beaches answers those against beach nourishment this way: "That's like saying it's a losing battle to pave streets because some day grass is going to poke through."

Other methods of saving eroding beaches are being tried. In places along the Great Lakes shores and coastal shores, one company has installed fabrics underwater to slow currents. By slowing currents, sand is naturally deposited and kept in place.

Another shore-saving device is a synthetic barrier that is shaped like a plastic snowflake.

A string of these barriers are secured just off-shore. They absorb the energy of incoming waves. Reducing wave energy can prevent sand from being eroded from the beach. New sand also might accumulate because the barriers slow down the currents that flow along the shore.

Many people believe that communities along the shore must restrict the beachfront building of homes, hotels, and stores. Since some estimates claim that by the year 2025, nearly 75 percent of the U.S. population will live in coastal areas, it's a tough solution. Says one geologist, "We can retreat now and save our beaches or we can retreat later and probably ruin the beaches in the process."

CONNECTIONS Debate Using the facts in this article and other research you have done in your school media center or the Glencoe Science Web site, make a list of methods that could be used to save beaches. Debate the issue with your classmates.

SCIENCE *Online*

For more information, visit science.glencoe.com

Reviewing Main Ideas

Section 1 Surface Water

1. Rainwater that does not soak into the ground is pulled down the slope by gravity. This water is called runoff.

2. Runoff has the ability to erode and carry sediment. Factors such as steepness of slope and number and type of plants affect the amount of erosion. Rill, gully, and sheet erosion are types of surface water erosion caused by runoff. *What type of erosion is occurring in this photograph?*

3. Runoff generally flows into streams that merge with larger and larger rivers until emptying into a lake or ocean. Major river systems usually contain several different types of streams.

4. In the mountains, young streams flow through steep valleys and have rapids and waterfalls. Mature streams flow through gentler terrain and have less energy. Old streams are often wide and snake back and forth across their floodplains.

Section 2 Groundwater

1. When water soaks into the ground, it becomes part of a vast groundwater system.

2. Although rock may seem solid, many types are filled with connected spaces called pores. Such rocks are permeable and can contain large amounts of groundwater. *What would happen to the permeability of this material if the pores filled with clay or some other material?*

Section 3 Ocean Shoreline

1. Ocean shorelines are always changing. *Would you expect the rocky coast, shown to the right, to erode slower or faster than a sandy coast? Why?*

2. Waves and currents have tremendous amounts of energy. Pounding waves break up rocks into tiny fragments called sediment. Over time, the waves and currents move this sediment and deposit it elsewhere constantly changing beaches, sandbars, and barrier islands.

FOLDABLES
Reading & Study Skills

After You Read

Use the information in your Main Ideas Study Fold to review the different characteristics of surface water, groundwater, and ocean shorelines.

Visualizing Main Ideas

Complete the following concept map on caves.

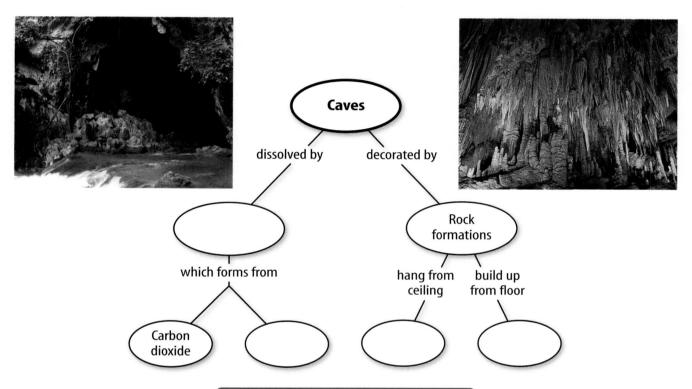

Vocabulary Review

Vocabulary Words

a. aquifer
b. beach
c. cave
d. channel
e. drainage basin
f. geyser
g. groundwater
h. impermeable

i. longshore current
j. meander
k. permeable
l. runoff
m. sheet erosion
n. spring
o. water table

Using Vocabulary

Explain the difference between the vocabulary words in each of the following sets.

1. runoff, sheet erosion

2. channel, drainage basin

3. aquifer, cave

4. spring, geyser

5. permeable, impermeable

6. sheet erosion, meander

7. groundwater, water table

8. permeable, aquifer

9. longshore current, beach

10. meander, channel

Study Tip

Don't just memorize definitions. Write complete sentences using new vocabulary words to be certain you understand what they mean.

Chapter 4 Assessment

Checking Concepts

Choose the word or phrase that best answers the question.

1. Identify an example of a structure created by deposition.
   A) beach
   B) rill
   C) cave
   D) geyser

2. Name the deposit that forms when a mountain river runs onto a plain.
   A) subsidence
   B) an alluvial fan
   C) infiltration
   D) water diversion

3. What is a layer of permeable rock that water flows through?
   A) an aquifer
   B) a pore
   C) a water table
   D) impermeable

4. What is the network formed by a river and all the smaller streams that contribute to it?
   A) groundwater system
   B) zone of saturation
   C) river system
   D) water table

5. Which term describes rock through which fluids can flow easily?
   A) impermeable
   B) meanders
   C) saturated
   D) permeable

6. Which stage of development are mountain streams in?
   A) young
   B) mature
   C) old
   D) meandering

7. What forms as a result of the water table meeting Earth's surface?
   A) meander
   B) spring
   C) aquifer
   D) stalactite

8. What contains heated groundwater that reaches Earth's surface?
   A) water table
   B) cave
   C) aquifer
   D) hot spring

9. Where are beaches most common?
   A) rocky shorelines
   B) flat shorelines
   C) aquifers
   D) young streams

10. Why does water rise in an artesian well?
    A) a pump
    B) erosion
    C) heat
    D) pressure

Thinking Critically

11. Explain why the Mississippi River has meanders along its course.

12. What determines whether a stream erodes its bottom or its sides?

13. Why might you be concerned if developers of a new housing project started drilling wells near your well?

14. Along what kind of shoreline would you find barrier islands? Explain.

15. Explain why beach sands collected from different locations will differ.

Developing Skills

16. **Interpreting Data** The rate of water flowing out of the Brahmaputra River in India, the La Plata River in South America, and the Mississippi River in North America are given in the table below. Infer which river carries the most sediment.

River Flow Rates	
River	Flow, m^3/s
Brahmaputra River, India	19,800
La Plata River, South America	79,300
Mississippi River, North America	175,000

17. **Forming Hypotheses** Hypothesize why most of the silt in the Mississippi delta is found farther out to sea than the sand-sized particles are.

18. Communicating Make an outline that explains the three stages of stream development. Share it with the class.

19. Concept Mapping Complete the concept map below using the following terms: *developed meanders, gentle curves, gentle gradient, old, rapids, steep gradient, wide floodplain,* and *young.*

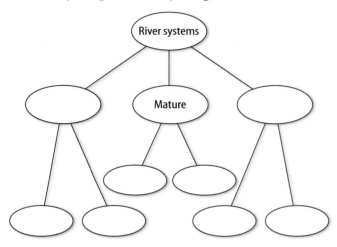

20. Using Variables, Constants, and Controls Explain how you could test the effect of slope on the amount of runoff produced.

Performance Assessment

21. Poster Do additional research about the distribution of water on Earth. Make a poster showing the different water reservoirs and what percentage of Earth's water is contained in each reservoir. Include processes such as erosion and deposition that are associated with each reservoir in your poster.

TECHNOLOGY

Go to the Glencoe Science Web site at **science.glencoe.com** or use the **Glencoe Science CD-ROM** for additional chapter assessment.

Test Practice

A scientist is gathering data and looking at trends in water erosion. The scientist's data are shown in the graph below.

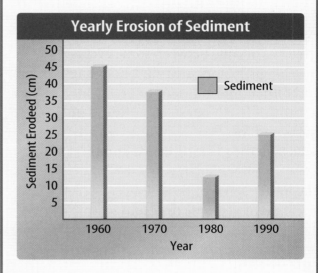

Study the graph and answer the following questions.

1. According to this information, which year had the most erosion?
A) 1960   **C)** 1980
B) 1970   **D)** 1990

2. According to the graph, between which years was erosion increasing?
F) 1960–1970   **H)** 1980–1990
G) 1970–1980   **J)** 1960–1980

3. According to the graph, which year had the least erosion?
A) 1960   **C)** 1980
B) 1970   **D)** 1990

4. According to the graph, how many centimeters of erosion were there in 1990?
F) 5   **H)** 15
G) 25   **J)** 20

Clues to Earth's Past

Studying the history of Earth is not as easy as studying the history of a country. This is because no people were around to record the events in Earth's past. Also, the long stretches of time between some events in geologic history are mind-boggling and difficult for humans to grasp. In a study of Earth's past, clues found in rocks and fossils of long-dead organisms take the place of words and pictures. In this chapter, you will encounter some of those long stretches of geologic time and learn how fossils form so that you can interpret some of Earth's past for yourself.

What do you think?

Science Journal Study the picture below. Discuss what you think this might be with a classmate. Here's a hint: *It lived in the ocean millions of years ago.* Write your answer or best guess in your Science Journal.

EXPLORE ACTIVITY

The process of fossil formation begins when dead plants or animals are buried in sediment. In time, if conditions are right, the sediment hardens into sedimentary rock. Parts of the organism are preserved along with the impressions of parts that don't survive. Any evidence of once-living things contained in the rock record is a fossil.

Make a model of a fossil

1. Fill a small jar (about 500 mL) one-third full of plaster of Paris. Add water until the jar is half full.
2. Drop in a few small shells.
3. To model a swift, muddy stream, cover the jar and shake it.
4. Now model the stream flowing into a lake by uncovering the jar and pouring the contents into a paper or plastic bowl. Let the mixture sit for an hour.
5. Crack open the hardened plaster to locate the model fossils.

Observe

Pick the shells out of the plaster and focus your attention on the impressions left by them. In your Science Journal, list what the impressions could tell you.

Before You Read

FOLDABLES
Reading & Study Skills

Making a Question Study Fold Asking yourself questions helps you stay focused and better understand Earth's past when you are reading the chapter.

1. Place a sheet of paper in front of you so the long side is at the top. Fold the paper in half from the left side to the right side and then unfold.
2. Fold each side in to the centerfold line to divide the paper into fourths. Fold the paper in half from top to bottom and unfold.
3. Through the top thickness of paper, cut along both of the middle fold lines to form four tabs. Write these questions on the tabs: *What are fossils? How do fossils form? How is the relative age of rocks determined? How is the absolute age of rocks determined?*
4. As you read the chapter, write answers to the questions under the tabs.

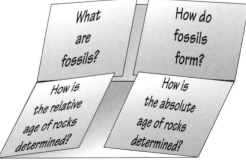

1 Fossils

As You Read

What You'll Learn

- **List** the conditions necessary for fossils to form.
- **Describe** several processes of fossil formation.
- **Explain** how fossil correlation is used to determine rock ages.

Vocabulary

fossil
permineralized remains
carbon film

mold
cast
index fossil

Why It's Important

Fossils help scientists find oil and other sources of energy necessary for society.

Traces of the Distant Past

A giant crocodile lurks in the shallow water of a river. A herd of *Triceratops* emerges from the edge of the forest and cautiously moves toward the river. The dinosaurs are thirsty, but they know danger waits for them in the water. A large bull *Triceratops* moves into the river. The others follow.

Does this scene sound familiar to you? It's likely that you've read about dinosaurs and other past inhabitants of Earth. But how do you know that they really existed or what they were like? What evidence do humans have of past life on Earth? The answer is fossils. Paleontologists, scientists who study fossils, can reconstruct what an animal looked like from its fossil remains, as shown in **Figure 1**.

Figure 1
Scientists and artists can reconstruct what dinosaurs looked like in life using fossil remains.

A A paleontologist carefully examines a fossil skeleton and prepares a reconstruction of what the animal might have looked like when it was alive.

B The reconstruction is finished and ready for display.

Formation of Fossils

Fossils are the remains, imprints, or traces of prehistoric organisms. Fossils have helped scientists determine approximately when life first appeared, when plants and animals first lived on land, and when organisms became extinct. Fossils are evidence of not only when and where organisms once lived, but also how they lived.

For the most part, the remains of dead plants and animals disappear quickly. Scavengers eat and scatter the remains of dead organisms. Fungi and bacteria invade, causing the remains to rot and disappear. If you've ever left a banana on the counter too long, you've seen this process begin. In time, compounds within the banana cause it to break down chemically and soften. Microorganisms, such as bacteria, cause it to decay. What keeps some plants and animals from disappearing before they become fossils? Which organisms are more likely to become fossils?

Conditions Needed for Fossil Formation Whether or not a dead organism becomes a fossil depends upon how well it is protected from scavengers and agents of physical destruction, such as waves and currents. One way a dead organism can be protected is for sediment to bury the body quickly. If a fish dies and sinks to the bottom of a lake, sediment carried into the lake by a stream can cover the fish rapidly. As a result, no waves or scavengers can get to it and tear it apart. The body parts then might be fossilized and included in a sedimentary rock like shale. However, quick burial alone isn't always enough to make a fossil.

Organisms have a better chance of becoming fossils if they have hard parts such as bones, shells, or teeth. One reason is that scavengers are less likely to eat these hard parts. Hard parts also decay more slowly than soft parts do. Most fossils are the hard parts of organisms, such as the fossil teeth in **Figure 2.**

Types of Preservation

Perhaps you've seen skeletal remains of *Tyrannosaurus rex* towering above you in a museum. You also have some idea of what this dinosaur looked like because you've seen illustrations. Artists who draw *Tyrannosaurus rex* and other dinosaurs base their illustrations on fossil bones. What preserves fossil bones?

Figure 2
These fossil shark teeth are hard parts. Soft parts of animals do not become fossilized as easily.

TRY AT HOME
Mini LAB

Predicting Fossil Preservation

Procedure
1. Take a brief walk outside and observe your neighborhood.
2. Look around and notice what kinds of plants and animals live nearby.

Analysis
1. Predict what remains from your time might be preserved far into the future.
2. Explain what conditions would need to exist for these remains to be fossilized.

Figure 3
Quartz and other minerals have replaced original materials and filled the hollow spaces in this permineralized dinosaur bone. *Why has this fossil retained the shape of the original bone?*

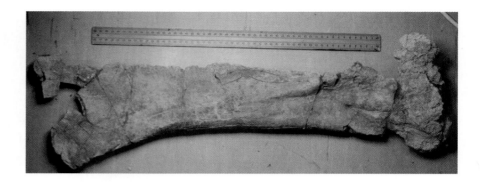

Mineral Replacment Most hard parts of organisms such as bones, teeth, and shells have tiny spaces within them. In life, these spaces can be filled with cells, blood vessels, nerves, or air. When the organism dies and the soft materials inside the hard parts decay, the tiny spaces become empty. If the hard part is buried, groundwater can seep in and deposit minerals in the spaces. **Permineralized remains** are fossils in which the spaces inside are filled with minerals from groundwater. In permineralized remains, some original material from the fossil organism's body might be preserved—encased within the minerals from groundwater. It is from these original materials that DNA, the chemical that contains an organism's genetic code, can sometimes be recovered.

Sometimes minerals replace the hard parts of fossil organisms. For example, a solution of water and dissolved silica (the compound SiO_2) might flow into and through the shell of a dead organism. If the water dissolves the shell and leaves silica in its place, the original shell is replaced.

Often people learn about past forms of life from bones, wood, and other remains that became permineralized or replaced with minerals from groundwater, as shown in **Figure 3,** but many other types of fossils can be found.

Figure 4
Graptolites lived hundreds of millions of years ago and drifted on currents in the oceans. These organisms often are preserved as carbon films.

Carbon Films The tissues of most organisms are made of compounds that contain carbon. Sometimes fossils contain only carbon. Fossils usually form when sediments bury a dead organism. As sediment piles up, the organism's remains are subjected to pressure and heat. These conditions force gases and liquids from the body. A thin film of carbon residue is left, forming a silhouette of the original organism called a **carbon film. Figure 4** shows the carbonized remains of graptolites, which are small marine animals. Graptolites have been found in rocks as old as 500 million years.

Coal In swampy regions, large volumes of plant matter accumulate. Over millions of years, these deposits become completely carbonized, forming coal. Coal is more important as a source of fuel than as a fossil because the structure of the original plant often is lost when coal forms.

✔ Reading Check *In what sort of environment does coal form?*

Molds and Casts In nature, impressions form when seashells or other hard parts of organisms fall into a soft sediment such as mud. The object and sediment then are buried by more sediment. Compaction and cementation, the deposition of minerals from water into the pore spaces between sediment particles, turn the sediment into rock. Other open pores in the rock then let water and air reach the shell or hard part. The hard part might decay or dissolve, leaving behind a cavity in the rock called a **mold.** Later, mineral-rich water or other sediment might wash into the cavity, harden into rock, and produce a copy or **cast** of the original object, as shown in **Figure 5.**

Chemistry
INTEGRATION

The bones of vertebrates contain calcium phosphate, and the shells of many invertebrates contain calcium carbonate. Calcium carbonate dissolves more easily in acid than calcium phosphate does. The ground water in some swampy environments is acidic. In your Science Journal, design an investigation to find out whether bones or shells would preserve best as fossils in a swamp.

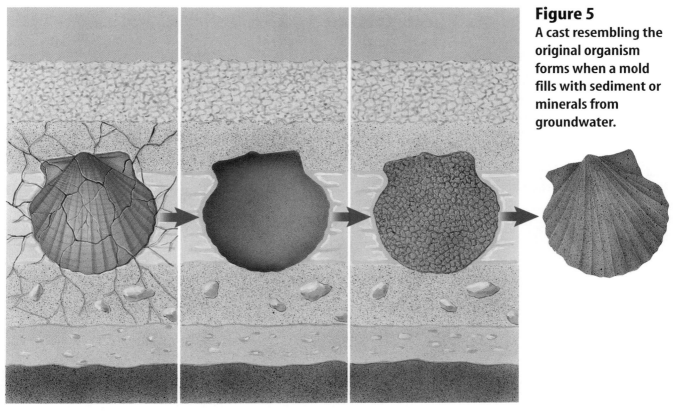

Figure 5
A cast resembling the original organism forms when a mold fills with sediment or minerals from groundwater.

A The fossil begins to dissolve as water moves through spaces in the rock layers.

B The fossil has been dissolved away. The harder rock once surrounding it forms a mold.

C Sediment washes into the mold and is deposited, or mineral crystals form.

D A cast forms.

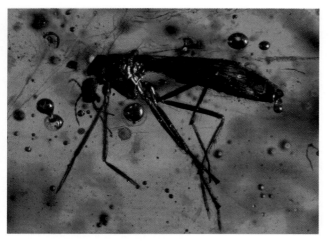

Original Remains Sometimes conditions allow original soft parts of organisms to be preserved for thousands or millions of years. For example, insects can be trapped in amber, a hardened form of sticky tree resin. The amber surrounds and protects the original material of the insect's exoskeleton from destruction, as shown in **Figure 6.** Some organisms, such as the mammoth, have been found preserved in frozen ground in Siberia. Original remains also have been found in natural tar deposits at Earth's surface, such as the La Brea tar pits in California.

Figure 6
The original soft parts of this mosquito have been preserved in amber for millions of years.

Trace Fossils Do you have a handprint in plaster that you made when you were in kindergarten? If so, it's a record that tells something about you. From it, others can guess your size and maybe your weight at that age. Animals walking on Earth long ago left similar tracks, such as those in **Figure 7.** Trace fossils are fossilized tracks and other evidence of the activity of organisms. In some cases, tracks can tell you more about how an organism lived than any other type of fossil. For example, from a set of tracks at Davenport Ranch, Texas, you might be able to learn something about the social life of sauropods, which were large, plant-eating dinosaurs. The largest tracks of the herd are on the outer edges and the smallest are on the inside. These tracks cause some scientists to hypothesize that adult sauropods surrounded their young as they traveled—probably to protect them from predators. A nearby set of tracks might mean that another type of dinosaur, an allosaur, was stalking the herd.

Figure 7
Tracks made in soft mud, and now preserved in solid rock, can provide information about animal size, speed, and behavior.

A This dinosaur track is from the Glen Rose Formation in north-central Texas.

B These tracks are located on a Navajo Reservation in Arizona.

Trails and Burrows Other trace fossils include trails and burrows made by worms and other animals. These, too, tell something about how these animals lived. For example, by examining fossil burrows you can sometimes tell how firm the sediment the animals lived in was. As you can see, fossils can tell a great deal about the organisms that have inhabited Earth.

 **Reading Check** *How are trace fossils different from fossils that are the remains of an organism's body?*

Index Fossils

One thing you can learn by studying fossils is that species of organisms have changed over time. Some species of organisms inhabited Earth for long periods of time without changing. Other species changed a lot in comparatively short amounts of time. It is these organisms that became index fossils.

Index fossils are the remains of species that existed on Earth for relatively short periods of time, were abundant, and were widespread geographically. Because the organisms that became index fossils lived only during specific intervals of geologic time, geologists can estimate the ages of rock layers based on the particular index fossils they contain. However, not all rocks contain index fossils. Another way to approximate the age of a rock layer is to compare the spans of time, or ranges, over which more than one fossil lived. The estimated age is the time interval where fossil ranges overlap, as shown in **Figure 8.**

What types of fossils can be found in your part of the country? To find out, see the **Fossils Field Guide** at the back of the book.

Figure 8
A The fossils in a sequence of sedimentary rock can be used to estimate the ages of each layer. **B** The chart shows when each organism inhabited Earth. *Why is it possible to say that the middle layer of rock was deposited between 438 million and 408 million years ago?*

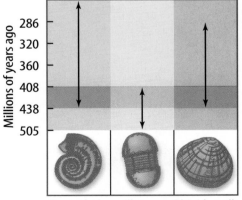

Fossil Range Chart

Millions of years ago

286
320
360
408
438
505

Euomphalus *Illaenus* *Rhipidomella*

Fossils and Ancient Environments

Scientists can use fossils to determine what the environment of an area was like long ago. Using fossils, you might be able to find out whether an area was land or whether it was covered by an ocean at a particular time. If the region was covered by ocean, it might even be possible to learn the depth of the water. What clues about the depth of water do you think fossils could provide?

Fossils also are used to determine the past climate of a region. For example, rocks in parts of the eastern United States contain fossils of tropical plants. The environment of this part of the United States today isn't tropical. However, because of the fossils, scientists know that it was tropical when these fossilized plants were living. **Figure 9** shows that North America was located near the equator when these fossils formed.

Figure 9
Because the continents on the surface of Earth slowly move, the climate of a given region changes through geologic time.

A The equator passed through North America 310 million years ago. At this time, warm shallow seas and coal swamps covered much of the continent.

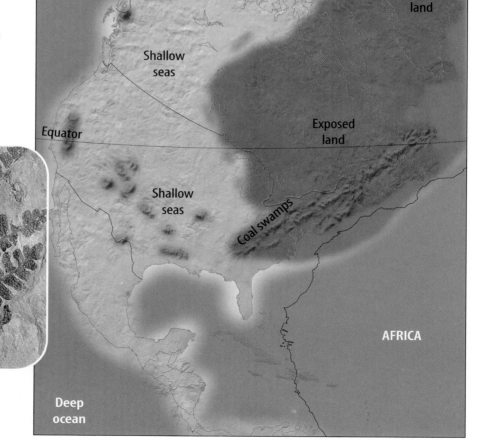

B *Neuropteris* was a common fern that grew in swamps during this time.

Shallow Seas How would you explain the presence of fossilized crinoids—animals that lived in shallow seas—in rocks just west of those containing the fern fossils? **Figure 10** shows a fossil crinoid and a living crinoid. When the fossil crinoids were alive, a shallow sea covered much of western and central North America. The crinoid hard parts were included in rocks that formed from the sediments at the bottom of this sea. Fossils provide information about past life on Earth and also about the history of the rock layers that contain them. Fossils can provide information about the ages of rocks and the climate and type of environment that existed when the rocks formed.

Figure 10
A This fossil crinoid lived in the warm, shallow seas that once covered part of North America.
B This crinoid lives in shallow water near Papua New Guinea. *How do the habitats of these crinoids compare?*

Section Assessment

1. What conditions must exist for most fossils to form?

2. Describe how a fossil mold could form. Explain how a fossil mold is different from a fossil cast.

3. What characteristics do the organisms that become index fossils have? How are these characteristics useful to geologists?

4. How do carbon films form?

5. **Think Critically** What can you say about the ages of two widely separated layers of rock that contain the same type of fossil? What can you say about the environments of these widely separated layers?

Skill Builder Activities

6. **Concept Mapping** Make a concept map that compares and contrasts permineralized remains and original remains. Use the following phrases: *types of fossils, original remains, evidence of former life, permineralized remains, replaced by minerals,* and *parts of organisms.* **For more help, refer to the** Science Skill Handbook.

7. **Communicating** Visit a museum that has fossils on display. In your Science Journal, make an illustration of each fossil. Write a brief description, noting key facts about each. Also, write about how each fossil might have formed. **For more help, refer to the** Science Skill Handbook.

Relative Ages of Rocks

Superposition

Imagine that you are walking to your favorite store and you happen to notice an interesting car go by. You're not sure what kind it is, but you remember that you read an article about it. You decide to look it up. At home you have a stack of magazines from the past year, as seen in **Figure 11.**

You know that the article you're thinking of came out in the January edition, so it must be near the bottom of the pile. As you dig downward, you find magazines from March, then February. January must be next. How did you know that the January issue of the magazine would be on the bottom? To find the older edition under newer ones, you applied the principle of superposition.

Oldest Rocks on the Bottom According to the **principle of superposition,** in undisturbed layers of rock, the oldest rocks are on the bottom and the rocks become progressively younger toward the top. Why is this the case?

Figure 11
The pile of magazines illustrates the principle of superposition. According to this principle, the oldest rock layer (or magazine) is on the bottom.

Rock Layers Sediment accumulates in horizontal beds, forming layers of sedimentary rock. The first layer to form is on the bottom. The next layer forms on top of the previous one. Because of this, the oldest rocks are at the bottom. However, forces generated by mountain formation sometimes can turn layers over. When layers have been turned upside down, it's necessary to use other clues in the rock layers to determine their original positions and relative ages.

Relative Ages

Now you want to look for another magazine. You're not sure how old it is, but you know it arrived after the January issue. You can find it in the stack by using the principle of relative age.

The **relative age** of something is its age in comparison to other things. Geologists determine the relative ages of rocks and other structures by examining their places in a sequence. For example, if layers of sedimentary rock are offset by a fault, which is a break in Earth's surface, you know that the layers had to be there before a fault could cut through them. The relative age of the rocks is older than the relative age of the fault. Relative age determination doesn't tell you anything about the age of rock layers in actual years. You don't know if a layer is 100 million or 10,000 years old. You only know that it's younger than the layers below it and older than the fault cutting through it.

Other Clues Help Determination of relative age is easy if the rocks haven't been faulted or turned upside down. For example, look at **Figure 12A.** Which layer is the oldest? In cases where rock layers have been disturbed as in **Figure 12B,** you might have to look for fossils and other clues to date the rocks. If you find a fossil in the top layer that's older than a fossil in a lower layer, you can hypothesize that layers have been turned upside down by folding during mountain building.

SCIENCE *Online*

Research Visit the Glencoe Science Web site at **science.glencoe.com** for more information about how geologists determine the relative ages of rocks. Communicate to your class what you learn.

Figure 12
A In a stack of undisturbed sedimentary rocks, the oldest rocks are at the bottom. **B** This similar stack of rocks has been folded by forces within Earth. *How can you tell if an older rock is above a younger one?*

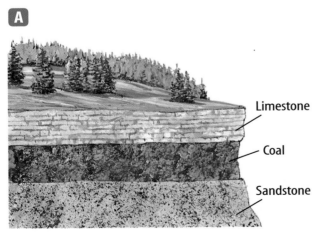

A

Limestone
Coal
Sandstone

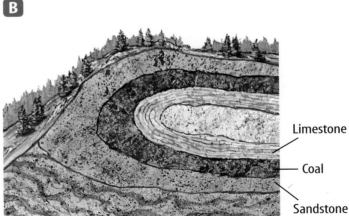

B

Limestone
Coal
Sandstone

Unconformities

A sequence of rock is a record of past events. But most rock sequences are incomplete—layers are missing. These gaps in rock layers are called **unconformities** (un kun FOR mih teez). Unconformities develop when agents of erosion such as running water or glaciers remove existing rock layers by washing or scraping them away. They also form when a period of time passes without any new deposition occurring to form new layers of rock.

 **Reading Check** *How do unconformities form?*

Angular Unconformities Horizontal layers of sedimentary rock often are tilted and uplifted. Erosion and weathering then wear down these tilted rock layers. Eventually, younger sediment layers are deposited horizontally on top of the eroded and tilted layers. Geologists call such an unconformity an angular unconformity. **Figure 13** shows how angular unconformities develop.

Disconformity Suppose you're looking at a stack of sedimentary rock layers. They look complete, but layers are missing. If you look closely you might find an old surface of erosion. This records a time when the rocks were exposed and eroded. Later, younger rocks formed above the erosion surface when deposition of sediment began again. Even though all the layers are parallel, the rock record still has a gap. This type of unconformity is called a disconformity.

Nonconformity Another type of unconformity, called a nonconformity, occurs when metamorphic or igneous rocks are uplifted and eroded. Sedimentary rocks are then deposited on top of this erosion surface. The surface between the two rock types is a nonconformity. Sometimes rock fragments from below are incorporated into sediments deposited above the nonconformity. All types of unconformities are shown in **Figure 14.**

Figure 13
An angular unconformity results when horizontal layers cover tilted, eroded layers.

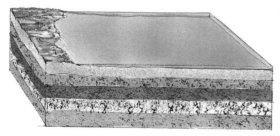

A Sedimentary rocks are deposited originally as horizontal layers.

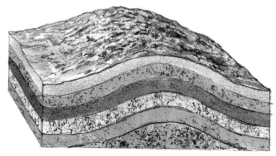

B The horizontal rock layers are tilted as forces within Earth deform them.

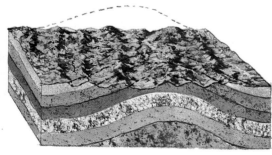

C The tilted layers erode.

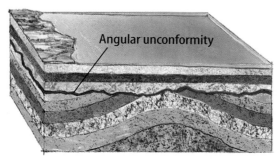

Angular unconformity

D An angular unconformity results when new layers form on the tilted layers as deposition resumes.

Figure 14

An unconformity is a gap in the rock record caused by erosion or a pause in deposition. There are three major kinds of unconformities—nonconformity, angular unconformity, and disconformity.

Nonconformity

▲ In a nonconformity, layers of sedimentary rock overlie older igneous or metamorphic rocks. A nonconformity in Big Bend National Park, Texas, is shown above.

Angular unconformity

▲ An angular unconformity develops when new horizontal layers of sedimentary rock form on top of older sedimentary rock layers that have been folded by compression. An example of an angular unconformity at Siccar Point in southeastern Scotland is shown above.

▼ A disconformity develops when horizontal rock layers are exposed and eroded, and new horizontal layers of rock are deposited on the eroded surface. The disconformity shown below is in the Grand Canyon.

Disconformity

Matching Up Rock Layers

Suppose you're studying a layer of sandstone in Bryce Canyon in Utah. Later, when you visit Canyonlands National Park, Utah, you notice that a layer of sandstone there looks just like the sandstone in Bryce Canyon, 250 km away. Above the sandstone in the Canyonlands is a layer of limestone and then another sandstone layer. You return to Bryce Canyon and find the same sequence—sandstone, limestone, and sandstone. What do you infer? It's likely that you're looking at the same layers of rocks in two different locations. **Figure 15** shows that these rocks are parts of huge deposits that covered this whole area of the western United States. Geologists often can match up, or correlate, layers of rocks over great distances.

Evidence Used for Correlation It's not always easy to say that a rock layer exposed in one area is the same as a rock layer exposed in another area. Sometimes it's possible to walk along the layer for kilometers and prove that it's continuous. In other cases, such as at the Canyonlands area and Bryce Canyon as seen in **Figure 16,** the rock layers are exposed only where rivers have cut through overlying layers of rock and sediment. How can you show that the limestone sandwiched between the two layers of sandstone in Canyonlands is likely the same limestone as at Bryce Canyon? One way is to use fossil evidence. If the same types of fossils were found in the limestone layer in both places, it's a good indication that the limestone at each location is the same age, and, therefore, one continuous deposit.

✓ **Reading Check** *How do fossils help show that rocks at different locations belong to the same rock layer?*

SCIENCE *Online*

Research Visit the Glencoe Science Web site at **science.glencoe.com** for a link to more information about the process of correlation.

Figure 15
These rock layers, exposed at Hopi Point in Grand Canyon National Park, Arizona, can be correlated, or matched up, with rocks from across large areas of the western United States.

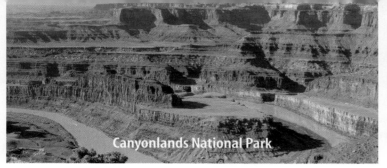

Canyonlands National Park

Bryce Canyon National Park

Date deposited (millions of years ago)

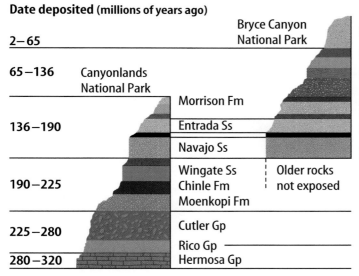

2–65	Bryce Canyon National Park	Wasatch Fm
65–136	Canyonlands National Park	Kaiparowits Fm
		Straight Cliffs Ss
	Morrison Fm	Dakota Ss
136–190	Entrada Ss	Winsor Fm
		Entrada Ss
	Navajo Ss	Navajo Ss
190–225	Wingate Ss / Chinle Fm / Moenkopi Fm	Older rocks not exposed
225–280	Cutler Gp	
	Rico Gp	
280–320	Hermosa Gp	

Figure 16
Geologists have named the many rock layers, or formations in Canyonlands and in Bryce Canyon, Utah. They also have correlated some formations between the two canyons. *Which layers are present at both canyons?*

Can layers of rock be correlated in other ways? Sometimes determining relative ages isn't enough, and other dating methods must be used. In Section 3, you'll see how the numerical ages of rocks can be determined, and how geologists have used this information to estimate the age of Earth.

Section 2 Assessment

1. Suppose you haven't cleaned out your locker all year. Where would you expect to find papers from the beginning of the year? What principle of geology would you use to find these old papers?

2. Explain the concept of relative age.

3. What is a disconformity?

4. What is one way to correlate similar rock layers in two different areas?

5. **Think Critically** Explain the relationship between the concept of relative age and the principle of superposition.

Skill Builder Activities

6. **Interpreting Data** A sandstone contains a 400-million-year-old fossil. A shale contains fossils that are over 500 million years old. A limestone, underlying a sandstone, contains fossils that are between 400 million and 500 million years old. Which rock bed is oldest? Explain. **For more help, refer to the** Science Skill Handbook.

7. **Using an Electronic Spreadsheet** Use this section to prepare a table comparing and contrasting types of unconformities. **For more help, refer to the** Technology Skill Handbook.

Activity

Relative Ages

Which of your two friends is older? To answer this question, you'd need to know their relative ages. You wouldn't need to know the exact age of either of your friends—just who was born first. The same is sometimes true for rock layers.

What You'll Investigate
Can you determine the relative ages of rock layers?

Materials
paper   pencil

Goals
■ **Interpret** illustrations of rock layers and other geological structures and determine the relative order of events.

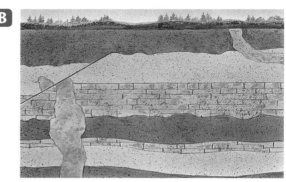

	Granite		Limestone
	Sandstone		Shale

Procedure

1. **Analyze Figures A** and **B.**
2. Make a sketch of **Figure A.** On it, identify the relative age of each rock layer, igneous intrusion, fault, and unconformity. For example, the shale layer is the oldest, so mark it with a 1. Mark the next-oldest feature with a 2, and so on.
3. Repeat question 2 for **Figure B.**

Conclude and Apply

Figure A

1. **Identify** the type of unconformity shown. Is it possible that there were originally more layers of rock than are shown?
2. **Describe** how the rocks left of the fault moved in relation to rocks on the right.
3. **Hypothesize** how the hill on the left side of the figure formed.

Figure B

4. Is it possible to conclude if the igneous intrusion on the left is older or younger than the unconformity nearest the surface?
5. **Describe** the relative ages of the two igneous intrusions. How did you know?
6. **Hypothesize** which two layers of rock might have been much thicker in the past.

Communicating
Your Data

Compare your results with other students' results. **For more help, refer to the** Science Skill Handbook.

Absolute Ages of Rocks

Absolute Ages

As you sort through your stack of magazines looking for that article about the car you saw, you decide that you need to restack them into a neat pile. By now, they're in a jumble and no longer in order of their relative age, as shown in **Figure 17.** How can you stack them so the oldest are on the bottom and the newest are on top? Fortunately, magazine dates are printed on the cover. Thus, stacking magazines in order is a simple process. Unfortunately, rocks don't have their ages stamped on them. Or do they? **Absolute age** is the age, in years, of a rock or other object. Geologists determine absolute ages by using properties of the atoms that make up materials.

Radioactive Decay

Physics
INTEGRATION

Atoms consist of a dense central region called the nucleus, which is surrounded by a cloud of negatively charged particles called electrons. The nucleus is made up of protons, which have a positive charge, and neutrons, which have no electric charge. The number of protons determines the identity of the element, and the number of neutrons determines the form of the element, or isotope. For example, every atom with a single proton is a hydrogen atom. Hydrogen atoms can have no neutrons, a single neutron, or two neutrons. This means that there are three isotopes of hydrogen.

✓ Reading Check *What particles make up an atom's nucleus?*

Some isotopes are unstable and break down into other isotopes and particles. Sometimes a lot of energy is given off during this process. The process of breaking down is called **radioactive decay.** In the case of hydrogen, atoms with one proton and two neutrons are unstable and tend to break down. Many other elements have stable and unstable isotopes.

Figure 17
The magazines that have been shuffled through no longer illustrate the principle of superposition.

Jelly Bean Carbon-14 Dating

Procedure:
1. Count out 80 **red jelly beans.**
2. Remove half the red jelly beans and replace them with **green jelly beans.**
3. Continue replacing half the red jelly beans with green jelly beans until only 5 red jelly beans remain. Count the number of times you replace half the red jelly beans.

Analysis
1. How did this activity model the decay of carbon-14 atoms?
2. How many half lives of carbon-14 did you model during this activity?
3. If the atoms in a bone experienced the same number of half lives as your jelly beans, how old would the bone be?

Alpha and Beta Decay In some isotopes, a neutron breaks down into a proton and an electron. This type of radioactive decay is called beta decay because the electron leaves the atom as a beta particle. The nucleus loses a neutron but gains a proton. When the number of protons in an atom is changed, a new element forms. Other isotopes give off two protons and two neutrons in the form of an alpha particle. Alpha and beta decay are shown in **Figure 18.**

Half-Life In radioactive decay, the parent isotope undergoes radioactive decay. The daughter product is produced by radioactive decay. Each radioactive parent isotope decays to its daughter product at a certain rate. Based on this decay rate, it takes a certain period of time for one half of the parent isotope to decay to its daughter product. The **half-life** of an isotope is the time it takes for half of the atoms in the isotope to decay. For example, the half-life of carbon-14 is 5,730 years. So it will take 5,730 years for half of the carbon-14 atoms in an object to change into nitrogen-14 atoms. You might guess that in another 5,730 years, all of the remaining carbon-14 atoms will decay to nitrogen-14. However, this is not the case. Only half of the atoms of carbon-14 remaining after the first 5,730 years will decay during the second 5,730 years. So, after two half-lives, one fourth of the original carbon-14 atoms still remain. Half of them will decay during another 5,730 years. After three half-lives, one eighth of the original carbon-14 atoms still remain. After many half-lives, such a small amount of the parent isotope remains that it might not be measurable.

Figure 18
A In beta decay, a neutron changes into a proton by giving off an electron. This electron has a lot of energy and is called a beta particle.

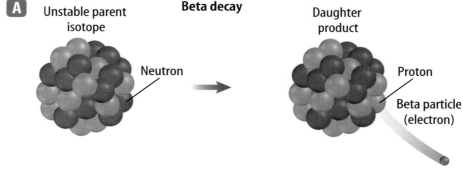

A Beta decay

Unstable parent isotope — Neutron → Daughter product — Proton, Beta particle (electron)

B In the process of alpha decay, an unstable parent isotope nucleus gives off an alpha particle and changes into a new daughter product. Alpha particles contain two neutrons and two protons.

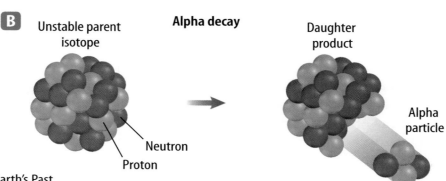

B Alpha decay

Unstable parent isotope — Neutron, Proton → Daughter product — Alpha particle

Radiometric Ages

Decay of radioactive isotopes is like a clock keeping track of time that has passed since rocks have formed. As time passes, the amount of parent isotope in a rock decreases as the amount of daughter product increases, as in **Figure 19.** By measuring the ratio of parent isotope to daughter product in a mineral and by knowing the half-life of the parent, in many cases you can calculate the absolute age of a rock. This process is called **radiometric dating.**

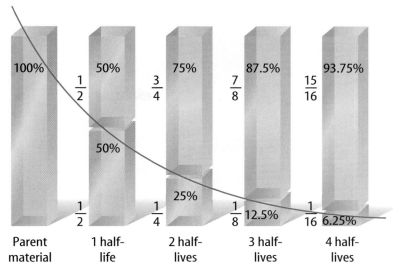

Figure 19
During each half-life, one half of the parent material decays to the daughter product.

A scientist must decide which parent isotope to use when measuring the age of a rock. If the object to be dated seems old, then the geologist will use an isotope with a long half-life. The half-life for the decay of potassium-40 to argon-40 is 1.25 billion years. As a result, this isotope can be used to date rocks that are many millions of years old. To avoid error, conditions must be met for the ratios to give a correct indication of age. For example, the rock being studied must still retain all of the argon-40 that was produced by the decay of potassium-40. Also, it cannot contain any contamination of daughter product from other sources. Potassium-argon dating is good for rocks containing potassium, but what about other things?

Radiocarbon Dating Carbon-14 is useful for dating bones, wood, and charcoal up to 75,000 years old. Living things take in carbon from the environment to build their bodies. After the organism dies, the carbon-14 slowly decays and escapes as nitrogen-14 gas. If scientists can determine the amount of carbon-14 remaining in a sample, they can determine its age. For example, during much of human history, people built campfires. The wood from these fires often is preserved as charcoal. Scientists can determine the amount of carbon-14 remaining in a sample of charcoal by measuring the amount of radiation emitted by the carbon-14 isotope in labs like the one in **Figure 20.** Once they know the amount of carbon-14 in a charcoal sample, scientists can determine the age of the wood used to make the fire.

Figure 20
Radiometric ages are determined in labs like this one.

Figure 21
Meteorites like this one are thought to be as old as Earth.

Age Determinations Aside from carbon-14 dating, rocks that can be radiometrically dated are mostly igneous and metamorphic rocks. Most sedimentary rocks cannot be dated by this method. This is because many sedimentary rocks are made up of particles eroded from older rocks. Dating these pieces only gives the age of the preexisting rock from which it came.

The Oldest Known Rocks Radiometric dating has been used to date the oldest rocks on Earth. These rocks are about 3.96 billion years old. By dating meteorites like the one shown in **Figure 21** and using other evidence, scientists have estimated the age of Earth to be about 4.6 billion years. Earth rocks greater than 3.96 billion years old probably were eroded or changed by heat and pressure.

☑ **Reading Check** *Why can't most sedimentary rocks be dated radiometrically?*

Problem-Solving Activity

When did the Iceman die?

Carbon-14 dating has been used to date charcoal, wood, bones, mummies from Egypt and Peru, the Dead Sea Scrolls, and the Italian Iceman. The Iceman was found in 1991 in the Italian Alps, near the Austrian border. Based on carbon-14 analysis, scientists determined that the Iceman is 5,300 years old. In approximately what year did the Iceman die?

Half-Life of Carbon-14	
Percent Carbon-14	Years Passed
100	0
50	5,730
25	11,460
12.5	17,190
6.25	22,920
3.125	

Reconstruction of Iceman

Identifying the Problem

The half-life chart shows the decay of carbon-14 over time. Half-life is the time it takes for half of a sample to decay. Fill in the years passed when only 3.125 percent of carbon-14 remain. Is there a point at which no carbon-14 would be present? Explain.

Solving the Problem

1. Estimate, using the data table, how much carbon-14 still was present in the Iceman's body that allowed scientists to determine his age.
2. If you had an artifact that contained 10.0 g of carbon-14, how many grams would remain after 17,190 years?

Uniformitarianism

Can you imagine trying to determine the age of Earth without some of the information you know today? Before the discovery of radiometric dating, many people estimated that Earth is only a few thousand years old. But in the 1700s, Scottish scientist James Hutton estimated that Earth is much older. He used the principle of **uniformitarianism.** This principle states that Earth processes occurring today are similar to those that occurred in the past. Hutton's principle is often paraphrased as "the present is the key to the past."

Hutton observed that the processes that changed the landscape around him were slow, and he inferred that they were just as slow throughout Earth's history. Hutton hypothesized that it took much longer than a few thousand years to form the layers of rock around him and to erode mountains that once stood kilometers high. **Figure 22** shows Hutton's native Scotland, a region shaped by millions of years of geologic processes.

Today, scientists recognize that Earth has been shaped by two types of change: slow, everyday processes that take place over millions of years, and violent, unusual events such as the collision of a comet or asteroid about 65 million years ago that might have caused the extinction of the dinosaurs.

Figure 22
The rugged highlands of Scotland were shaped by erosion and uplift.

Section Assessment

1. You discover three rock layers that have not been turned upside down. The absolute age of the middle layer is 120 million years. What can you say about the ages of the layers above and below it?

2. How old would a fossil be if it had only one eighth of its original carbon-14 content remaining?

3. Explain the concept of uniformitarianism.

4. How do radioactive isotopes decay?

5. **Think Critically** Why can't scientists use carbon-14 to determine the age of an igneous rock?

Skill Builder Activities

6. **Making and Using Tables** Make a table that shows the amounts of parent and daughter material of a radioactive element that is left after four half-lives if the original parent material had a mass of 100 g. **For more help, refer to the Science Skill Handbook.**

7. **Using Fractions** You know that after every half-life, one half of the parent isotope changes to daughter product. In general, how would you determine how much parent isotope remains after any specified number of half-lives? **For more help, refer to the Math Skill Handbook.**

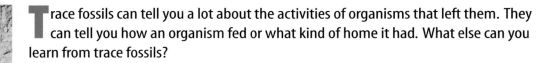

Trace Fossils

Trace fossils can tell you a lot about the activities of organisms that left them. They can tell you how an organism fed or what kind of home it had. What else can you learn from trace fossils?

Recognize the Problem

How can you model trace fossils that can provide information about the behavior of organisms?

Thinking Critically

What can you use to model trace fossils? What types of behavior could you show with your trace fossil model?

Goals

■ **Construct** a model of trace fossils.
■ **Describe** the information that you can learn from looking at your model.

Possible Materials

construction paper	wire
plastic (a fairly rigid type)	scissors
plaster of Paris	toothpicks
sturdy cardboard	clay
pipe cleaners	glue

Data Source

SCIENCE *Online* Go to the Glencoe Science Web site at **science.glencoe.com** for more information about trace fossils and what can be learned from them.

Safety Precautions

Wash your hands after the activity.

Planning the Model

1. **Decide** how you are going to make your model. What materials will you need?

2. **Decide** what types of activities you will demonstrate with your model. Were the organisms feeding? Resting? Traveling? Were they predators? Prey? How will your model indicate the activities you chose?

3. What is the setting of your model? Are you modeling the organism's home? Feeding areas? Is your model on land or water? How can the setting affect the way you build your model?

4. Will you only show trace fossils from a single species or multiple species? If you include more than one species, how will you provide evidence of any interaction between the species?

Check the Model Plans

1. Compare your plans with those of others in your class. Did other groups mention details that you had forgotten to think about? Are there any changes you would like to make to your plan before you continue?

2. Make sure your teacher approves your plan before you continue.

Making the Model

1. Following your plan, **construct** your model of trace fossils.

2. Have you included evidence of all the behaviors you intended to model?

Analyzing and Applying Results

1. Now that your model is complete, do you think that it adequately shows the behaviors you planned to demonstrate? Is there anything that you think you might want to do differently if you were going to make the model again?

2. Describe how using different kinds of materials might have affected your model. Can you think of other materials that would have allowed you to show more detail that you did?

3. Compare and contrast your model of trace fossils with trace fossils left by real organisms. Is one more easily interpreted than the other? Explain.

Communicating Your Data

Ask other students in your class or another class to look at your model and describe what information they can learn from the trace fossils. Did their interpretations agree with what you intended to show?

The World's Oldest Fish Story

A catch-of-the-day set science on its ears

Second Dorsal Fin

Anal Fin

Pelvic Fin

On a December day in 1938, just before Christmas, Marjorie Courtenay-Latimer went to say hello to her friends on board a fishing boat that had just returned to port in South Africa. Courtenay-Latimer, who worked at a museum, often went aboard her friends' ship to check out the catch. On this visit, she received a surprise Christmas present—an odd-looking fish. As soon as the woman spotted its strange blue fins among the piles of sharks and rays, she knew it was special.

Courtenay-Latimer took the fish back to her museum to study it. "It was the most beautiful fish I had ever seen, five feet long, and a pale mauve blue with iridescent silver markings," she later wrote. Courtenay-Latimer sketched it and sent the drawing to a friend of hers, J. L. B. Smith.

Smith was a chemistry teacher who was passionate about fish. After a time, he realized it was a coelacanth (SEE luh kanth). Fish experts knew that coelacanths had first appeared on Earth 400 million years ago. But the experts thought the fish were extinct. People had found fossils of coelacanths, but no one had seen one alive. It was assumed that the last coelacanth species had died out 65 million years ago. They were wrong. The ship's crew had caught one by accident.

Smith figured there might be more living coelacanths. So he decided to offer a reward for anyone who could find a living specimen.

TANZANIA
INDIAN OCEAN
Comoros Islands
MADAGASCAR
Europe
MOZAMBIQUE
Africa
South America

First Dorsal Fin

Camouflage Marks

Marjorie Courtenay-Latimer poses with her fish (above).

Courtenay-Latimer's original sketch of the fish

Pectoral Fin

Some scientists call the coelacanth "Old Four Legs." It got its nickname because the fish has paired fins that look something like legs.

After 14 years of silence, a report came in that a coelacanth had been caught off the east coast of Africa.

Today, scientists know that there are at least several hundred coelacanths living in the Indian Ocean, just east of central Africa. Many of these fish live near the Comoros Islands. The coelacanths live in underwater caves during the day but move out at night to feed. The rare fish are now a protected species. With any luck, they will survive for another hundred million years.

CONNECTIONS Write Find out how people responded to the discovery of living coelacanths. Why do you think people were so fascinated by this fish? Use the Glencoe Science Web site to find out more about the coelacanth.

SCIENCE Online

For more information, visit science.glencoe.com

Reviewing Main Ideas

Section 1 Fossils

1. Fossils are more likely to form if hard parts of the dead organisms are buried quickly.

2. Some fossils form when original materials that made up the organisms are replaced with minerals. Other fossils form when remains are subjected to heat and pressure, leaving only a carbonaceous film behind. Some fossils are the tracks or traces left by ancient organisms. *What type of fossil is shown to the right?*

3. A rock layer can be no older than the age of the fossils embedded in it.

Section 2 Relative Ages of Rocks

1. The principle of superposition states that older rocks lie underneath younger rocks in areas where the rocks haven't been disturbed. Faults and igneous intrusions are always younger than the rocks they cut across. *Which of the rock layers shown below is youngest?*

2. Unconformities, or gaps in the rock record, are due to erosion or periods of time during which no deposition occurred.

3. Rock layers can be correlated using rock types and fossils.

Section 3 Absolute Ages of Rocks

1. Absolute dating of rocks and minerals, unlike relative age determination, provides an age in years for the rocks.

2. The half-life of a radioactive isotope is the time it takes for half of the atoms of the isotope to decay into another isotope. *Which isotope could be used to date the buried tree shown below?*

3. Because half-lives don't change, scientists can determine absolute ages of rocks and minerals containing radioactive elements.

FOLDABLES
Reading & Study Skills

After You Read

To help review fossils and how to determine the age of rocks, use the Foldable you made at the beginning of the chapter.

Chapter (5) Study Guide

Visualizing Main Ideas

Complete the following concept map on fossils.

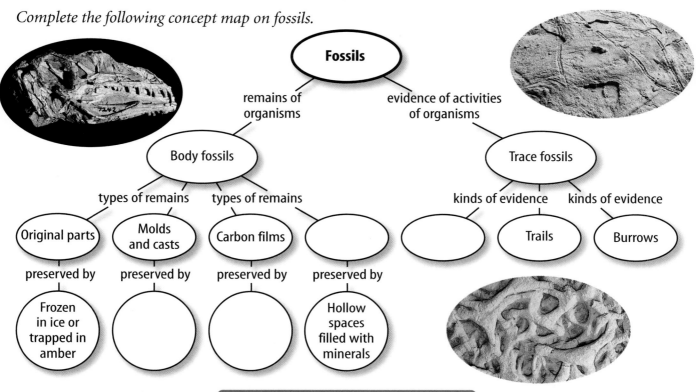

Concept map:

Fossils
- remains of organisms → **Body fossils**
  - types of remains → **Original parts** → preserved by → Frozen in ice or trapped in amber
  - types of remains → **Molds and casts** → preserved by → ( )
  - **Carbon films** → preserved by → ( )
  - ( ) → preserved by → Hollow spaces filled with minerals
- evidence of activities of organisms → **Trace fossils**
  - kinds of evidence → ( )
  - kinds of evidence → **Trails**
  - **Burrows**

Vocabulary Review

Vocabulary Words

a. absolute age
b. carbon film
c. cast
d. fossil
e. half-life
f. index fossil
g. mold
h. permineralized remains
i. principle of superposition
j. radioactive decay
k. radiometric dating
l. relative age
m. unconformity
n. uniformitarianism

Using Vocabulary

Write an original sentence using the vocabulary word to which each phrase refers.

1. thin film of carbon preserved as a fossil
2. older rocks lie under younger rocks
3. processes occur today as they did in the past
4. gap in the rock record
5. time needed for half the atoms to decay
6. fossil organism that lived for a short time
7. gives the age of rocks in years
8. minerals fill spaces inside fossil
9. a copy of a fossil produced by filling a mold with sediment or crystals
10. evidence of ancient life

THE PRINCETON REVIEW **Study Tip**

Reading material before your teacher explains it gives you a better understanding and provides you with an opportunity to ask questions.

Checking Concepts

Choose the word or phrase that best answers the question.

1. What is any evidence of ancient life called?
   - **A)** half-life
   - **B)** a fossil
   - **C)** unconformity
   - **D)** disconformity

2. Which of the following conditions makes fossil formation more likely?
   - **A)** buried slowly
   - **B)** attacked by scavengers
   - **C)** made of hard parts
   - **D)** composed of soft parts

3. What are cavities left in rocks when a shell or bone dissolves called?
   - **A)** casts
   - **B)** original remains
   - **C)** molds
   - **D)** carbon films

4. When the tiny spaces inside a fossil are filled in with minerals, you have what kind of preservation?
   - **A)** original remains
   - **B)** permineralized remains
   - **C)** molds and casts
   - **D)** carbonaceous films

5. To say "the present is the key to the past" is a way to describe which of the following principles?
   - **A)** superposition
   - **B)** succession
   - **C)** radioactivity
   - **D)** uniformitarianism

6. A fault can be useful in determining which of the following for a group of rocks?
   - **A)** absolute age
   - **B)** radiometric age
   - **C)** index age
   - **D)** relative age

7. Which of the following is an unconformity between parallel rock layers?
   - **A)** angular unconformity
   - **B)** fault
   - **C)** disconformity
   - **D)** nonconformity

8. Which process forms new elements?
   - **A)** superposition
   - **B)** uniformitarianism
   - **C)** permineralization
   - **D)** radioactive decay

9. In one type of radioactive decay, which of the following breaks down, releasing an electron?
   - **A)** alpha particle
   - **B)** proton
   - **C)** beta particle
   - **D)** neutron

10. About how old is Earth, based on radiometric dating?
    - **A)** 2,000 years
    - **B)** 5,000 years
    - **C)** 3.5 billion years
    - **D)** 4.6 billion years

Thinking Critically

11. How do relative and absolute ages differ?

12. How many half-lives have passed in a rock containing one eighth of the original radioactive material and seven eighths of the daughter product?

13. The fossil record of life on Earth is incomplete. Give some reasons why.

14. Suppose a lava flow were found between two sedimentary rock layers. How could you use the lava flow to learn about the ages of the sedimentary rock layers? (Hint: Most lava contains radioactive isotopes.)

15. Suppose you're correlating rock layers in the western United States. You find a layer of volcanic ash deposits. How can this layer help you in your correlation over a large area?

Developing Skills

16. **Recognizing Cause and Effect** Explain how some woolly mammoths could have been preserved intact in frozen ground. What conditions must have persisted since the deaths of these animals?

17. Classifying Copy the table below, and place each of the following fossils in the correct category: *dinosaur footprint, worm burrow, dinosaur skull, insect in amber, fossil woodpecker hole,* and *fish tooth.*

Types of Fossils	
Trace Fossils	**Body Fossils**

18. Concept Mapping Make a concept map using the following possible steps in the process of making a cast of a fossil: *organism dies, burial, protection from scavengers and bacteria, replacement by minerals, fossil erodes away,* and *mineral crystals form from solution.*

19. Communicating Make an outline of Section 1 that discusses the ways in which fossils form.

Performance Assessment

20. Write a Poem Write a poem explaining the principle of uniformitarianism.

21. Use a Classification System Start your own fossil collection. Label each find as to type, approximate age, and the place where it was found. Most state geological surveys can provide you with reference materials on local fossils.

TECHNOLOGY

Go to the Glencoe Science Web site at **science.glencoe.com** or use the **Glencoe Science CD-ROM** for additional chapter assessment.

THE PRINCETON REVIEW — Test Practice

A group of scientists found several different fossils. The scientists listed the different fossils in the table below.

Type of Fossils	
Fossils A	**Fossils B**
Large footprint	Frozen mammoth
Trackway with small footprints	Dinosaur bones
Animal burrow	?

Study the table and answer the following questions.

1. Fossils A are different from Fossils B because only Fossils A are _____ .
   A) index fossils
   B) trace fossils
   C) permineralized fossils
   D) original remains

2. Which of these belongs with Fossils B?
   F) An imprint of a leaf in mud
   G) A footprint in cement
   H) An insect in amber
   J) A fossilized nest

3. All of the fossils in the table above are _____ .
   A) evidence of past life
   B) types of rocks
   C) softparts
   D) hardparts

Geologic Time

The discovery of a new fossil often changes scientists' ideas about how ancient organisms looked and lived. Pictured here is Sue, the most complete *Tyrannosaurus rex* fossil ever found. Discovered in 1990, Sue has provided evidence indicating that this type of dinosaur relied heavily on a very good sense of smell. In this chapter, you will learn how dinosaurs and other types of organisms changed over time. You also will come to appreciate the long span of geologic time.

What do you think?

Science Journal Look at the picture below with a classmate. Discuss what you think this might be or what is happening. Here's a hint: *Sue couldn't have survived without them.* Write your answer or best guess in your Science Journal.

Environments include the living and nonliving things that surround and affect organisms. Whether or not an organism survives in its environment depends upon the characteristics that it has. Only if an organism survives until adulthood can it reproduce and pass on its characteristics to its offspring. In this activity, you will use a model to find out how one characteristic can determine whether individuals can compete and survive in an environment.

Make a model environment

1. Cut 15 pieces each of green, orange, and blue yarn into 3-cm lengths.

2. Scatter them on a sheet of green construction paper.

3. Have your partner use a pair of tweezers to pick up as many pieces as possible in 15 s.

Observe

In your Science Journal, discuss which colors your partner selected. Which color was least selected? Suppose that the construction paper represents grass, the yarn pieces represent insects, and the tweezers represent an insect-eating bird. Which color of insect do you predict would survive to adulthood?

Before You Read

FOLDABLES
Reading & Study Skills

Making an Organizational Study Fold Make the following Foldable to help you organize your thoughts into clear categories about geological time.

1. Place a sheet of paper in front of you so the long side is at the top. Fold the paper in half from top to bottom.

2. Fold both sides in. Unfold the paper so three sections show.

| Paleozoic Era | Mesozoic Era | Cenozoic Era |

3. Through the top thickness of paper, cut along each of the fold lines to the topfold, forming three tabs. Label the tabs *Paleozoic Era, Mesozoic Era,* and *Cenozoic Era.*

4. Before you read the chapter, find an example of an animal from each era and write it on the front of the tabs. As you read the chapter, write information about each era under the tabs.

1 Life and Geologic Time

As You Read

What You'll Learn

- **Explain** how geologic time can be divided into units.
- **Relate** changes of Earth's organisms to divisions on the geologic time scale.
- **Describe** how plate tectonics affects species.

Vocabulary

trilobite
geologic
  time scale
eon
era
period

epoch
organic evolution
species
natural selection
Pangaea

Why It's Important

The life and landscape around you are the products of change through geologic time.

Geologic Time

A group of students is searching for fossils. By looking in rocks that are hundreds of millions of years old, they hope to find many examples of **trilobites** (TRI loh bites) so that they can help piece together a puzzle. That puzzle is to find out what caused the extinction of these organisms. **Figure 1** shows some examples of what they are finding. The fossils are small, and their bodies are divided into segments. Some of them seem to have eyes. Could these be trilobites?

Trilobites are interesting fossils to search for. These small, hard-shelled organisms crawled on the seafloor and sometimes swam through the water. Most ranged in size from 2 cm to 7 cm in length and from 1 cm to 3 cm in width. They are considered to be index fossils because they lived over vast regions of the world during specific periods of geologic time.

The Geologic Time Scale The appearance or disappearance of types of organisms throughout Earth's history marks important occurrences in geologic time. Paleontologists have been able to divide Earth's history into time units based on the life-forms that lived only during certain periods. This division of Earth's history makes up the **geologic time scale.** However, sometimes fossils are not present, so certain divisions of the geologic time scale are based on other criteria.

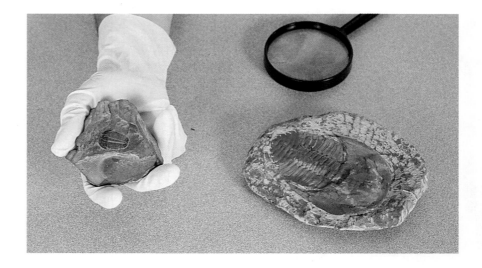

Figure 1
Many sedimentary rocks in the United States are rich in invertebrate fossils such as these trilobites.

Major Subdivisions of Geologic Time The oldest rocks on Earth contain no fossils. Then, for many millions of years after the first appearance of fossils, the fossil record remained sparse. Later in Earth's history came an explosion in the abundance and diversity of fossil organisms. These organisms created a rich fossil record. As shown in **Figure 2,** four major subdivisions of geologic time are used—eons, eras, periods, and epochs. The longest subdivisions—**eons**—are based upon the abundance of fossils.

Figure 2
Scientists have divided the geologic time scale into subunits based upon the appearance and disappearance of types of organisms.

> ☑ **Reading Check** *What are the major subdivisions of geologic time?*

Next to eons, the longest subdivisions are the **eras,** which are marked by major, striking, and worldwide changes in the types of fossils present. For example, at the end of the Mesozoic Era, many kinds of invertebrates, birds, mammals, and reptiles became extinct.

Eras are subdivided into periods. **Periods** are units of geologic time characterized by the types of life existing worldwide at the time. Periods can be divided into smaller units of time called **epochs.** Epochs also are characterized by differences in life-forms, but some of these differences can vary regionally such as from continent to continent. Epochs of the Cenozoic Era have been given specific names. Epochs of other periods usually are referred to simply as early, middle, or late. Epochs are further subdivided into units of shorter duration.

Dividing Geologic Time There is a limit to how finely geologic time can be subdivided. It depends upon the kind of rock record that is being studied. Sometimes it is possible to distinguish layers of rock that formed during a single year or season. In other cases, thick stacks of rock that have no fossils provide little information that could help in subdividing geologic time.

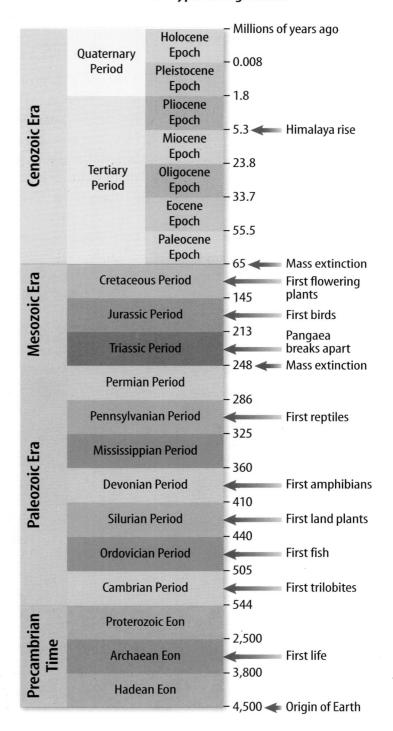

			Millions of years ago
Cenozoic Era	Quaternary Period	Holocene Epoch	
			0.008
		Pleistocene Epoch	
			1.8
	Tertiary Period	Pliocene Epoch	
			5.3 ← Himalaya rise
		Miocene Epoch	
			23.8
		Oligocene Epoch	
			33.7
		Eocene Epoch	
			55.5
		Paleocene Epoch	
			65 ← Mass extinction
Mesozoic Era	Cretaceous Period		First flowering plants
			145
	Jurassic Period		First birds
			213
	Triassic Period		Pangaea breaks apart
			248 ← Mass extinction
Paleozoic Era	Permian Period		
			286
	Pennsylvanian Period		First reptiles
			325
	Mississippian Period		
			360
	Devonian Period		First amphibians
			410
	Silurian Period		First land plants
			440
	Ordovician Period		First fish
			505
	Cambrian Period		First trilobites
			544
Precambrian Time	Proterozoic Eon		
			2,500
	Archaean Eon		First life
			3,800
	Hadean Eon		
			4,500 ← Origin of Earth

Organic Evolution

The fossil record shows that species have changed over geologic time. This change through time is known as **organic evolution**. According to most theories about organic evolution, environmental changes can affect an organism's survival. Those organisms that are not adapted to changes are less likely to survive or reproduce. Over time, the elimination of individuals that are not adapted can cause changes to species of organisms.

Species Many ways of defining the term **species** (SPEE sheez) have been proposed. Life scientists often define a **species** as a group of organisms that normally reproduces only with other members of their group. For example, dogs are a species because dogs mate and reproduce only with other dogs. In some rare cases, members of two different species, such as lions and tigers, can mate and produce offspring. These offspring, however, are usually sterile and cannot produce offspring of their own. Even though two organisms look nearly alike, if the populations they each come from do not interbreed naturally and produce offspring that can reproduce, the two individuals do not belong to the same species. **Figure 3** shows an example of two species that look similar to each other but live in different areas and do not mate naturally with each other.

Figure 3
Just because two organisms look alike does not mean that they belong to the same species.

A The coast horned lizard lives along the coast of central and southern California.

B The desert horned lizard lives in arid regions of the southwestern United States.

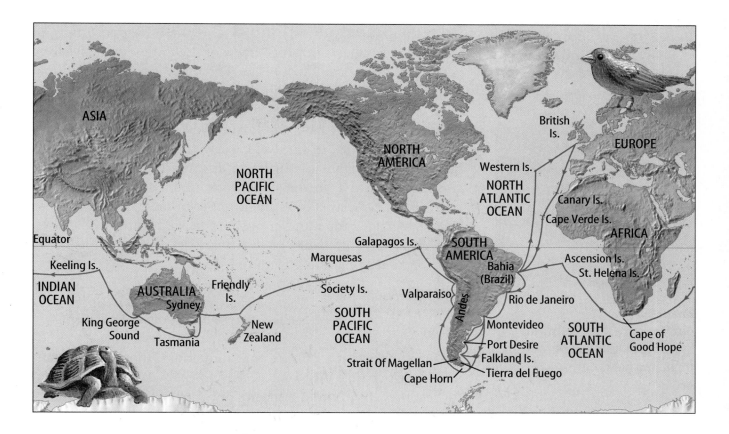

Figure 4
Charles Darwin sailed around the world between 1831 and 1836 aboard the HMS *Beagle* as a naturalist. On his journey he saw an abundance of evidence for natural selection, especially on the Galápagos Islands off the western coast of South America.

Natural Selection Charles Darwin was a naturalist who sailed around the world from 1831 to 1836 to study biology and geology. **Figure 4** shows a map of his journey. With some of the information about the plants and animals he observed on this trip in mind, he later published a book about the theory of evolution by natural selection.

In his book, he proposed that **natural selection** is a process by which organisms with characteristics that are suited to a certain environment have a better chance of surviving and reproducing than organisms that do not have these characteristics. Darwin knew that many organisms are capable of producing more offspring than can survive. This means that organisms compete with each other for resources necessary for life, such as food and living space. He also knew that individual organisms within the same species could be different, or show variations, and that these differences could help or hurt the individual organism's chance of surviving.

Some organisms that were well suited to their environment lived longer and had a better chance of producing offspring. Organisms that were poorly adapted to their environment produced few or no offspring. Because many characteristics are inherited, the characteristics of organisms that are better adapted to the environment get passed on to offspring more often. According to Darwin, this can cause a species to change over time.

Figure 5
Giraffes can eat leaves off the branches of tall trees because of their long necks.

Figure 6
Cat breeders have succeeded in producing a great variety of cats by using the principle of artificial selection.

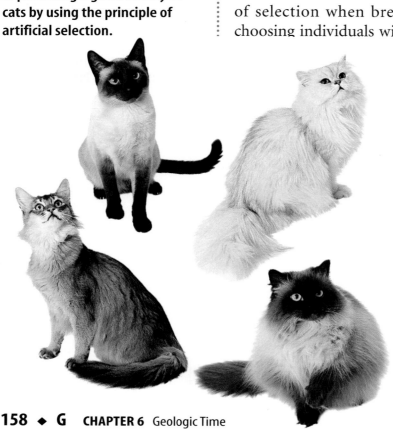

Natural Selection Within a Species Suppose that an animal species exists in which a few of the individuals have long necks, but most have short necks. The main food for the animal is the leafy foliage on trees in the area. What happens if the climate changes and the area becomes dry? The lower branches of the trees might not have any leaves. Now which of the animals will be better suited to survive? Clearly, the long-necked animals have a better chance of surviving and reproducing. Their offspring will have a greater chance of inheriting the important characteristic. Gradually, as the number of long-necked animals becomes greater, the number of short-necked animals decreases. The species might change so that nearly all of its members have long necks as the giraffe in **Figure 5** does.

☑ **Reading Check** *What might happen to the population of animals if the climate became wet again?*

It is important to notice that individual, short-necked animals didn't change into long-necked animals. A new characteristic becomes common in a species only if some members already possess that characteristic, and if the trait increases the animal's chance of survival. If no animal in the species possessed a long neck in the first place, a long-necked species could not have evolved by means of natural selection.

Artificial Selection Humans have long used the principle of selection when breeding domestic animals. By carefully choosing individuals with desired characteristics, animal breeders have created many breeds of cats, dogs, cattle, and chickens. **Figure 6** shows the great variety of cats produced by artificial selection.

The Evolution of New Species Natural selection explains how characteristics change and how new species arise. For example, if the short-necked animals migrated to a different location, they might have survived. They could have continued to reproduce in the new location, eventually developing enough different characteristics from the long-necked animals that they might not be able to breed with each other. At this point, at least one new species would have evolved.

Trilobites

Remember the trilobites? The term *trilobite* comes from the structure of the animal's hard outer skeleton or exoskeleton. The exoskeleton of a trilobite consists of three lobes that run the length of the body. As shown in **Figure 7,** the trilobite's body also has a head (cephalon), a segmented middle section (thorax), and a tail (pygidium).

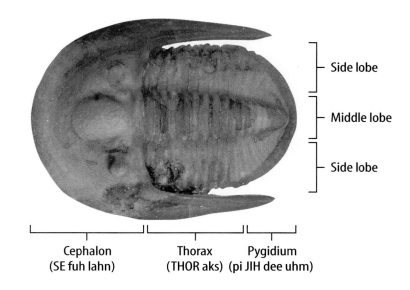

Cephalon
(SE fuh lahn)

Thorax
(THOR aks)

Pygidium
(pi JIH dee uhm)

Figure 7
The trilobite's body was divided into three lobes that run the length of the body—two side lobes and one middle lobe.

Changing Characteristics of Trilobites Trilobites inhabited Earth's oceans for more than 200 million years. Throughout the Paleozoic Era, some species of trilobites became extinct and other new species evolved. Species of trilobites that lived during one period of the Paleozoic Era showed different characteristics than species from other periods of this era. As **Figure 8** shows, paleontologists can use these different characteristics to demonstrate changes in trilobites through geologic time. These changes can tell you about how different trilobites from different periods lived and responded to changes in their environments.

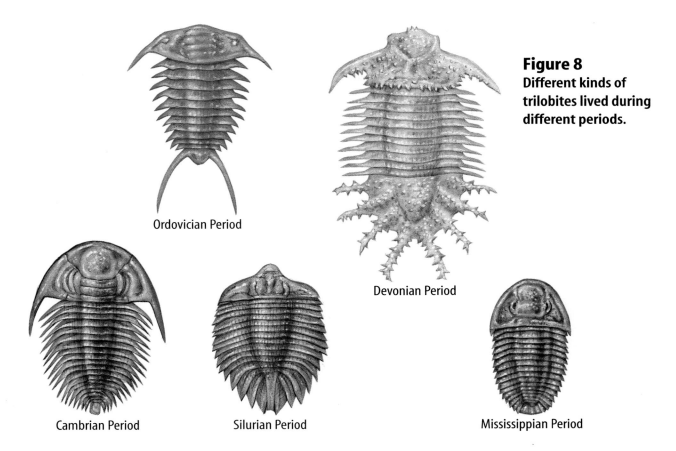

Ordovician Period

Devonian Period

Cambrian Period

Silurian Period

Mississippian Period

Figure 8
Different kinds of trilobites lived during different periods.

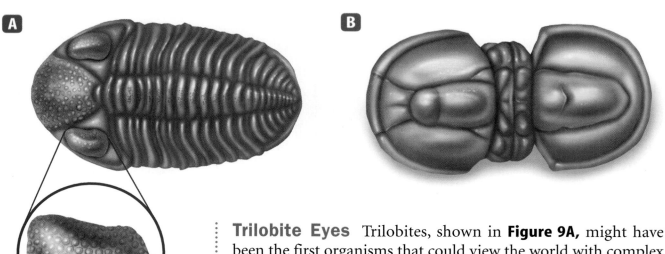

A

B

Figure 9
Trilobites had many different types of eyes. **A** Some had eyes that contained hundreds of small circular lenses, somewhat like an insect. **B** This blind trilobite had no eyes.

Figure 10
Olenellus is one of the most primitive trilobite species.

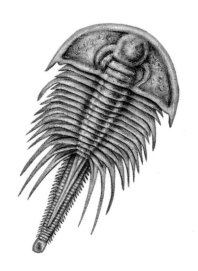

Trilobite Eyes Trilobites, shown in **Figure 9A,** might have been the first organisms that could view the world with complex eyes. Trilobite eyes show the result of natural selection. The position of the eyes on an organism gives clues about where it must have lived. Eyes that are located toward the front of the head indicate an organism that was adapted for active swimming. If the eyes are located toward the back of the head, the organism could have been a bottom dweller. In most species of trilobites, the eyes were located midway on the head—a compromise for an organism that was adapted for crawling on the seafloor and swimming in the water.

Over time, the eyes in trilobites changed. In many trilobite species, the eyes became progressively smaller until they completely disappeared. Blind trilobites, such as the one shown in **Figure 9B,** might have burrowed into sediments on the seafloor or lived deeper than light could penetrate. In other species, however, the eyes became more complex. One kind of trilobite, *Aeglina,* developed large compound eyes that had numerous individual lenses. Some trilobites developed stalks that held the eyes upward. Where would this be useful?

Trilobite Bodies The trilobite body and tail also underwent significant changes in form through time, as you can see in **Figure 8.** A special case is *Olenellus,* shown in **Figure 10.** This trilobite, which lived during the Early Cambrian Period, had an extremely segmented body—perhaps more so than any other known species of trilobite. It is thought that *Olenellus,* and other species that have so many body segments, are primitive trilobites.

Fossils Show Changes Trilobite exoskeletons changed as trilobites adapted to changing environments. Species that could not adapt became extinct. What processes on Earth caused environments to change so drastically that species adapted or became extinct?

Plate Tectonics and Earth History

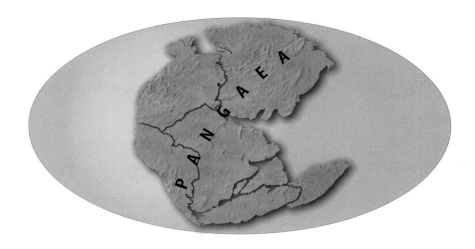

Plate tectonics is one possible answer to the riddle of trilobite extinction. Earth's moving plates caused continents to collide and separate many times. Continental collisions formed mountains and closed seas. Continental separations created wider, deeper seas between continents. By the end of the Paleozoic Era, sea levels had dropped and the continents had come together to form one giant landmass, the supercontinent **Pangaea** (pan JEE uh). Because trilobites lived in the oceans, their environment was changed or destroyed. **Figure 11** shows the arrangement of continents at the end of the Paleozoic Era. What effect might these changes have had on the trilobite populations?

Not all scientists accept the above explanation for the extinctions at the end of the Paleozoic Era, and other possibilities—such as climate change—have been proposed. As in all scientific debates, you must consider the evidence carefully and come to conclusions based on the evidence.

Figure 11
The amount of shallow water environment was reduced when Pangaea formed. *How do you think this change affected organisms that lived along the coasts of continents?*

Section 1 Assessment

1. Discuss how fossils relate to the geologic time scale.

2. How might plate tectonics affect species of organisms?

3. Relate trilobite eye type to lifestyle type.

4. Why can paleontologists use some trilobite fossils as index fossils for the Cambrian Period and other trilobite fossils as index fossils for other geologic time periods?

5. **Think Critically** Aside from moving continents, what other factors could cause an organism's environment to change? What effects could changing environments have on species?

Skill Builder Activities

6. **Recognizing Cause and Effect** Answer the questions below. **For more help, refer to the** Science Skill Handbook.
   a. How does natural selection cause evolutionary change to take place?
   b. How could the evolution of a characteristic within one species affect the evolution of a characteristic within another species? Give an example.

7. **Communicating** Write a short poem in your Science Journal that describes a day in the life of a trilobite. **For more help, refer to the** Science Skill Handbook.

2 Early Earth History

Figure 12
During the early Precambrian, Earth was a lifeless planet with many volcanoes.

Precambrian Time

Can you imagine a barren Earth with only rock and sea, as shown in **Figure 12?** This seems strange, but it's probably an accurate picture of Earth's first billion years. Over the next 3 billion years, simple life-forms began to colonize the oceans.

Look again at the geologic time scale shown in **Figure 2. Precambrian** (pree KAM bree un) **time** is the longest part of Earth's history and includes the Hadean, Archean, and Proterozoic Eons. Precambrian time lasted from about 4.5 billion years ago to about 544 million years ago. The oldest rocks that have been found on Earth are about 4 billion years old. However, rocks older than about 3.5 billion years are rare. This probably is due to remelting and erosion. Although the Precambrian was the longest interval of geologic time, relatively little is known about the organisms that lived during this time.

Why is the fossil record from Precambrian time so sparse? One reason is that many Precambrian rocks have been so deeply buried that they have been changed by heat and pressure. Many fossils can't withstand these conditions. In addition, most Precambrian organisms didn't have hard parts that otherwise would have increased their chances to be preserved as fossils.

Lava flow

Lava flow

Ash

Ash deposits

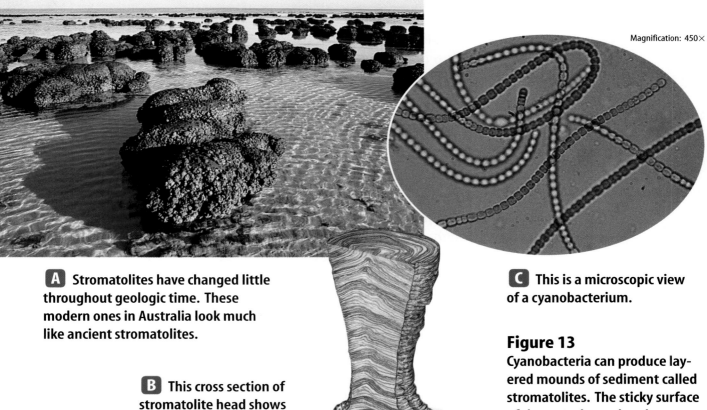

A Stromatolites have changed little throughout geologic time. These modern ones in Australia look much like ancient stromatolites.

B This cross section of stromatolite head shows their layered appearance.

C This is a microscopic view of a cyanobacterium.

Figure 13
Cyanobacteria can produce layered mounds of sediment called stromatolites. The sticky surface of the cyanobacteria colony traps grains of sediment. The surface of the sediment then becomes colonized with cyanobacteria again, and the cycle repeats, producing the layers inside the stromatolite.

Early Life Many studies of the early history of life involve ancient stromatolites (stroh MAT oh lytes). **Figure 13** shows stromatolites, which are layered mats formed by cyanobacteria colonies. **Cyanobacteria** are blue-green algae thought to be one of the earliest forms of life on Earth. Cyanobacteria first appeared about 3.5 billion years ago. They contained chlorophyll and photosynthesized. This is important because during photosynthesis, they produced oxygen, which helped change Earth's atmosphere. For the few billion years following the appearance of cyanobacteria, oxygen became a major atmospheric gas. Also of importance was that the ozone layer in the atmosphere began to develop, shielding Earth from ultraviolet rays. It is hypothesized that these changes allowed species of single-celled organisms to evolve into more complex organisms.

Reading Check *What atmospheric gas is produced by photosynthesis?*

Animals without backbones, called invertebrates (in VURT uh brayts), appeared toward the end of Precambrian time. A few imprints of jellyfish and marine worms have been found in late Precambrian rocks, but because these early invertebrates were soft bodied, they weren't often preserved as fossils. Because of this, many Precambrian fossils are trace fossils.

Chemistry
INTEGRATION

Cyanobacteria are thought to have been one of the mechanisms by which Earth's early atmosphere became richer in oxygen. Research the composition of Earth's early atmosphere and where these gases probably came from. Record your findings in your Science Journal.

Dating Rock Layers with Fossils

Procedure

1. Draw three rock layers.
2. Number the layers 1 to 3, bottom to top.
3. Layer 1 contains fossil A. Layer 2 contains fossils A and B. Layer 3 contains fossil C.
4. Fossil A lived from the Cambrian through the Ordovician. Fossil B lived from the Ordovician through the Silurian. Fossil C lived in the Silurian and Devonian.

Analysis

1. Which layers were you able to date to a specific period?
2. Why isn't it possible to determine during which specific period the other layers formed?

Figure 14

This giant predatory fish lived in North America during the Devonian Period. It grew to about 6 m in length.

Unusual Life-Forms Living late in Precambrian time was a group of animals with shapes similar to modern jellyfish, worms, and soft corals. Fossils of these organisms were first found in the Ediacara Hills in southern Australia. This group of organisms has become known as the Ediacaran (eed ee uh KAR un) fauna. **Figure 15** shows some of these organisms.

✔ **Reading Check** *What modern organisms do some Ediacaran organisms resemble?*

Ediacaran animals were bottom dwellers and might have had tough outer coverings like air mattresses. Trilobites and other invertebrates might have outcompeted the Ediacarans and caused them to become extinct, but nobody knows for sure why these creatures disappeared.

The Paleozoic Era

As you have learned, fossils are unlikely to form if organisms have only soft parts. An abundance of organisms with hard parts, such as shells, marks the beginning of the Paleozoic (pay lee uh ZOH ihk) Era. The **Paleozoic Era,** or era of ancient life, began about 544 million years ago and ended about 248 million years ago. Traces of life are much easier to find in Paleozoic rocks than in Precambrian rocks.

Paleozoic Life Warm, shallow seas covered large parts of the continents during much of the Paleozoic Era, so many of the life-forms scientists know about were marine, meaning they lived in the ocean. Trilobites were common, especially early in the Paleozoic. Other organisms developed shells that were easily preserved as fossils. Therefore, the fossil record of this era contains abundant shells. However, invertebrates were not the only animals to live in the shallow, Paleozoic seas.

Vertebrates, or animals with backbones, also evolved during this era. The first vertebrates were fishlike creatures without jaws. Armoured fish with jaws such as the one shown in **Figure 14** lived during the Devonian Period. Some of these fish were so huge that they could eat large sharks with their powerful jaws. By the Devonian Period, forests had appeared, and vertebrates began to adapt to land environments, as well.

Figure 15

A variety of 600-million-year-old fossils—known as Ediacaran (eed ee uh KAR un) fauna—have been found on every continent except Antarctica. These unusual organisms were originally thought to be descendants of early animals such as jellyfish, worms, and coral. Today, paleontologists debate whether these organisms were part of the animal kingdom or belonged to an entirely new kingdom whose members became extinct about 545 million years ago.

DICKENSONIA (dihk un suh NEE uh) Impressions of *Dickensonia,* a bottom-dwelling wormlike creature, have been discovered. Some are nearly one meter long.

RANGEA (rayn JEE uh) As it lay rooted in sea-bottom sediments, *Rangea* may have snagged tiny bits of food by filtering water through its body.

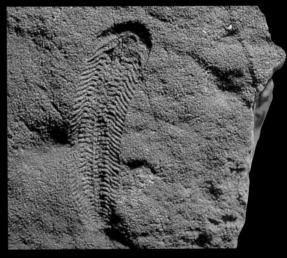

SPRIGGINA (sprih GIHN uh) Some scientists hypothesize that the four-centimeter-long *Spriggina* was a type of crawling, segmented organism. Others suggest that it sat upright while attached to the sea floor.

CYCLOMEDUSA (si kloh muh DEW suh) Although it looks a lot like a jellyfish, *Cyclomedusa* may have had more in common with modern sea anemones. Some paleontologists, however, hypothesize that it is unrelated to any living organism.

Life on Land Based on their structure, paleontologists know that many ancient fish had lungs as well as gills. Lungs enabled these fish to live in water with low oxygen levels—when needed they could swim to the surface and breathe air. Today's lungfish also can get oxygen from the water through gills and from the air through lungs.

One kind of ancient fish had lungs and leglike fins, which were used to swim and crawl around on the bottom. Paleontologists hypothesize that amphibians might have evolved from this kind of fish, shown in **Figure 16.** The characteristics that helped animals survive in oxygen-poor waters also made living on land possible. Today, amphibians live in a variety of habitats in water and on land. They all have at least one thing in common, though. They must lay their eggs in water or moist places.

Figure 16
Amphibians probably evolved from fish like *Panderichthys* (pan dur IHK theez), which had leglike fins and lungs.

 **Reading Check** *What are some characteristics of the fish from which amphibians might have evolved?*

By the Pennsylvanian Period, some amphibians evolved an egg with a membrane that protected it from drying out. Because of this, these animals, called reptiles, no longer needed to lay eggs in water. Reptiles also have skin with hard scales that prevent loss of body fluids. This adaptation enables them to survive farther from water and in relatively dry climates, as shown in **Figure 17,** where many amphibians cannot live.

Figure 17
Reptiles have scaly skins that allow them to live in dry places.

Figure 18
The Appalachian Mountains formed in several steps.

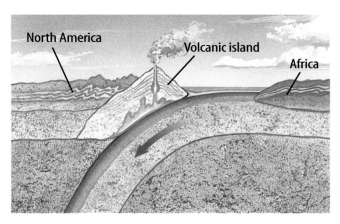

A More than 375 million years ago, volcanic island chains formed in the ocean and were pushed against the coast as Africa moved toward North America.

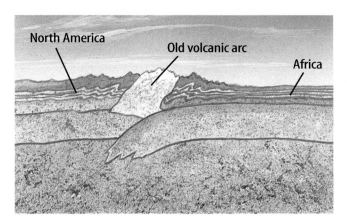

B About 375 million years ago, the African plate collided with the North American plate, forming mountains on both continents.

C About 200 million years ago, the Atlantic Ocean opened up, separating the two continents.

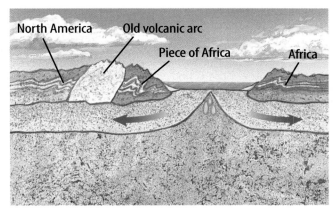

Mountain Building Several mountain-building episodes occurred during the Paleozoic Era. The Appalachian Mountains, for example, formed during this time. This happened in several stages, as shown in **Figure 18.** The first mountain-building episode occurred as the ocean separating North America from Europe and Africa closed. Several volcanic island chains that had formed in the ocean collided with the North American Plate, as shown in **Figure 18A.** The collision of the island chains generated high mountains.

The next mountain-building episode was a result of the African Plate colliding with the North American Plate, as shown in **Figure 18B.** When Africa and North America collided, rock layers were folded and faulted. Some rocks originally deposited near the eastern coast of the North American Plate were pushed along faults as much as 65 km westward by the collision. Sediments were uplifted to form an immense mountain belt, part of which still remains today.

Figure 19
Hyoliths were organisms that became extinct at the end of the Paleozoic Era.

End of an Era At the end of the Paleozoic Era, as many as 85 percent of all marine species and 70 percent of all land species died off. **Figure 19** shows one such animal. The cause of these extinctions might have been changes in climate and a lowering of sea level.

Near the end of the Permian Period, all of the continental plates came together and formed Pangaea, and glaciers formed over most of its southern part. The slow, gradual collision of continental plates caused mountain building. Mountain-building processes caused seas to close and deserts to spread over North America and Europe. Many species, especially marine organisms, couldn't adapt to these changes, so they became extinct.

Other Hypotheses Other explanations also have been proposed for this mass extinction. During the late Paleozoic Era, volcanoes were extremely active. If the volcanic activity was great enough, it could have affected the entire globe. Another recent theory is similar to the one proposed to explain the extinction of dinosaurs. Perhaps a large asteroid or comet collided with Earth some 248 million years ago. This event could have caused widespread extinctions just as many paleontologists suggest happened at the end of the Mesozoic Era, 65 million years ago. Perhaps the extinction at the end of the Paleozoic Era was caused by several or all of these events happening at about the same time.

Section 2 Assessment

1. What geologic events occurred at the end of the Paleozoic Era?
2. How might geologic events at the end of the Paleozoic Era have caused extinctions?
3. What advance allowed reptiles to reproduce away from water? Why was this an advantage?
4. What major change in life-forms occurred at the end of Precambrian time?
5. **Think Critically** How, and through what process, did cyanobacteria contribute to the evolution of complex life on land? Do you think cyanobacteria are as significant to this process today as they were during Precambrian time?

Skill Builder Activities

6. **Making and Using Tables** Use **Figure 2** to answer these questions. **For more help, refer to the** Science Skill Handbook.
   a. When did the Paleozoic Era begin?
   b. How long did the Silurian Period last?
   c. When did vertebrates invade dry land?

7. **Using a Database** Research trilobites in a geology book or computer database. Write a paragraph in your Science Journal describing these organisms and their habitat. Include hand-drawn illustrations and compare them with the illustrations in the computer database on geology. **For more help, refer to the** Technology Skill Handbook.

Activity

Changing Species

In this activity, you will observe how adaptation within a species might cause the evolution of a particular trait, leading to the development of a new species.

What You'll Investigate
How might adaptation within a species cause the evolution of a particular trait?

Materials
Deck of playing cards

Goals
- **Model** adaptation within a species.

Procedure

1. **Remove** all of the kings, queens, jacks, and aces from a deck of playing cards.

2. Each remaining card represents an individual in a population of animals called "varimals." The number on each card represents the height of the individual. For example, the 5 of diamonds is a varimal that's 5 units tall.

3. **Calculate** the average height of the population of varimals represented by your cards.

4. Suppose varimals eat grass, shrubs, and leaves from trees. A drought causes many of these plants to die. All that's left are a few tall trees. Only varimals at least 6 units tall can reach the leaves on these trees.

5. All the varimals under 6 units leave the area to seek food elsewhere or die from starvation. Discard all of the cards with a number value less than 6. Calculate the new average height of the population of varimals.

6. Shuffle the deck of remaining cards.

7. **Draw** two cards at a time. Each pair represents a pair of varimals that will mate.

8. The offspring of each pair reaches a height equal to the average height of his or her parents. Calculate and record the height of each offspring.

9. Repeat by discarding all parents and offspring under 8 units tall. Now calculate the new average height of varimals. Include both the parents and offspring in your calculation.

Conclude and Apply

1. How did the height of the population change?

2. If you hadn't discarded the shortest varimals, would the average height of the population have changed as much? **Explain.**

3. Why didn't every member of the original population reproduce?

4. If there had been no varimals over 6 units tall in step 5, what would have happened to the population?

5. If there had been no variation in height in the population before the droughts occurred, would the species have been able to evolve into a taller species? **Explain.**

6. How does this activity demonstrate that traits evolve in species?

Middle and Recent Earth History

The Mesozoic Era

Dinosaurs have captured people's imaginations since their bones first were unearthed more than 150 years ago. Dinosaurs and other interesting animals lived during the Mesozoic Era, which was between 248 and 65 million years ago. The Mesozoic Era also was marked by rapid movement of Earth's continents.

The Breakup of Pangaea The **Mesozoic** (meh zuh ZOH ihk) **Era,** or era of middle life, was a time of many changes on Earth. At the beginning of the Mesozoic Era, all continents were joined as a single landmass called Pangaea, as shown in **Figure 11.**

Pangaea separated into two large landmasses during the Triassic Period, as shown in **Figure 20.** The northern mass was Laurasia (law RAY zhuh), and Gondwanaland (gahn DWAH nuh land) was the southern landmass. As the Mesozoic Era continued, Laurasia and Gondwanaland broke apart and eventually formed the present-day continents.

Species adapted to the new environments survived the mass extinction at the end of the Paleozoic Era. Recall that a reptile's skin helps it retain bodily fluids. This characteristic, along with their shelled eggs, enabled reptiles to adapt readily to the drier climate of the Mesozoic Era. Reptiles became the most conspicuous animals on land by the Triassic Period.

Figure 20
The supercontinent Pangaea formed at the end of the Paleozoic Era. At the end of the Triassic Period, it began to break up into the northern supercontinent, Laurasia, and the southern supercontinent, Gondwanaland.

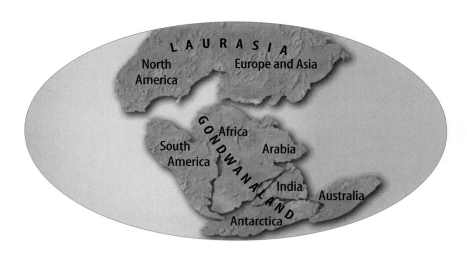

Dinosaurs What were the dinosaurs like? Dinosaurs ranged in height from less than 1 m to enormous creatures like *Apatosaurus* and *Tyrannosaurus*. The first small dinosaurs appeared during the Triassic Period. Larger species appeared during the Jurassic and Cretaceous Periods. Throughout the Mesozoic Era, new species of dinosaurs evolved and other species became extinct.

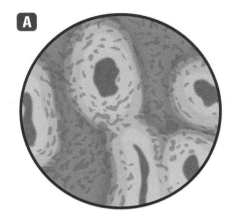
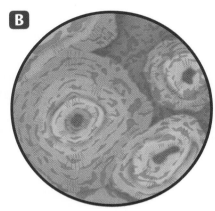

Dinosaurs Were Active Studying fossil footprints sometimes allows paleontologists to calculate how fast animals walked or ran. Some dinosaur tracks that have been found indicate that these animals were much faster runners than you might think. *Gallimimus* was 4 m long and could reach speeds of 65 km/h—as fast as a modern race horse.

Some studies also indicate that dinosaurs might have been warm blooded, not cold blooded like present-day reptiles. The evidence that leads to this conclusion has to do with their bone structure. Slices through some cold blooded animal bones show rings similar to growth rings in trees. The bones of some dinosaurs don't show this ring structure. Instead, they are similar to bones found in modern mammals, as you can see in **Figure 21.**

Figure 21
Some dinosaur bones show structural features that are like mammal bones, leading some paleontologists to think that dinosaurs were warm blooded like mammals. **A** This shows the structure of a dinosaur bone. **B** This shows the structure of a mammal bone.

✔ **Reading Check** *Why do some paleontologists think that dinosaurs were warm blooded?*

These observations indicate that some dinosaurs might have been warm-blooded, fast-moving animals somewhat like present-day mammals and birds. They might have been quite different from present-day reptiles.

Good Mother Dinosaurs The fossil record also indicates that some dinosaurs nurtured their young and traveled in herds in which the adults surrounded their young.

One such dinosaur is *Maiasaura*. This dinosaur built nests in which it laid its eggs and raised its offspring. Nests have been found in relatively close clusters, indicating that more than one family of dinosaurs built in the same area. Some fossils of hatchlings have been found near adult animals, leading paleontologists to think that some dinosaurs nurtured their young. In fact, *Maiasaura* hatchlings might have stayed in the nest while they grew in length from about 35 cm to more than 1 m.

SCIENCE *Online*

Research Visit the Glencoe Science Web site at **science.glencoe.com** for more information about dinosaurs. Communicate to your class what you learn.

Figure 22
Birds might have evolved from dinosaurs.

A *Bambiraptor feinberger* is a 75-million-year-old member of a family of meat-eating dinosaurs thought by some paleontologists to be closely related to birds.

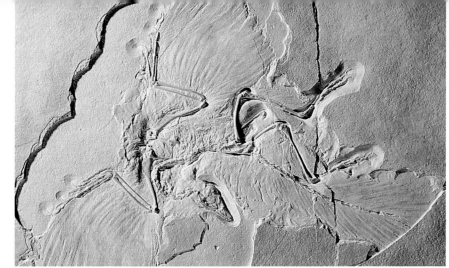

B Considered one of the world's most priceless fossils, *Archaeopteryx* was first found in a limestone quarry in Germany in 1861.

Birds Birds appeared during the Jurassic Period. Some paleontologists think that birds evolved from small, meat-eating dinosaurs much like *Bambiraptor feinberger* in **Figure 22A.** The earliest bird, *Archaeopteryx*, shown in **Figure 22B,** had wings and feathers. However, because *Archaeopteryx* had features not shared with modern birds, scientists know it was not a direct ancestor of today's birds.

Mammals Mammals first appeared in the Triassic Period. The earliest mammals were small, mouselike creatures, as shown in **Figure 23.** Mammals are warm-blooded vertebrates that have hair or fur covering their bodies. The females produce milk to feed their young. These two characteristics have enabled mammals to survive in many changing environments.

Gymnosperms During most of the Mesozoic Era, gymnosperms (JIHM nuh spurmz), which first appeared in the Paleozoic Era, dominated the land. Gymnosperms are plants that produce seeds but not flowers. Many gymnosperms are still around today. These include pines and ginkgo trees.

Figure 23
The earliest mammals were small creatures that resembled today's mice and shrews.

Angiosperms Angiosperms (AN jee uh spurmz), or flowering plants, first evolved during the Cretaceous Period. Angiosperms produce seeds with hard outer coverings.

Because their seeds are enclosed and protected, angiosperms can live in many environments. Angiosperms are the most diverse and abundant land plants today. Present-day angiosperms that evolved during the Mesozoic Era include magnolia and oak trees.

End of an Era The Mesozoic Era ended about 65 million years ago with a major extinction of land and marine species. Many groups of animals, including the dinosaurs, disappeared suddenly at this time. Many paleontologists hypothesize that a comet or asteroid collided with Earth, causing a huge cloud of dust and smoke to rise into the atmosphere, blocking out the Sun. Without sunlight the plants died, and all the animals that depended on these plants also died. Not everything died, however. All the organisms that you see around you today are descendants of the survivors of the great extinction at the end of the Mesozoic Era.

Math Skills Activity

Calculating Extinction Using Percentages

Example Problem

At the end of the Cretaceous Period, large numbers of animals became extinct. Scientists still are trying to understand why some types of animals survived while others died. Looking at animals such as amphibians, reptiles, and mammals that lived during the Cretaceous Period, can you determine what percentage of amphibians died during the extinction?

Solution

1 *This is what you know:*

Animal Extinctions		
Animal Type	**Groups Living Before Extinction Event (n)**	**Groups Left After Extinction Event (t)**
Amphibians	12	4
Reptiles	63	30
Mammals	24	8

2 *This is what you need to find out:* p = the percentage of amphibian groups that died during the Cretaceous extinction

3 *This is the equation you need to use:* $p = t / n \times 100$

Both t and n are shown on the above chart.

Check your answer by multiplying n *by the percentage you calculated, divide by 100, and you should get a number close to* t.

Practice Problem

Using the same equation, calculate the percentage of reptiles and then the percentage of mammals that died. Which group lost the greatest percentage of animals?

For more help, refer to the Math Skill Handbook.

Calculating the Age of the Atlantic Ocean

Procedure

1. On a **world map** or **globe**, measure the distance in kilometers between a point on the east coast of South America and a point on the west coast of Africa.
2. Measure in SI several times and take the average of your results.
3. Assuming that Africa has been moving away from South America at a rate of 3.5 cm per year, calculate how many years it took to create the Atlantic Ocean.

Analysis

1. Did the values used to obtain your average value vary much?
2. How close did your age come to the accepted estimate for the beginning of the breakup of Pangaea in the Triassic Period?

The Cenozoic Era

The **Cenozoic** (sen uh ZOH ihk) **Era,** or era of recent life, began about 65 million years ago and continues today. Many mountain ranges in North and South America and Europe began to form in the Cenozoic Era. In the late Cenozoic, the climate became much cooler and ice ages occurred. The Cenozoic Era is subdivided into two periods. The first of these is the Tertiary Period. The present-day period is the Quaternary Period. It began about 1.8 million years ago.

✔ **Reading Check** *What happened to the climate during the late Cenozoic Era?*

Times of Mountain Building Many mountain ranges formed during the Cenozoic Era. These include the Alps in Europe and the Andes in South America. The Himalaya, shown in **Figure 24,** formed as India moved northward and collided with Asia. The collision crumpled and thickened Earth's crust, raising the highest mountains presently on Earth. Many people think the growth of these mountains has helped create cooler climates worldwide.

A

B

Figure 24

A The Himalaya extend along the India-Tibet border and contain some of the world's tallest mountains. **B** India drifted north and finally collided with Asia, forming the Himalaya.

Further Evolution of Mammals

Throughout much of the Cenozoic Era, expanding grasslands favored grazing plant eaters like horses, camels, deer, and some elephants. Many kinds of mammals became larger. Horses evolved from small, multi-toed animals into the large, hoofed animals of today. However, not all mammals remained on land. Ancestors of the present-day whales and dolphins evolved to make their lives in the sea.

As Australia and South America separated from Antarctica during the continuing breakup of the continents, many species became isolated. They evolved separately from life-forms in other parts of the world. Evidence of this can be seen today in Australia's marsupials. Marsupials are mammals such as kangaroos, koalas, and wombats (shown in **Figure 25**) that carry their young in a pouch.

Your species, *Homo sapiens,* probably appeared about 140,000 years ago. Some people suggest that the appearance of humans could have led to the extinction of many other mammals. As their numbers grew, humans competed for food that other animals relied upon. Also, fossil bones and other evidence indicate that early humans were hunters.

Figure 25
The wombat is one of many Australian marsupials. As a result of human activities, the number and range of wombats have diminished.

Section 3 Assessment

1. In which era, period, and epoch did *Homo sapiens* first appear?

2. Did mammals become more or less abundant after the extinction of the dinosaurs? Explain why.

3. How did the development of seeds with a hard outer covering enable angiosperms to survive in a wide variety of climates?

4. Give two reasons why some paleontologists hypothesize that dinosaurs were warm-blooded animals.

5. **Think Critically** How could two species that evolved on separate continents have many similarities?

Skill Builder Activities

6. **Researching Information** Arrange these organisms in sequence according to when they first appeared on Earth: *mammals, reptiles, dinosaurs, fish, angiosperms, birds, insects, amphibians, land plants,* and *bacteria.* **For more help, refer to the** Science Skill Handbook.

7. **Converting Units** A fossil mosasaur, a giant marine reptile, measured 9 m in lenth and had a skull that measured 45 cm in length. What fraction of the mosasaur's total length did the skull account for? Compare your length with the mosasaur's length. **For more help, refer to the** Math Skill Handbook.

Discovering the Past

I magine what your state was like millions of years ago. What animals might have been roaming around the spot where you now sit? Can you picture a Tyrannosaurus rex roaming the area that is now your school? The animals and plants that once inhabited your region might have left some clues to their identity—fossils. Scientists use fossils to piece together what Earth looked like in the geologic past. Fossils can help determine whether an area used to be dry land or was underwater. Fossils can help uncover clues about how plants and animals have evolved over the course of time. Using the resources of the Internet and by sharing data with your peers, you can start to discover how North America has changed through time.

Recognize the Problem

How has your area changed over geologic time?

Form a Hypothesis

How might the area where you are now living have looked thousands or millions of years ago? Do you think that the types of animals and plants have changed much over time? Form a hypothesis concerning the change in organisms and geography from long ago to the present day in your area.

Goals
■ **Gather** information about fossils found in your area.
■ **Communicate** details about fossils found in your area.
■ **Synthesize** information from sources about the fossil record and the changes in your area over time.

SCIENCE *Online* Go to the Glencoe Science Web site at **science.glencoe.com** to get more information about fossils and changes over geologic time and for data collected by other students.

Fossils in Your Area					
Fossil Name	Plant or Animal Fossil	Age of Fossils	Details About Plant or Animal Fossil	Location of Fossil	Additional Information

Test Your Hypothesis

Plan

1. **Determine** the age of the rocks that make up your area. Were they formed during Precambrian time, the Paleozoic Era, the Mesozoic Era, or the Cenozoic Era?

2. Gather information about the fossil plants and animals found in your area during one of the above geologic time intervals. Find specific information on when, where and how the fossil organisms lived. If no fossils are known from your area, find out information about the fossils found nearest your area.

Do

1. Make sure your teacher approves your plan before you start.

2. Go to the Glencoe Science Web site at **science.glencoe.com** to post your data in the table. Add any additional information you think is important to understanding the fossils found in your area.

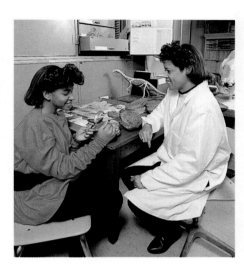

Analyze Your Data

1. What present-day relatives of prehistoric animals or plants exist in your area?

2. How have the organisms in your area changed over time? Is your hypothesis supported? Why or why not?

3. What other information did you discover about your area's climate or environment from the geologic time period you investigated?

Draw Conclusions

1. Find this *Use the Internet* activity on the Glencoe Science Web site at **science.glencoe.com.** Compare your data to those of other students. Study other students' data to compare information about the geologic time periods and fossils that you investigated. Review data that other students have entered about fossils they have researched.

2. **Describe** the plant and animal fossils that have been discovered in your area. What clues did you discover about the environment of your fossil organisms? How do these compare to the environment of your area today?

3. **Infer** from the fossil organisms found in your area what the geography and climate were like during the geologic time period you chose.

Science Stats

Extinct!

Did you know...

...In 1865, when Lewis Carroll

wrote about the dodo in his famous book *Alice in Wonderland*, the bird had been gone for almost two hundred years from the island of Mauritius in the Indian Ocean. First seen by European settlers in 1598, the dodo was hunted for food. The birds were extinct by 1681.

...The earliest known gliding reptile

had "wings" with a span of 30 cm that were wide flaps of flesh not attached to its limbs. From fossils found in Madagascar, scientists believe that the *Coelurosauravus* (see lor oh SOR uh vuhs) lived between 260 and 246 million years ago.

Coelurosauravus

Saber-toothed cat

...The saber-toothed cat lived

in the Americas from about 1.6 million to 8,000 years ago. Smilodon, the best-known saber-toothed cat, was among the most ferocious carnivores. It had large canine teeth, about 15 cm long, which it used to pierce the flesh of its prey.

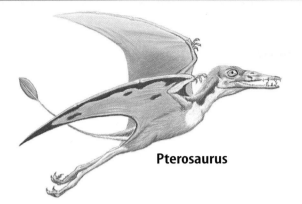

...The first vertebrates to fly were reptiles called pterosaurs (TER uh sawrz). The front limbs of these reptiles developed into wings during the Triassic Period. Their wingspans ranged from 1.8 m to more than 12 m. Some pterosaurs were fish eaters, flying low over water to catch fish with their narrow jaws.

Pterosaurus

Great Mass Extinctions of Species

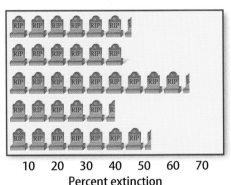

Woolly mammoth

...The woolly mammoth lived in the cold tundra regions during the Ice Age. It looked rather like an elephant with long hair, weighed between 5,300 kg and 7,300 kg, and was between 3 m and 4 m tall.

Do the Math

1. If 75 species of organisms become extinct each day, how many would become extinct during a leap year?
2. How many years did it take from the first sighting of the dodo bird by humans until it became extinct?
3. What is the range between the smallest and largest wingspans among pterosaurs?

Go Further

Use the Glencoe Science Web site at **science.glencoe.com** to research extinct animals, fish, birds, plants, and other life-forms. Trace the origins of each of the species and learn how long its kind existed on Earth.

Reviewing Main Ideas

Section 1 Life and Geologic Time

1. Geologic time is divided into eons, eras, periods, and epochs.

2. Divisions within the geologic time scale are based largely on major evolutionary changes in organisms.

3. Plate movements cause changes that affect organic evolution. *How can the building of mountains like those shown here affect the evolution of species?*

Section 2 Early Earth History

1. Cyanobacteria were an early form of life that evolved during Precambrian time. Trilobites, fish, and corals were abundant during the Paleozoic Era.

2. Plants and animals began to move onto land during the middle of the Paleozoic Era. Land plants and animals then evolved rapidly and colonized the land.

3. The Paleozoic Era was a time of mountain building. The Appalachian Mountains formed when several islands and finally Africa collided with North America.

4. At the end of the Paleozoic Era, many marine invertebrates became extinct. *What kind of marine organism is shown here?*

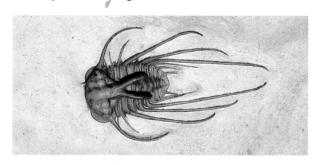

Section 3 Middle and Recent Earth History

1. Reptiles and gymnosperms were dominant land life-forms in the Mesozoic Era. Mammals and angiosperms began to dominate the land in the Cenozoic Era.

2. Pangaea broke apart during the Mesozoic Era. Many mountain ranges formed during the Cenozoic.

3. *Homo sapiens* appeared during the Pleistocene Epoch. *How might Homo sapiens have contributed to the extinction of animals like the one shown here?*

FOLDABLES
Reading & Study Skills

After You Read

To help you review geological time, use the Organizational Study Fold you made at the beginning of the chapter.

Visualizing Main Ideas

Complete the concept map on geologic time using the following choices: Cenozoic, Trilobites in oceans, mammals common, Paleozoic, Dinosaurs roam Earth, and Abundant gymnosperms.

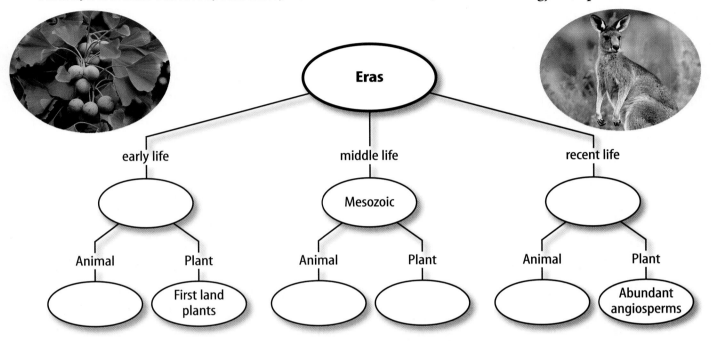

Vocabulary Review

Vocabulary Words

a. Cenozoic Era
b. cyanobacteria
c. eon
d. epoch
e. era
f. geologic time scale
g. Mesozoic Era
h. natural selection
i. organic evolution
j. Paleozoic Era
k. Pangaea
l. period
m. Precambrian time
n. species
o. trilobite

Study Tip

Outline the chapters to make sure that you're understanding the key ideas. Writing down the main points of the chapter will help you remember important details and understand larger themes.

Using Vocabulary

The sentences below include vocabulary words that have been used incorrectly. Change the incorrect word so that the sentence reads correctly.

1. A change in the hereditary features of a species over a long period is extinction.

2. A record of events in Earth history is natural selection.

3. The largest subdivision of geologic time is the period.

4. The process by which the best-suited individuals survive in their environment is organic evolution.

5. A group of individuals that normally breed only among themselves is an epoch.

Chapter 6 Assessment

Checking Concepts

Choose the word or phrase that best completes the sentence.

1. How many millions of years ago did the era in which you live begin?
   A) 650
   C) 1.6
   B) 245
   D) 65

2. What is the process by which better-suited organisms survive and reproduce?
   A) endangerment
   C) gymnosperm
   B) extinction
   D) natural selection

3. What is the next smaller division of geologic time after the era?
   A) period
   C) epoch
   B) stage
   D) eon

4. When did the most recent ice age occur?
   A) Pennsylvanian
   C) Tertiary
   B) Triassic
   D) Quaternary

5. What was one of the earliest forms of life on Earth?
   A) gymnosperm
   C) angiosperm
   B) cyanobacterium
   D) dinosaur

6. Which group of organisms evolved from the same ancestors as amphibians?
   A) reptiles
   C) angiosperms
   B) lungfish
   D) gymnosperms

7. During which era did the dinosaurs live?
   A) Mesozoic
   C) Miocene
   B) Paleozoic
   D) Cenozoic

8. Which type of plant has seeds without protective coverings?
   A) angiosperms
   C) gymnosperms
   B) flowering plants
   D) magnolias

9. Which group of plants evolved during the Mesozoic Era and is the dominant plant group today?
   A) gymnosperms
   C) ginkgoes
   B) angiosperms
   D) algae

10. When did the Ediacaran animals live?
    A) Precambrian time
    C) Mesozoic Era
    B) Paleozoic Era
    D) Cenozoic Era

Thinking Critically

11. Why couldn't plants move onto land until an ozone layer formed?

12. Why are trilobites classified as index fossils?

13. What is the most significant difference between Precambrian life-forms and Paleozoic life-forms?

14. How is natural selection related to organic evolution?

15. In the early 1800s, a naturalist proposed that the giraffe species has a long neck as a result of years of stretching their necks to reach leaves in tall trees. Explain why this isn't true.

Developing Skills

16. **Interpreting Scientific Illustrations** The circle graph below represents geologic time. Determine which interval of geologic time is represented by each portion of the graph. Which interval was longest? Which do we know the least about?

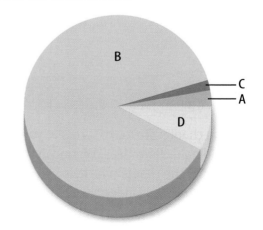

17. Interpreting Data The Cenozoic Era has lasted 65 million years. What percentage of Earth's 4.6-billion-year history is that?

18. Comparing and Contrasting Use the outlines of the present-day continents to make a sketch of Pangaea.

19. Forming Hypotheses Suggest some reasons why trilobites might have become extinct at the end of the Paleozoic Era?

20. Interpreting Data A student found what he thought was a piece of dinosaur bone in Pleistocene sediment. How likely is it that he is right? Explain.

Performance Assessment

21. Make a Model In the Activity, you learned how a particular characteristic might evolve within a species. Modify the experimental model by using color instead of height as a characteristic. Design your activity with the understanding that varimals live in a dark-colored forest environment.

TECHNOLOGY

Go to the Glencoe Science Web site at **science.glencoe.com** or use the **Glencoe Science CD-ROM** for additional chapter assessment.

THE PRINCETON REVIEW — Test Practice

Many animals have inhabited Earth. Some of these animals have been divided into groups below.

Group A	Group B	Group C
Saber-toothed cat	*Apatosaurus*	Frog
Giant ground sloth	*Maiasaura*	Turtle
Woolly mammoth	*Tyrannosaurus*	Salamander

Study the table and answer the following questions.

1. The animals in Group A are different from the animals in Group B because only the animals in Group A are _____ .
A) mammals   **C)** amphibians
B) reptiles   **D)** birds

2. The animals in Group B are different from the animals in Group C because only the animals in Group B are _____ .
F) dinosaurs   **H)** amphibians
G) reptiles   **J)** herbivores

3. The animals in all three groups are similar because _____ .
A) They make their own food.
B) They have hair.
C) They must eat other organisms.
D) They are meat eaters.

Reading Comprehension

Read the passage carefully. Then read the questions that follow the passage. Decide which is the best answer to each question.

Shorelines

A recent study on shoreline erosion completed by the Federal Emergency Management Agency (FEMA) has determined that about one quarter of man-made structures that are within 500 feet of the United States' shorelines will be damaged by erosion during the next 60 years. If development of coasts continues and the level of the oceans continues to rise, the situation could be even worse.

Scientists predict that the Atlantic and Gulf of Mexico coastlines will experience the most erosion. The cost to homeowners is predicted to be about a half billion dollars per year. With yearly average erosion rates of 1m on the Atlantic Coast and 2m on the Gulf of Mexico coastlines, many homes will be lost forever. In fact, these areas will account for approximately 60 percent of nationwide losses.

The grain size of sediment is one factor that accounts for some of the difference in erosion rates between coasts. The sediment on the shores of the Gulf of Mexico generally is fine grained and easily picked up and carried away by wave action. On the Atlantic coast, the sediment generally is more coarse grained and therefore erodes at a slower rate. Along the Pacific Coast, rates of erosion vary from one area to another. Erosion rates of 2.4 m per year have been recorded along parts of the Alaskan coast, while the state of Washington's shoreline actually is growing in some places.

Test-Taking Tip   After reading a passage, quickly glance over the questions and then skim the passage again, looking for important information.

1. Based on the passage, which of the following is most likely true?
   A) Building a summer home along the Gulf of Mexico would be more secure than building one along the Atlantic Coast.
   B) Erosion is a major threat to shorelines in many parts of the country.
   C) All man-made structures within 500 feet of the Atlantic Coast will disappear.
   D) Ocean water levels will decrease during the next 60 years.

2. The main purpose of the Federal Emergency Management Agency's study was most likely to _____.
   F) discourage people from building homes near the coastline
   G) explain how coastline erosion of various types of sediment occurs
   H) help to limit erosion and protect property
   I) figure out the costs of coastline erosion in the United States

Reasoning and Skills

Read each question and choose the best answer.

Group R

Group S

1. The weathering examples in Group R are different from weathering examples in Group S because only the weathering examples in Group R have been caused by _____.
   A) chemical weathering
   B) ice wedging
   C) mechanical weathering
   D) oxidation

Test-Taking Tip Think about the different kinds of weathering and how they affect Earth.

2. Which of these facts best explains why the oldest fossils have been discovered in sediments that were deposited in ancient oceans?
   F) Only aquatic animals leave fossils.
   G) Fossils from land organisms have been destroyed.
   H) The first life on Earth began in the oceans.
   J) All living organisms need water.

Test-Taking Tip Some answer choices might be true statements but not the *best* explanation to a particular question.

3. Which of the following is most responsible for the development of these landscapes?
   A) ice wedging
   B) the movement of wind
   C) the effects of acid rain
   D) the movement of water

Test-Taking Tip Consider what you know about erosion and specific examples of erosion, such as the Grand Canyon.

Consider this question carefully before writing your answer on a separate sheet of paper.

4. Earth's surface has been shaped by erosion. Discuss some of the different agents of erosion that affect Earth's surface. How do these agents of erosion reshape the landscape?

Test-Taking Tip Think about the different features of Earth's landscape. Then, decide how agents of erosion might have affected them.

Student Resources

Student Resources

Field GUIDE

Suppose you live hundreds of miles from the ocean. One day, you find a rock with a clear imprint of a seashell on its surface. What might this imprint, or fossil, tell you about the area in which you live?

Fossils are the traces or remains of organisms that lived long ago. Fossils provide a record of the vast array of life-forms that have lived on Earth, and they show how these life-forms have changed over time. Fossils also can give clues about how the rock formed over millions of years.

Common Fossils

The most easily found fossils are shells, or casts of shells, from the sea animals that once lived in them. Some fossils might have been well preserved, but most are only fragments of the ancient organism. Fossils of soft-bodied animals and plants are not so easily found because they decay more quickly. However, some rare fossils of soft-bodied organisms have been found and have provided a wealth of information about the organisms.

This field guide shows examples of common fossils belonging to some of the major fossil groups. When you find a fossil, you can use this guide to help identify the group to which the fossil belongs.

Fossils

Fossil Groups

Coral

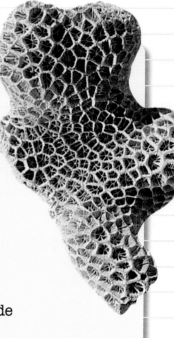

Coral fossil

Corals are small sea creatures that live attached to the ocean floor in warm, shallow waters. The animals build structures that have a honeycomb-like appearance. These structures commonly are found as fossils. The first corals appeared during the Paleozoic Era of geologic time. Use the key on the fourth page of this field guide to identify these symbols.

Field Activity

Go on an Internet fossil hunt at **science.glencoe.com**. Find five different fossils and make a sketch of each in your Science Journal. Then, below each illustration, write a description of the fossil and explain what kind of organism the fossil came from.

Trilobite

Trilobites (TRI loh bites) are now extinct, but they once were common in ancient seas. Their bodies were divided into three parts—one slightly raised center lobe flanked by two flatter lobes. Trilobites measured from less than 1 cm long to more than 20 cm long.

Trilobite fossil

Snail fossil

Gastropod or Snail

Gastropods (GAS troh pahdz), or snails, have a head with eyes and mouth, one flat foot for crawling, and a spiral shell. They can be found in oceans, in freshwater ponds and lakes, and on land.

Crinoid or Sea Lily

In spite of its name, the sea lily is an animal. Most crinoids (KRI noydz) attach themselves to the soft, muddy floor of the ocean and then use their long arms to catch prey.

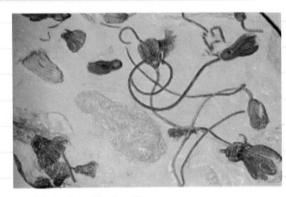

Multiple Sea lily fossils

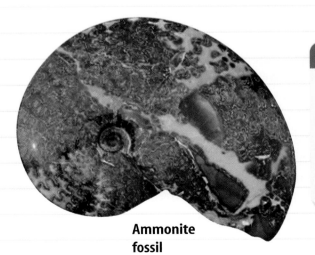

Ammonite fossil

Ammonoid

Ammonoids (A muh noydz) were free-swimming shellfish, related to squid. Ammonites appeared during the Devonian Era, long before dinosaurs roamed Earth. They became extinct when dinosaurs did.

Echinoid

Echinoids (ih KI noydz)—sea urchins and sand dollars—can be ball shaped, cone shaped, or flat. The sea urchin that left this fossil was cone shaped. It used its mouth, located on the flat bottom side, to swallow sand from which it took its nourishment.

Echinoid fossil

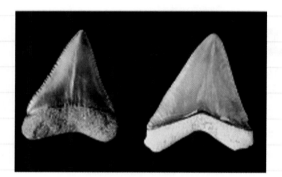

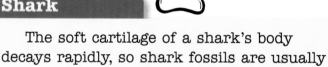

Shark

The soft cartilage of a shark's body decays rapidly, so shark fossils are usually teeth or scales. Sharks are abundant in today's oceans.

Shark's tooth fossils

Seed fern fossils

Plant (Leaves)

Some plant fossils show leaves, fronds, or stems. Fern trees thrived during the Carboniferous Period (360 million to 286 million years ago). Seed ferns can be identified by their fronds, or branches, which are divided into smaller leaflets.

Plant (Wood)

Some plant fossils are pieces of wood. This petrified wood fossil is from the Petrified Forest in Arizona. Growth rings in wood indicate changing growth rates during each year. Growth rings often are clear enough to be counted.

Petrified wood fossil

FOSSIL MAP OF THE UNITED STATES

The key below provides a symbol for each fossil group shown in this guide. Use the key to find out which fossils can be found in your region.

Key

Coral		Crinoid		Shark	
Trilobite		Ammonoid		Plant (leaves)	
Gastropod		Echinoid		Plant (wood)	

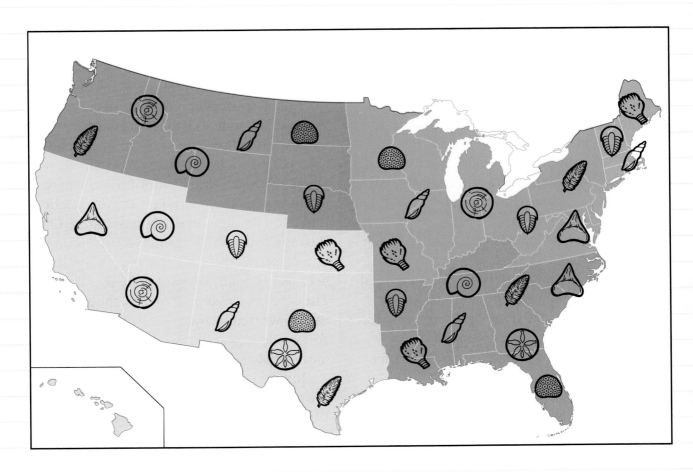

As you study science, you will make many observations and conduct investigations and experiments. You will also research information that is available from many sources. These activities will involve organizing and recording data. The quality of the data you collect and the way you organize it will determine how well others can understand and use it. In **Figure 1,** the student is obtaining and recording information using a thermometer.

Putting your observations in writing is an important way of communicating to others the information you have found and the results of your investigations and experiments.

Researching Information

Scientists work to build on and add to human knowledge of the world. Before moving in a new direction, it is important to gather the information that already is known about a subject. You will look for such information in various reference sources. Follow these steps to research information on a scientific subject:

Step 1 Determine exactly what you need to know about the subject. For instance, you might want to find out what happened when Mount St. Helens erupted in 1980.

Step 2 Make a list of questions, such as: When did the eruption begin? How long did it last? What kind of material was expelled and how much?

Step 3 Use multiple sources such as textbooks, encyclopedias, government documents, professional journals, science magazines, and the Internet.

Step 4 List where you found the sources. Make sure the sources you use are reliable and the most current available.

Figure 1
Collecting data is one way to gather information directly.

Evaluating Print and Nonprint Sources

Not all sources of information are reliable. Evaluate the sources you use for information, and use only those you know to be dependable. For example, suppose you live in an area where earthquakes are common and you want to know what to do to keep safe. You might find two Web sites on earthquake safety. One Web site contains "Earthquake Tips" written by a company that sells metal scrapings to help secure your hot-water tank to the wall. The other is a Web page on "Earthquake Safety" written by the U.S. Geological Survey. You would choose the second Web site as the more reliable source of information.

In science, information can change rapidly. Always consult the most current sources. A 1985 source about the Moon would not reflect the most recent research and findings.

Skill Handbooks

Interpreting Scientific Illustrations

As you research a science topic, you will see drawings, diagrams, and photographs. Illustrations help you understand what you read. Some illustrations are included to help you understand an idea that you can't see easily by yourself. For instance, you can't see the layers of Earth, but you can look at a diagram of Earth's layers, as labeled in **Figure 2,** that helps you understand what the layers are and where they are located. Visualizing a drawing helps many people remember details more easily. Illustrations also provide examples that clarify difficult concepts or give additional information about the topic you are studying.

Most illustrations have a label or caption. A label or caption identifies the illustration or provides additional information to better explain it. Can you find the caption or labels in **Figure 2?**

Figure 2
This cross section shows a slice through Earth's interior and the positions of its layers.

Concept Mapping

If you were taking a car trip, you might take some sort of road map. By using a map, you begin to learn where you are in relation to other places on the map.

A concept map is similar to a road map, but a concept map shows relationships among ideas (or concepts) rather than places. It is a diagram that visually shows how concepts are related. Because a concept map shows relationships among ideas, it can make the meanings of ideas and terms clear and help you understand what you are studying.

Overall, concept maps are useful for breaking large concepts down into smaller parts, making learning easier.

Venn Diagram

Although it is not a concept map, a Venn diagram illustrates how two subjects compare and contrast. In other words, you can see the characteristics that the subjects have in common and those that they do not.

The Venn diagram in **Figure 3** shows the relationship between two types of rocks made from the same basic chemical. Both rocks share the chemical calcium carbonate. However, due to the way they are formed, one rock is the sedimentary rock limestone, and the other is the metamorphic rock marble.

Figure 3
A Venn diagram shows how objects or concepts are alike and how they are different.

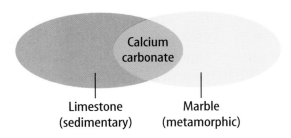

Calcium carbonate

Limestone (sedimentary)   Marble (metamorphic)

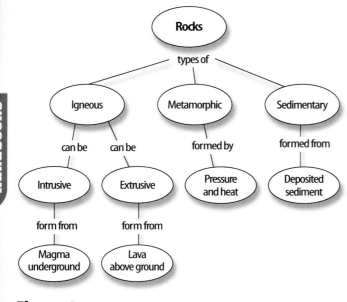

Figure 4
A network tree shows how concepts or objects are related.

Network Tree Look at the concept map in **Figure 4,** that shows the three main types of rock. This is called a network tree concept map. Notice how some words are in ovals while others are written across connecting lines. The words inside the ovals are science terms or concepts. The words written on the connecting lines describe the relationships between the concepts.

When constructing a network tree, write the topic on a note card or piece of paper. Write the major concepts related to that topic on separate note cards or pieces of paper. Then arrange them in order from general to specific. Branch the related concepts from the major concept and describe the relationships on the connecting lines. Continue branching to more specific concepts. Write the relationships between the concepts on the connecting lines until all concepts are mapped. Then examine the concept map for relationships that cross branches, and add them to the concept map.

Events Chain An events chain is another type of concept map. It models the order of items or their sequence. In science, an events chain can be used to describe a sequence of events, the steps in a procedure, or the stages of a process.

When making an events chain, first find the one event that starts the chain. This event is called the *initiating event.* Then, find the next event in the chain and continue until you reach an outcome. Suppose you are asked to describe why and how a sound might make an echo. You might draw an events chain such as the one in **Figure 5.** Notice that connecting words are not necessary in an events chain.

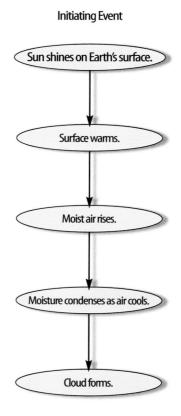

Figure 5
Events chains show the order of steps in a process or event.

Cycle Map A cycle concept map is a specific type of events chain map. In a cycle concept map, the series of events does not produce a final outcome. Instead, the last event in the chain relates back to the beginning event.

You first decide what event will be used as the beginning event. Once that is decided, you list events in order that occur after it. Words are written between events that describe what happens from one event to the next. The last event in a cycle concept map relates back to the beginning event. The number of events in a cycle concept varies, but is usually three or more. Look at the cycle map, as shown in **Figure 6.**

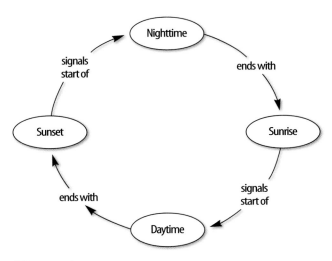

Figure 6
A cycle map shows events that occur in a cycle.

Spider Map A type of concept map that you can use for brainstorming is the spider map. When you have a central idea, you might find you have a jumble of ideas that relate to it but are not necessarily clearly related to each other. The spider map on sound in **Figure 7** shows that if you write these ideas outside the main concept, then you can begin to separate and group un-related terms so they become more useful.

Figure 7
A spider map allows you to list ideas that relate to a central topic but not necessarily to one another.

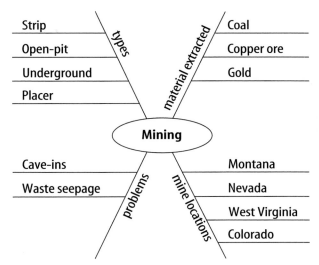

Writing a Paper

You will write papers often when researching science topics or reporting the results of investigations or experiments. Scientists frequently write papers to share their data and conclusions with other scientists and the public. When writing a paper, use these steps.

Step 1 Assemble your data by using graphs, tables, or a concept map. Create an outline.

Step 2 Start with an introduction that contains a clear statement of purpose and what you intend to discuss or prove.

Step 3 Organize the body into paragraphs. Each paragraph should start with a topic sentence, and the remaining sentences in that paragraph should support your point.

Step 4 Position data to help support your points.

Step 5 Summarize the main points and finish with a conclusion statement.

Step 6 Use tables, graphs, charts, and illustrations whenever possible.

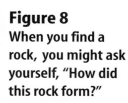

You might say the work of a scientist is to solve problems. When you decide to find out why one corner of your yard is always soggy, you are problem solving, too. You might observe the corner is lower than the surrounding area and has less vegetation growing in it. You might decide to see whether planting some grass will keep the corner drier.

Scientists use orderly approaches to solve problems. The methods scientists use include identifying a question, making observations, forming a hypothesis, testing a hypothesis, analyzing results, and drawing conclusions.

Scientific investigations involve careful observation under controlled conditions. Such observation of an object or a process can suggest new and interesting questions about it. These questions sometimes lead to the formation of a hypothesis. Scientific investigations are designed to test a hypothesis.

Identifying a Question

The first step in a scientific investigation or experiment is to identify a question to be answered or a problem to be solved. You might be interested in knowing why a rock like the one in **Figure 8** looks the way it does.

Figure 8
When you find a rock, you might ask yourself, "How did this rock form?"

Forming Hypotheses

Hypotheses are based on observations that have been made. A hypothesis is a possible explanation based on previous knowledge and observations.

Perhaps a scientist has observed that thunderstorms happen more often on hot days than on cooler days. Based on these observations, the scientist can make a statement that he or she can test. The statement is a hypothesis. The hypothesis could be: *Warm temperatures cause thunderstorms.* A hypothesis has to be something you can test by using an investigation. A testable hypothesis is a valid hypothesis.

Predicting

When you apply a hypothesis, or general explanation, to a specific situation, you predict something about that situation. First, you must identify which hypothesis fits the situation you are considering. People use predictions to make everyday decisions. Based on previous observations and experiences, you might form a prediction that if warm temperatures cause thunderstorms, then more thunderstorms will occur in summer months than in spring months. Someone could use these predictions to plan when to take a camping trip or when to schedule an outdoor activity.

Testing a Hypothesis

To test a hypothesis, you need a procedure. A procedure is the plan you follow in your experiment. A procedure tells you what materials to use, as well as how and in what order to use them. When you follow a procedure, data are generated that support or do not support the original hypothesis statement.

For example, premium gasoline costs more than regular gasoline. Does premium gasoline increase the efficiency or fuel mileage of your family car? You decide to test the hypothesis: "If premium gasoline is more efficient, then it should increase the fuel mileage of my family's car." Then you write the procedure shown in **Figure 9** for your experiment and generate the data presented in the table below.

Figure 9
A procedure tells you what to do step by step.

> **Procedure**
> 1. Use regular gasoline for two weeks.
> 2. Record the number of kilometers between fill-ups and the amount of gasoline used.
> 3. Switch to premium gasoline for two weeks.
> 4. Record the number of kilometers between fill-ups and the amount of gasoline used.

Gasoline Data			
Type of Gasoline	Kilometers Traveled	Liters Used	Liters per Kilometer
Regular	762	45.34	0.059
Premium	661	42.30	0.064

These data show that premium gasoline is less efficient than regular gasoline in one particular car. It took more gasoline to travel 1 km (0.064) using premium gasoline than it did to travel 1 km using regular gasoline (0.059). This conclusion does not support the hypothesis.

Are all investigations alike? Keep in mind as you perform investigations in science that a hypothesis can be tested in many ways. Not every investigation makes use of all the ways that are described on these pages, and not all hypotheses are tested by investigations. Scientists encounter many variations in the methods that are used when they perform experiments. The skills in this handbook are here for you to use and practice.

Identifying and Manipulating Variables and Controls

In any experiment, it is important to keep everything the same except for the item you are testing. The one factor you change is called the independent variable. The factor that changes as a result of the independent variable is called the dependent variable. Always make sure you have only one independent variable. If you allow more than one, you will not know what causes the changes you observe in the dependent variable. Many experiments also have controls—individual instances or experimental subjects for which the independent variable is not changed. You can then compare the test results to the control results.

For example, in the fuel-mileage experiment, you made everything the same except the type of gasoline that was used. The driver, the type of automobile, and the type of driving were the same throughout. In this way, you could be sure that any mileage differences were caused by the type of fuel—the independent variable. The fuel mileage was the dependent variable.

If you could repeat the experiment using several automobiles of the same type on a standard driving track with the same driver, you could make one automobile a control by using regular gasoline over the four-week period.

Collecting Data

Whether you are carrying out an investigation or a short observational experiment, you will collect data, or information. Scientists collect data accurately as numbers and descriptions and organize it in specific ways.

Observing Scientists observe items and events, then record what they see. When they use only words to describe an observation, it is called qualitative data. For example, a scientist might describe the color, texture, or odor of a substance produced in a chemical reaction. Scientists' observations also can describe how much there is of something. These observations use numbers, as well as words, in the description and are called quantitative data. For example, if a sample of the element gold is described as being "shiny and very dense," the data are clearly qualitative. Quantitative data on this sample of gold might include "a mass of 30 g and a density of 19.3 g/cm^3." Quantitative data often are organized into tables. Then, from information in the table, a graph can be drawn. Graphs can reveal relationships that exist in experimental data.

When you make observations in science, you should examine the entire object or situation first, then look carefully for details. If you're looking at a rock sample, for instance, check the general color and pattern of the rock before using a hand lens to examine the small mineral grains that make up its underlying structure. Remember to record accurately everything you see.

Scientists try to make careful and accurate observations. When possible, they use instruments such as microscopes, metric rulers, graduated cylinders, thermometers, and balances. Measurements provide numerical data that can be repeated and checked.

Sampling When working with large numbers of objects or a large population, scientists usually cannot observe or study every one of them. Instead, they use a sample or a portion of the total number. To *sample* is to take a small, representative portion of the objects or organisms of a population for research. By making careful observations or manipulating variables within a portion of a group, information is discovered and conclusions are drawn that might apply to the whole population.

Estimating Scientific work also involves estimating. To *estimate* is to make a judgment about the amount or the number of something without measuring every part of an object or counting every member of a population. Scientists first measure or count the amount or number in a small sample. A chemist, for example, might remove a 10-g piece of a large rock that is rich in copper ore, such as the one shown in **Figure 10.** Then the chemist can determine the percentage of copper by mass and multiply that percentage by the mass of the rock to get an estimate of the total mass of copper in the rock.

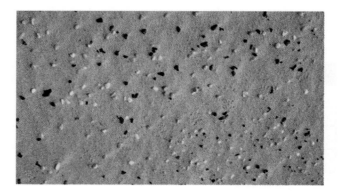

Figure 10
In a 1-meter frame positioned on a beach, count the pebbles that are longer than 2.5 cm. Multiply this number by the area of the beach. This will give you an estimate for the total number of pebbles on the beach.

Measuring in SI

The metric system of measurement was developed in 1795. A modern form of the metric system, called the International System, or SI, was adopted in 1960. SI provides standard measurements that all scientists around the world can understand.

The metric system is convenient because unit sizes vary by multiples of 10. When changing from smaller units to larger units, divide by a multiple of 10. When changing from larger units to smaller, multiply by a multiple of 10. To convert millimeters to centimeters, divide the millimeters by 10. To convert 30 mm to centimeters, divide 30 by 10 (30 mm equal 3 cm).

Prefixes are used to name units. Look at the table below for some common metric prefixes and their meanings. Do you see how the prefix *kilo-* attached to the unit *gram* is *kilogram*, or 1,000 g?

Metric Prefixes			
Prefix	**Symbol**	**Meaning**	
kilo-	k	1,000	thousand
hecto-	h	100	hundred
deka-	da	10	ten
deci-	d	0.1	tenth
centi-	c	0.01	hundredth
milli-	m	0.001	thousandth

Now look at the metric ruler shown in **Figure 11.** The centimeter lines are the long, numbered lines, and the shorter lines are millimeter lines.

When using a metric ruler, line up the 0-cm mark with the end of the object being measured, and read the number of the unit where the object ends, in this instance it would be 4.5 cm.

Figure 11
This metric ruler shows centimeters and millimeter divisions.

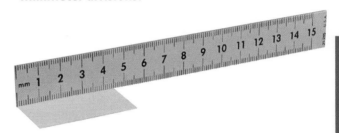

Liquid Volume In some science activities, you will measure liquids. The unit that is used to measure liquids is the liter. A liter has the volume of 1,000 cm³. The prefix *milli-* means "thousandth (0.001)." A milliliter is one thousandth of 1 L, and 1 L has the volume of 1,000 mL. One milliliter of liquid completely fills a cube measuring 1 cm on each side. Therefore, 1 mL equals 1 cm³.

You will use beakers and graduated cylinders to measure liquid volume. A graduated cylinder, as illustrated in **Figure 12,** is marked from bottom to top in milliliters. This one contains 79 mL of a liquid.

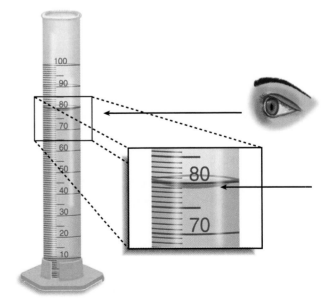

Figure 12
Graduated cylinders measure liquid volume.

Mass Scientists measure mass in grams. You might use a beam balance similar to the one shown in **Figure 13.** The balance has a pan on one side and a set of beams on the other side. Each beam has a rider that slides on the beam.

Before you find the mass of an object, slide all the riders back to the zero point. Check the pointer on the right to make sure it swings an equal distance above and below the zero point. If the swing is unequal, find and turn the adjusting screw until you have an equal swing.

Place an object on the pan. Slide the largest rider along its beam until the pointer drops below zero. Then move it back one notch. Repeat the process on each beam until the pointer swings an equal distance above and below the zero point. Sum the masses on each beam to find the mass of the object. Move all riders back to zero when finished.

Figure 13
A triple beam balance is used to determine the mass of an object.

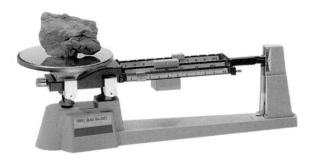

You should never place a hot object on the pan or pour chemicals directly onto the pan. Instead, find the mass of a clean container. Remove the container from the pan, then place the chemicals in the container. Find the mass of the container with the chemicals in it. To find the mass of the chemicals, subtract the mass of the empty container from the mass of the filled container.

Making and Using Tables

Browse through your textbook and you will see tables in the text and in the activities. In a table, data, or information, are arranged so that they are easier to understand. Activity tables help organize the data you collect during an activity so results can be interpreted.

Making Tables To make a table, list the items to be compared in the first column and the characteristics to be compared in the first row. The title should clearly indicate the content of the table, and the column or row heads should tell the reader what information is found in there. The table below lists materials collected for recycling on three weekly pick-up days. The inclusion of kilograms in parentheses also identifies for the reader that the figures are mass units.

Recyclable Materials Collected During Week			
Day of Week	**Paper (kg)**	**Aluminum (kg)**	**Glass (kg)**
Monday	5.0	4.0	12.0
Wednesday	4.0	1.0	10.0
Friday	2.5	2.0	10.0

Using Tables How much paper, in kilograms, is being recycled on Wednesday? Locate the column labeled "Paper (kg)" and the row "Wednesday." The information in the box where the column and row intersect is the answer. Did you answer "4.0"? How much aluminum, in kilograms, is being recycled on Friday? If you answered "2.0," you understand how to read the table. How much glass is collected for recycling each week? Locate the column labeled "Glass (kg)" and add the figures for all three rows. If you answered "32.0," then you know how to locate and use the data provided in the table.

Recording Data

To be useful, the data you collect must be recorded carefully. Accuracy is key. A well-thought-out experiment includes a way to record procedures, observations, and results accurately. Data tables are one way to organize and record results. Set up the tables you will need ahead of time so you can record the data right away.

Record information properly and neatly. Never put unidentified data on scraps of paper. Instead, data should be written in a notebook like the one in **Figure 14.** Write in pencil so information isn't lost if your data gets wet. At each point in the experiment, record your data and label it. That way, your information will be accurate and you will not have to determine what the figures mean when you look at your notes later.

Figure 14
Record data neatly and clearly so it is easy to understand.

Recording Observations

It is important to record observations accurately and completely. That is why you always should record observations in your notes immediately as you make them. It is easy to miss details or make mistakes when recording results from memory. Do not include your personal thoughts when you record your data. Record only what you observe to eliminate bias. For example, when you record the time required for five students to climb the same set of stairs, you would note which student took the longest time. However, you would not refer to that student's time as "the worst time of all the students in the group."

Making Models

You can organize the observations and other data you collect and record in many ways. Making models is one way to help you better understand the parts of a structure you have been observing or the way a process for which you have been taking various measurements works.

Models often show things that are too large or too small for normal viewing. For example, you normally won't see the inside of an atom. However, you can understand the structure of the atom better by making a three-dimensional model of an atom. The relative sizes, the positions, and the movements of protons, neutrons, and electrons can be explained in words. An atomic model made of a plastic-ball nucleus and pipe-cleaner electron shells can help you visualize how the parts of the atom relate to each other.

Other models can be devised on a computer. Some models, such as those that illustrate the chemical combinations of different elements, are mathematical and are represented by equations.

Science Skill Handbook

Making and Using Graphs

After scientists organize data in tables, they might display the data in a graph that shows the relationship of one variable to another. A graph makes interpretation and analysis of data easier. Three types of graphs are the line graph, the bar graph, and the circle graph.

Line Graphs A line graph like in **Figure 15** is used to show the relationship between two variables. The variables being compared go on two axes of the graph. For data from an experiment, the independent variable always goes on the horizontal axis, called the *x*-axis. The dependent variable always goes on the vertical axis, called the *y*-axis. After drawing your axes, label each with a scale. Next, plot the data points.

A data point is the intersection of the recorded value of the dependent variable for each tested value of the independent variable. After all the points are plotted, connect them.

Bar Graphs Bar graphs compare data that do not change continuously. Vertical bars show the relationships among data.

To make a bar graph, set up the *y*-axis as you did for the line graph. Draw vertical bars of equal size from the *x*-axis up to the point on the *y*-axis that represents value of *x*.

Figure 16
The amount of aluminum collected for recycling during one week can be shown as a bar graph or circle graph.

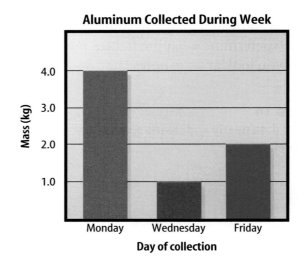

Circle Graphs A circle graph uses a circle divided into sections to display data as parts (fractions or percentages) of a whole. The size of each section corresponds to the fraction or percentage of the data that the section represents. So, the entire circle represents 100 percent, one-half represents 50 percent, one-fifth represents 20 percent, and so on.

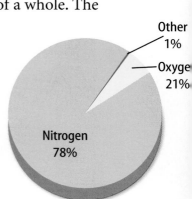

Figure 15
This line graph shows the relationship between degree of slope and the loss of soil in grams from a container during an experiment.

Analyzing Results

To determine the meaning of your observations and investigation results, you will need to look for patterns in the data. You can organize your information in several of the ways that are discussed in this handbook. Then you must think critically to determine what the data mean. Scientists use several approaches when they analyze the data they have collected and recorded. Each approach is useful for identifying specific patterns in the data.

Forming Operational Definitions

An operational definition defines an object by showing how it functions, works, or behaves. Such definitions are written in terms of how an object works or how it can be used; that is, they describe its job or purpose.

For example, a ruler can be defined as a tool that measures the length of an object (how it can be used). A ruler also can be defined as something that contains a series of marks that can be used as a standard when measuring (how it works).

Classifying

Classifying is the process of sorting objects or events into groups based on common features. When classifying, first observe the objects or events to be classified. Then select one feature that is shared by some members in the group but not by all. Place those members that share that feature into a subgroup. You can classify members into smaller and smaller subgroups based on characteristics.

How might you classify a group of rocks? You might first classify them by color, putting all of the black, white, and red rocks into separate groups. Within each group, you

could then look for another common feature to classify further, such as size or whether the rocks have sharp or smooth edges.

Remember that when you classify, you are grouping objects or events for a purpose. For example, classifying rocks can be the first step in identifying them. You might know that obsidian is a black, shiny rock with sharp edges. To find it in a large group of rocks, you might start with the classification scheme mentioned. You'll locate obsidian within the group of black, sharp-edged rocks that you separate from the rest. Pumice could be located by its white color and by the fact that it contains many small holes called vesicles. Keep your purpose in mind as you select the features to form groups and subgroups.

Figure 17
Color is one of many characteristics that are used to classify rocks.

Science Skill Handbook

Comparing and Contrasting

Observations can be analyzed by noting the similarities and differences between two or more objects or events that you observe. When you look at objects or events to see how they are similar, you are comparing them. Contrasting is looking for differences in objects or events. The table below compares and contrasts the characteristics of two minerals.

Mineral Characteristics		
Mineral	Graphite	Gold
Color	black	bright yellow
Hardness	1–2	2.5–3
Luster	metallic	metallic
Uses	pencil "lead"	jewelry, electronics

Recognizing Cause and Effect

Have you ever heard a loud pop right before the power went out and then suggested that an electric transformer probably blew out? If so, you have observed an effect and inferred a cause. The event is the effect, and the reason for the event is the cause.

When scientists are unsure of the cause of a certain event, they design controlled experiments to determine what caused it.

Interpreting Data

The word *interpret* means "to explain the meaning of something." Look at the problem originally being explored in an experiment and figure out what the data show. Identify the control group and the test group so you can see whether or not changes in the independent variable have had an effect. Look for differences in the dependent variable between the control and test groups.

These differences you observe can be qualitative or quantitative. You would be able to describe a qualitative difference using only words, whereas you would measure a quantitative difference and describe it using numbers. If there are differences, the independent variable that is being tested could have had an effect. If no differences are found between the control and test groups, the variable that is being tested apparently had no effect.

For example, suppose that three beakers each contain 100 mL of water. The beakers are placed on hot plates, and two of the hot plates are turned on, but the third is left off for a period of 5 min. Suppose you are then asked to describe any differences in the water in the three beakers. A qualitative difference might be the appearance of bubbles rising to the top in the water that is being heated but no rising bubbles in the unheated water. A quantitative difference might be a difference in the amount of water that is present in the beakers.

Inferring Scientists often make inferences based on their observations. An inference is an attempt to explain, or interpret, observations or to indicate what caused what you observed. An inference is a type of conclusion.

When making an inference, be certain to use accurate data and accurately described observations. Analyze all of the data that you've collected. Then, based on everything you know, explain or interpret what you've observed.

Drawing Conclusions

When scientists have analyzed the data they collected, they proceed to draw conclusions about what the data mean. These conclusions are sometimes stated using words similar to those found in the hypothesis formed earlier in the process.

Conclusions To analyze your data, you must review all of the observations and measurements that you made and recorded. Recheck all data for accuracy. After your data are rechecked and organized, you are almost ready to draw a conclusion such as "salt water boils at a higher temperature than freshwater."

Before you can draw a conclusion, however, you must determine whether the data allow you to come to a conclusion that supports a hypothesis. Sometimes that will be the case, other times it will not.

If your data do not support a hypothesis, it does not mean that the hypothesis is wrong. It means only that the results of the investigation did not support the hypothesis. Maybe the experiment needs to be redesigned, but very likely, some of the initial observations on which the hypothesis was based were incomplete or biased. Perhaps more observation or research is needed to refine the hypothesis.

Avoiding Bias Sometimes drawing a conclusion involves making judgments. When you make a judgment, you form an opinion about what your data mean. It is important to be honest and to avoid reaching a conclusion if there were no supporting evidence for it or if it were based on a small sample. It also is important not to allow any expectations of results to bias your judgments. If possible, it is a good idea to collect additional data. Scientists do this all the time.

For example, the *Hubble Space Telescope* was sent into space in April, 1990, to provide scientists with clearer views of the universe. The *Hubble* is the size of a school bus and has a 2.4-m-diameter mirror. The *Hubble* helped scientists answer questions about the planet Pluto.

For many years, scientists had only been able to hypothesize about the surface of the planet Pluto. The *Hubble* has now provided pictures of Pluto's surface that show a rough texture with light and dark regions on it. This might be the best information about Pluto scientists will have until they are able to send a space probe to it.

Evaluating Others' Data and Conclusions

Sometimes scientists have to use data that they did not collect themselves, or they have to rely on observations and conclusions drawn by other researchers. In cases such as these, the data must be evaluated carefully.

How were the data obtained? How was the investigation done? Was it carried out properly? Has it been duplicated by other researchers? Were they able to follow the exact procedure? Did they come up with the same results? Look at the conclusion, as well. Would you reach the same conclusion from these results? Only when you have confidence in the data of others can you believe it is true and feel comfortable using it.

Communicating

The communication of ideas is an important part of the work of scientists. A discovery that is not reported will not advance the scientific community's understanding or knowledge. Communication among scientists also is important as a way of improving their investigations.

Scientists communicate in many ways, from writing articles in journals and magazines that explain their investigations and experiments, to announcing important discoveries on television and radio, to sharing ideas with colleagues on the Internet or presenting them as lectures.

Computer Skills

People who study science rely on computers to record and store data and to analyze results from investigations. Whether you work in a laboratory or just need to write a lab report with tables, good computer skills are a necessity.

Using a Word Processor

Suppose your teacher has assigned a written report. After you've completed your research and decided how you want to write the information, you need to put all that information on paper. The easiest way to do this is with a word processing application on a computer.

A computer application that allows you to type your information, change it as many times as you need to, and then print it out so that it looks neat and clean is called a word processing application. You also can use this type of application to create tables and columns, add bullets or cartoon art to your page, include page numbers, and check your spelling.

Helpful Hints

- If you aren't sure how to do something using your word processing program, look in the help menu. You will find a list of topics there to click on for help. After you locate the help topic you need, just follow the step-by-step instructions you see on your screen.
- Just because you've spell checked your report doesn't mean that the spelling is perfect. The spell check feature can't catch misspelled words that look like other words. If you've accidentally typed *mind* instead of *mine*, the spell checker won't know the difference. Always reread your report to make sure you didn't miss any mistakes.

Figure 18
You can use computer programs to make graphs and tables.

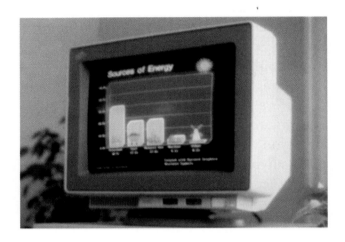

Using a Database

Imagine you're in the middle of a research project, busily gathering facts and information. You soon realize that it's becoming more difficult to organize and keep track of all the information. The tool to use to solve information overload is a database. Just as a file cabinet organizes paper records, a database organizes computer records. However, a database is more powerful than a simple file cabinet because at the click of a mouse, the contents can be reshuffled and reorganized. At computer-quick speeds, databases can sort information by any characteristics and filter data into multiple categories.

Helpful Hints

- Before setting up a database, take some time to learn the features of your database software by practicing with established database software.
- Periodically save your database as you enter data. That way, if something happens such as your computer malfunctions or the power goes off, you won't lose all of your work.

Doing a Database Search

When searching for information in a database, use the following search strategies to get the best results. These are the same search methods used for searching internet databases.

- Place the word *and* between two words in your search if you want the database to look for any entries that have both the words. For example, "Earth *and* Mars" would give you information that mentions both Earth and Mars.

- Place the word *or* between two words if you want the database to show entries that have at least one of the words. For example "Earth *or* Mars" would show you information that mentions either Earth or Mars.

- Place the word *not* between two words if you want the database to look for entries that have the first word but do not have the second word. For example, "Moon *not* phases" would show you information that mentions the Moon but does not mention its phases.

In summary, databases can be used to store large amounts of information about a particular subject. Databases allow biologists, Earth scientists, and physical scientists to search for information quickly and accurately.

Using an Electronic Spreadsheet

Your science fair experiment has produced lots of numbers. How do you keep track of all the data, and how can you easily work out all the calculations needed? You can use a computer program called a spreadsheet to record data that involve numbers. A spreadsheet is an electronic mathematical worksheet.

Type your data in rows and columns, just as they would look in a data table on a sheet of paper. A spreadsheet uses simple math to do data calculations. For example, you could add, subtract, divide, or multiply any of the values in the spreadsheet by another number. You also could set up a series of math steps you want to apply to the data. If you want to add 12 to all the numbers and then multiply all the numbers by 10, the computer does all the calculations for you in the spreadsheet. Below is an example of a spreadsheet that records weather data.

Helpful Hints

- Before you set up the spreadsheet, identify how you want to organize the data. Include any formulas you will need to use.

- Make sure you have entered the correct data into the correct rows and columns.

- You also can display your results in a graph. Pick the style of graph that best represents the data with which you are working.

Figure 19

A spreadsheet allows you to display large amounts of data and do calculations automatically.

	A	B	C	D	E
	Readings	Temperature	Wind speed	Precipitation	
2	10:00 A.M.	21°C	24 km/h	–	
3	12:00 noon	23°C	26 km/h	–	
4	2:00 P.M.	25°C	24 km/h	light drizzle (.5cm)	

Using a Computerized Card Catalog

When you have a report or paper to research, you probably go to the library. To find the information you need in the library, you might have to use a computerized card catalog. This type of card catalog allows you to search for information by subject, by title, or by author. The computer then will display all the holdings the library has on the subject, title, or author requested.

A library's holdings can include books, magazines, databases, videos, and audio materials. When you have chosen something from this list, the computer will show whether an item is available and where in the library to find it.

Helpful Hints

- Remember that you can use the computer to search by subject, author, or title. If you know a book's author but not the title, you can search for all the books the library has by that author.
- When searching by subject, it's often most helpful to narrow your search by using specific search terms, such as *and, or,* and *not*. If you don't find enough sources, you can broaden your search.
- Pay attention to the type of materials found in your search. If you need a book, you can eliminate any videos or other resources that come up in your search.
- Knowing how your library is arranged can save you a lot of time. If you need help, the librarian will show you where certain types of materials are kept and how to find specific items.

Using Graphics Software

Are you having trouble finding that exact piece of art you're looking for? Do you have a picture in your mind of what you want but can't seem to find the right graphic to represent your ideas? To solve these problems, you can use graphics software. Graphics software allows you to create and change images and diagrams in almost unlimited ways. Typical uses for graphics software include arranging clip art, changing scanned images, and constructing pictures from scratch. Most graphics software applications work in similar ways. They use the same basic tools and functions. Once you master one graphics application, you can use other graphics applications.

Figure 20
Graphics software can use your data to draw bar graphs.

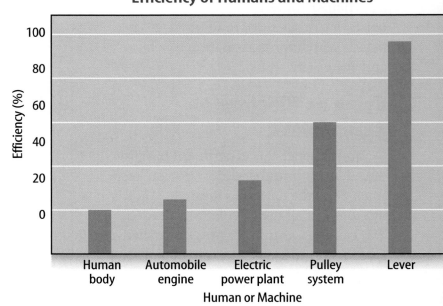

Efficiency of Humans and Machines

Figure 21
You can use this circle graph to find the names of the major gases that make up Earth's atmosphere.

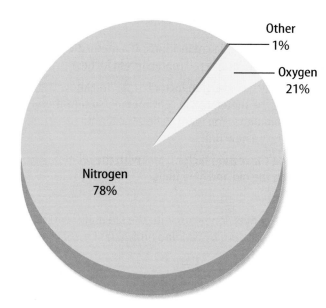

Other
1%

Oxygen
21%

Nitrogen
78%

Helpful Hints

- As with any method of drawing, the more you practice using the graphics software the better your results will be.
- Start by using the software to manipulate existing drawings. Once you master this, making your own illustrations will be easier.
- Clip art is available on CD-ROMs and the Internet. With these resources, finding a piece of clip art to suit your purposes is simple.
- As you work on a drawing, save it often.

Developing Multimedia Presentations

It's your turn—you have to present your science report to the entire class. How do you do it? You can use many different sources of information to get the class excited about your presentation. Posters, videos, photographs, sound, computers, and the Internet can help show your ideas.

First, determine what important points you want to make in your presentation. Then, write an outline of what materials and types of media would best illustrate those points. Maybe you could start with an outline on an overhead projector, then show a video, followed by something from the Internet or a slide show accompanied by music or recorded voices. You might choose to use a presentation builder computer application that can combine all these elements into one presentation. Make sure the presentation is well constructed to make the most impact on the audience.

Figure 21
Multimedia presentations use many types of print and electronic materials.

Helpful Hints

- Carefully consider what media will best communicate the point you are trying to make.
- Make sure you know how to use any equipment you will be using in your presentation.
- Practice the presentation several times.
- If possible, set up all of the equipment ahead of time. Make sure everything is working correctly.

Math Skill Handbook

Use this Math Skill Handbook to help solve problems you are given in this text. You might find it useful to review topics in this Math Skill Handbook first.

Converting Units

In science, quantities such as length, mass, and time sometimes are measured using different units. Suppose you want to know how many miles are in 12.7 km?

Conversion factors are used to change from one unit of measure to another. A conversion factor is a ratio that is equal to one. For example, there are 1,000 mL in 1 L, so 1,000 mL equals 1 L, or:

$$1{,}000 \text{ mL} = 1 \text{ L}$$

If both sides are divided by 1 L, this equation becomes:

$$\frac{1{,}000 \text{ mL}}{1 \text{ L}} = 1$$

The **ratio** on the left side of this equation is equal to one and is a conversion factor. You can make another conversion factor by dividing both sides of the top equation by 1,000 mL:

$$1 = \frac{1 \text{ L}}{1{,}000 \text{ mL}}$$

To **convert units,** you multiply by the appropriate conversion factor. For example, how many milliliters are in 1.255 L? To convert 1.255 L to milliliters, multiply 1.255 L by a conversion factor.

Use the **conversion factor** with new units (mL) in the numerator and the old units (L) in the denominator.

$$1.255 \text{ L} \times \frac{1{,}000 \text{ mL}}{1 \text{ L}} = 1{,}255 \text{ mL}$$

The unit L divides in this equation, just as if it were a number.

Example 1 There are 2.54 cm in 1 inch. If a meterstick has a length of 100 cm, how long is the meterstick in inches?

Step 1 Decide which conversion factor to use. You know the length of the meterstick in centimeters, so centimeters are the old units. You want to find the length in inches, so inch is the new unit.

Step 2 Form the conversion factor. Start with the relationship between the old and new units.

$$2.54 \text{ cm} = 1 \text{ inch}$$

Step 3 Form the conversion factor with the old unit (centimeter) on the bottom by dividing both sides by 2.54 cm.

$$1 = \frac{2.54 \text{ cm}}{2.54 \text{ cm}} = \frac{1 \text{ inch}}{2.54 \text{ cm}}$$

Step 4 Multiply the old measurement by the conversion factor.

$$100 \text{ cm} \times \frac{1 \text{ inch}}{2.54 \text{ cm}} = 39.37 \text{ inches}$$

The meter stick is 39.37 inches long.

Example 2 There are 365 days in one year. If a person is 14 years old, what is his or her age in days? (Ignore leap years)

Step 1 Decide which conversion factor to use. You want to convert years to days.

Step 2 Form the conversion factor. Start with the relation between the old and new units.

$$1 \text{ year} = 365 \text{ days}$$

Step 3 Form the conversion factor with the old unit (year) on the bottom by dividing both sides by 1 year.

$$1 = \frac{1 \text{ year}}{1 \text{ year}} = \frac{365 \text{ days}}{1 \text{ year}}$$

Step 4 Multiply the old measurement by the conversion factor:

$$14 \text{ years} \times \frac{365 \text{ days}}{1 \text{ year}} = 5{,}110 \text{ days}$$

The person's age is 5,110 days.

Practice Problem A book has a mass of 2.31 kg. If there are 1,000 g in 1 kg, what is the mass of the book in grams?

Using Fractions

A **fraction** is a number that compares a part to the whole. For example, in the fraction $\frac{2}{3}$, the 2 represents the part and the 3 represents the whole. In the fraction $\frac{2}{3}$, the top number, 2, is called the numerator. The bottom number, 3, is called the denominator.

Sometimes fractions are not written in their simplest form. To determine a fraction's **simplest form,** you must find the greatest common factor (GCF) of the numerator and denominator. The greatest common factor is the largest common factor of all the factors the two numbers have in common.

For example, because the number 3 divides into 12 and 30 evenly, it is a common factor of 12 and 30. However, because the number 6 is the largest number that evenly divides into 12 and 30, it is the **greatest common factor.**

After you find the greatest common factor, you can write a fraction in its simplest form. Divide both the numerator and the denominator by the greatest common factor. The number that results is the fraction in its **simplest form.**

Example Twelve of the 20 peaks in a mountain range have elevations over 10,000 m. What fraction of the peaks in the mountain range are over 10,000 m? Write the fraction in simplest form.

Step 1 Write the fraction.

$$\frac{\text{part}}{\text{whole}} = \frac{12}{20}$$

Step 2 To find the GCF of the numerator and denominator, list all of the factors of each number.

Factors of 12: 1, 2, 3, 4, 6, 12 (the numbers that divide evenly into 12)

Factors of 20: 1, 2, 4, 5, 10, 20 (the numbers that divide evenly into 20)

Step 3 List the common factors.

1, 2, 4.

Step 4 Choose the greatest factor in the list of common factors.

The GCF of 12 and 20 is 4.

Step 5 Divide the numerator and denominator by the GCF.

$$\frac{12 \div 4}{20 \div 4} = \frac{3}{5}$$

In the mountain range, $\frac{3}{5}$ of the peaks are over 10,000 m.

Practice Problem There are 90 rides at an amusement park. Of those rides, 66 have a height restriction. What fraction of the rides has a height restriction? Write the fraction in simplest form.

Math Skill Handbook

Calculating Ratios

A **ratio** is a comparison of two numbers by division.

Ratios can be written 3 to 5 or 3:5. Ratios also can be written as fractions, such as $\frac{3}{5}$. Ratios, like fractions, can be written in simplest form. Recall that a fraction is in **simplest form** when the greatest common factor (GCF) of the numerator and denominator is 1.

Example A particular geologic sample contains 40 kg of shale and 64 kg of granite. What is the ratio of shale to granite as a fraction in simplest form?

Step 1 Write the ratio as a fraction. $\frac{\text{shale}}{\text{granite}} = \frac{40}{64}$

Step 2 Express the fraction in simplest form. The GCF of 40 and 64 is 8.

$$\frac{40}{64} = \frac{40 \div 8}{64 \div 8} = \frac{5}{8}$$

The ratio of shale to granite in the sample is $\frac{5}{8}$.

Practice Problem Two metal rods measure 100 cm and 144 cm in length. What is the ratio of their lengths in simplest fraction form?

Using Decimals

A **decimal** is a fraction with a denominator of 10, 100, 1,000, or another power of 10. For example, 0.854 is the same as the fraction $\frac{854}{1,000}$.

In a decimal, the decimal point separates the ones place and the tenths place. For example, 0.27 means twenty-seven hundredths, or $\frac{27}{100}$, where 27 is the **number of units** out of 100 units. Any fraction can be written as a decimal using division.

Example Write $\frac{5}{8}$ as a decimal.

Step 1 Write a division problem with the numerator, 5, as the dividend and the denominator, 8, as the divisor. Write 5 as 5.000.

Step 2 Solve the problem.

```
      0.625
  8)5.000
    48
    ──
     20
     16
     ──
      40
      40
      ──
       0
```

Therefore, $\frac{5}{8} = 0.625$.

Practice Problem Write $\frac{19}{25}$ as a decimal.

Using Percentages

The word *percent* means "out of one hundred." A **percent** is a ratio that compares a number to 100. Suppose you read that 77 percent of Earth's surface is covered by water. That is the same as reading that the fraction of Earth's surface covered by water is $\frac{77}{100}$. To express a fraction as a percent, first find an equivalent decimal for the fraction. Then, multiply the decimal by 100 and add the percent symbol. For example, $\frac{1}{2} = 1 \div 2 = 0.5$. Then $0.5 = 0.50 = 50\%$.

Example Express $\frac{13}{20}$ as a percent.

Step 1 Find the equivalent decimal for the fraction.

$$\begin{array}{r} 0.65 \\ 20\overline{)13.00} \\ \underline{12\,0} \\ 100 \\ \underline{100} \\ 0 \end{array}$$

Step 2 Rewrite the fraction $\frac{13}{20}$ as 0.65.

Step 3 Multiply 0.65 by 100 and add the % sign.

$$0.65 \cdot 100 = 65 = 65\%$$

So, $\frac{13}{20} = 65\%$.

Practice Problem In one year, 73 of 365 days were rainy in one city. What percent of the days in that city were rainy?

Using Precision and Significant Digits

When you make a **measurement,** the value you record depends on the precision of the measuring instrument. When adding or subtracting numbers with different precision, the answer is rounded to the smallest number of decimal places of any number in the sum or difference. When multiplying or dividing, the answer is rounded to the smallest number of significant figures of any number being multiplied or divided. When counting the number of **significant figures,** all digits are counted except zeros at the end of a number with no decimal such as 2,500, and zeros at the beginning of a decimal such as 0.03020.

Example The lengths 5.28 and 5.2 are measured in meters. Find the sum of these lengths and report the sum using the least precise measurement.

Step 1 Find the sum.

$$\begin{array}{rl} 5.28\ \text{m} & \text{2 digits after the decimal} \\ \underline{+\ 5.2\ \ \text{m}} & \text{1 digit after the decimal} \\ 10.48\ \text{m} & \end{array}$$

Step 2 Round to one digit after the decimal because the least number of digits after the decimal of the numbers being added is 1.

The sum is 10.5 m.

Practice Problem Multiply the numbers in the example using the rule for multiplying and dividing. Report the answer with the correct number of significant figures.

Math Skill Handbook

Solving One-Step Equations

An **equation** is a statement that two things are equal. For example, $A = B$ is an equation that states that A is equal to B.

Sometimes one side of the equation will contain a **variable** whose value is not known. In the equation $3x = 12$, the variable is x.

The equation is solved when the variable is replaced with a value that makes both sides of the equation equal to each other. For example, the solution of the equation $3x = 12$ is $x = 4$. If the x is replaced with 4, then the equation becomes $3 \cdot 4 = 12$, or $12 = 12$.

To solve an equation such as $8x = 40$, divide both sides of the equation by the number that multiplies the variable.

$$8x = 40$$
$$\frac{8x}{8} = \frac{40}{8}$$
$$x = 5$$

You can check your answer by replacing the variable with your solution and seeing if both sides of the equation are the same.

$$8x = 8 \cdot 5 = 40$$

The left and right sides of the equation are the same, so $x = 5$ is the solution.

Sometimes an equation is written in this way: $a = bc$. This also is called a **formula.** The letters can be replaced by numbers, but the numbers must still make both sides of the equation the same.

Example 1 Solve the equation $10x = 35$.

Step 1 Find the solution by dividing each side of the equation by 10.

$$10x = 35 \qquad \frac{10x}{10} = \frac{35}{10} \qquad x = 3.5$$

Step 2 Check the solution.

$$10x = 35 \qquad 10 \times 3.5 = 35 \qquad 35 = 35$$

Both sides of the equation are equal, so $x = 3.5$ is the solution to the equation.

Example 2 In the formula $a = bc$, find the value of c if $a = 20$ and $b = 2$.

Step 1 Rearrange the formula so the unknown value is by itself on one side of the equation by dividing both sides by b.

$$a = bc$$
$$\frac{a}{b} = \frac{bc}{b}$$
$$\frac{a}{b} = c$$

Step 2 Replace the variables a and b with the values that are given.

$$\frac{a}{b} = c$$
$$\frac{20}{2} = c$$
$$10 = c$$

Step 3 Check the solution.

$$a = bc$$
$$20 = 2 \times 10$$
$$20 = 20$$

Both sides of the equation are equal, so $c = 10$ is the solution when $a = 20$ and $b = 2$.

Practice Problem In the formula $h = gd$, find the value of d if $g = 12.3$ and $h = 17.4$.

Using Proportions

A **proportion** is an equation that shows that two ratios are equivalent. The ratios $\frac{2}{4}$ and $\frac{5}{10}$ are equivalent, so they can be written as $\frac{2}{4} = \frac{5}{10}$. This equation is an example of a proportion.

When two ratios form a proportion, the **cross products** are equal. To find the cross products in the proportion $\frac{2}{4} = \frac{5}{10}$, multiply the 2 and the 10, and the 4 and the 5. Therefore $2 \cdot 10 = 4 \cdot 5$, or $20 = 20$.

Because you know that both proportions are equal, you can use cross products to find a missing term in a proportion. This is known as **solving the proportion.** Solving a proportion is similar to solving an equation.

Example The heights of a tree and a pole are proportional to the lengths of their shadows. The tree casts a shadow of 24 m at the same time that a 6-m pole casts a shadow of 4 m. What is the height of the tree?

Step 1 Write a proportion.

$$\frac{\text{height of tree}}{\text{height of pole}} = \frac{\text{length of tree's shadow}}{\text{length of pole's shadow}}$$

Step 2 Substitute the known values into the proportion. Let h represent the unknown value, the height of the tree.

$$\frac{h}{6} = \frac{24}{4}$$

Step 3 Find the cross products.

$$h \cdot 4 = 6 \cdot 24$$

Step 4 Simplify the equation.

$$4h = 144$$

Step 5 Divide each side by 4.

$$\frac{4h}{4} = \frac{144}{4}$$

$$h = 36$$

The height of the tree is 36 m.

Practice Problem The ratios of the weights of two objects on the Moon and on Earth are in proportion. A rock weighing 3 N on the Moon weighs 18 N on Earth. How much would a rock that weighs 5 N on the Moon weigh on Earth?

Math Skill Handbook

Using Statistics

Statistics is the branch of mathematics that deals with collecting, analyzing, and presenting data. In statistics, there are three common ways to summarize the data with a single number—the mean, the median, and the mode.

The **mean** of a set of data is the arithmetic average. It is found by adding the numbers in the data set and dividing by the number of items in the set.

The **median** is the middle number in a set of data when the data are arranged in numerical order. If there were an even number of data points, the median would be the mean of the two middle numbers.

The **mode** of a set of data is the number or item that appears most often.

Another number that often is used to describe a set of data is the range. The **range** is the difference between the largest number and the smallest number in a set of data.

A **frequency table** shows how many times each piece of data occurs, usually in a survey. The frequency table below shows the results of a student survey on favorite color.

Color	Tally	Frequency
red	IIII	4
blue	HHI	5
black	II	2
green	III	3
purple	HHI II	7
yellow	HHI I	6

Based on the frequency table data, which color is the favorite?

Example The high temperatures (in °C) on five consecutive days at a desert observation station are 39°, 37°, 44°, 36°, and 44°. Find the mean, median, mode, and range of this set.

To find the mean:
Step 1 Find the sum of the numbers.

$$39 + 37 + 44 + 36 + 44 = 200$$

Step 2 Divide the sum by the number of items, which is 5.

$$200 \div 5 = 40$$

The mean high temperature is 40°C.

To find the median:
Step 1 Arrange the temperatures from least to greatest.

$$36, \ 37, \ \underline{39}, \ 44, \ 44$$

Step 2 Determine the middle temperature.

The median high temperature is 39°C.

To find the mode:
Step 1 Group the numbers that are the same together.

44, 44, 36, 37, 39

Step 2 Determine the number that occurs most in the set.

<u>44, 44</u>, 36, 37, 39

The mode measure is 44°C.

To find the range:
Step 1 Arrange the temperatures from largest to smallest.

44, 44, 39, 37, 36

Step 2 Determine the largest and smallest temperature in the set.

<u>44</u>, 44, 39, 37, <u>36</u>

Step 3 Find the difference between the largest and smallest temperatures.

$$44 - 36 = 8$$

The range is 8°C.

Practice Problem Find the mean, median, mode, and range for the data set 8, 4, 12, 8, 11, 14, 16.

216 ◆ G STUDENT RESOURCES

Safety in the Science Classroom

1. Always obtain your teacher's permission to begin an investigation.

2. Study the procedure. If you have questions, ask your teacher. Be sure you understand any safety symbols shown on the page.

3. Use the safety equipment provided for you. Goggles and a safety apron should be worn during most investigations.

4. Always slant test tubes away from yourself and others when heating them or adding substances to them.

5. Never eat or drink in the lab, and never use lab glassware as food or drink containers. Never inhale chemicals. Do not taste any substances or draw any material into a tube with your mouth.

6. Report any spill, accident, or injury, no matter how small, immediately to your teacher, then follow his or her instructions.

7. Know the location and proper use of the fire extinguisher, safety shower, fire blanket, first aid kit, and fire alarm.

8. Keep all materials away from open flames. Tie back long hair and tie down loose clothing.

9. If your clothing should catch fire, smother it with the fire blanket, or get under a safety shower. NEVER RUN.

10. If a fire should occur, turn off the gas then leave the room according to established procedures.

Follow these procedures as you clean up your work area

1. Turn off the water and gas. Disconnect electrical devices.

2. Clean all pieces of equipment and return all materials to their proper places.

3. Dispose of chemicals and other materials as directed by your teacher. Place broken glass and solid substances in the proper containers. Make sure never to discard materials in the sink.

4. Clean your work area. Wash your hands thoroughly after working in the laboratory.

First Aid	
Injury	**Safe Response** ALWAYS NOTIFY YOUR TEACHER IMMEDIATELY
Burns	Apply cold water.
Cuts and Bruises	Stop any bleeding by applying direct pressure. Cover cuts with a clean dressing. Apply ice packs or cold compresses to bruises.
Fainting	Leave the person lying down. Loosen any tight clothing and keep crowds away.
Foreign Matter in Eye	Flush with plenty of water. Use eyewash bottle or fountain.
Poisoning	Note the suspected poisoning agent.
Any Spills on Skin	Flush with large amounts of water or use safety shower.

Reference Handbook

SI—Metric/English, English/Metric Conversions

	When you want to convert:	To:	Multiply by:
Length	inches	centimeters	2.54
	centimeters	inches	0.39
	yards	meters	0.91
	meters	yards	1.09
	miles	kilometers	1.61
	kilometers	miles	0.62
Mass and Weight*	ounces	grams	28.35
	grams	ounces	0.04
	pounds	kilograms	0.45
	kilograms	pounds	2.2
	tons (short)	tonnes (metric tons)	0.91
	tonnes (metric tons)	tons (short)	1.10
	pounds	newtons	4.45
	newtons	pounds	0.22
Volume	cubic inches	cubic centimeters	16.39
	cubic centimeters	cubic inches	0.06
	liters	quarts	1.06
	quarts	liters	0.95
	gallons	liters	3.78
Area	square inches	square centimeters	6.45
	square centimeters	square inches	0.16
	square yards	square meters	0.83
	square meters	square yards	1.19
	square miles	square kilometers	2.59
	square kilometers	square miles	0.39
	hectares	acres	2.47
	acres	hectares	0.40
Temperature	To convert °Celsius to °Fahrenheit		°C × 9/5 + 32
	To convert °Fahrenheit to °Celsius		5/9 (°F − 32)

*Weight is measured in standard Earth gravity.

Topographic Map Symbols

══════	Primary highway, hard surface	∿∿	Index contour
══-══	Secondary highway, hard surface	··········	Supplementary contour
════	Light-duty road, hard or improved surface	∿	Intermediate contour
==========	Unimproved road	⬭	Depression contours
┼─┼─┼─┼	Railroad: single track		
╪═╪═╪	Railroad: multiple track	▬ ▬ ▬	Boundaries: national
╪┼╪┼╪	Railroads in juxtaposition	▬ ▬ ▬	State
		─ ─ ──	County, parish, municipal
▪▫▪■	Buildings	── ── ──	Civil township, precinct, town, barrio
⚎ ⊞ [cem]	Schools, church, and cemetery	─·─ ─·─	Incorporated city, village, town, hamlet
▪▭ ▨▨	Buildings (barn, warehouse, etc)	·─·─·─·	Reservation, national or state
∘ ∘	Wells other than water (labeled as to type)	──────────	Small park, cemetery, airport, etc.
●●● ⊘	Tanks: oil, water, etc. (labeled only if water)	─··─··─	Land grant
⊙ ꙮ	Located or landmark object; windmill	────────	Township or range line, U.S. land survey
⤬ ⤬	Open pit, mine, or quarry; prospect	── ── ──	Township or range line, approximate location
▦	Marsh (swamp)		
▦	Wooded marsh	∿∿	Perennial streams
▭	Woods or brushwood	→─── ←──	Elevated aqueduct
▦	Vineyard	∘ ⌒	Water well and spring
▦	Land subject to controlled inundation	∿⤬	Small rapids
▦	Submerged marsh	∿	Large rapids
▦	Mangrove	▨▨	Intermittent lake
▦	Orchard	∿⤬∿	Intermittent stream
▦	Scrub	→=====←─	Aqueduct tunnel
▦	Urban area	▨▨	Glacier
		∿⤬	Small falls
x7369	Spot elevation	▬	Large falls
670	Water elevation	▨▨	Dry lake bed

REFERENCE HANDBOOK D

PERIODIC TABLE OF THE ELEMENTS

Columns of elements are called groups. Elements in the same group have similar chemical properties.

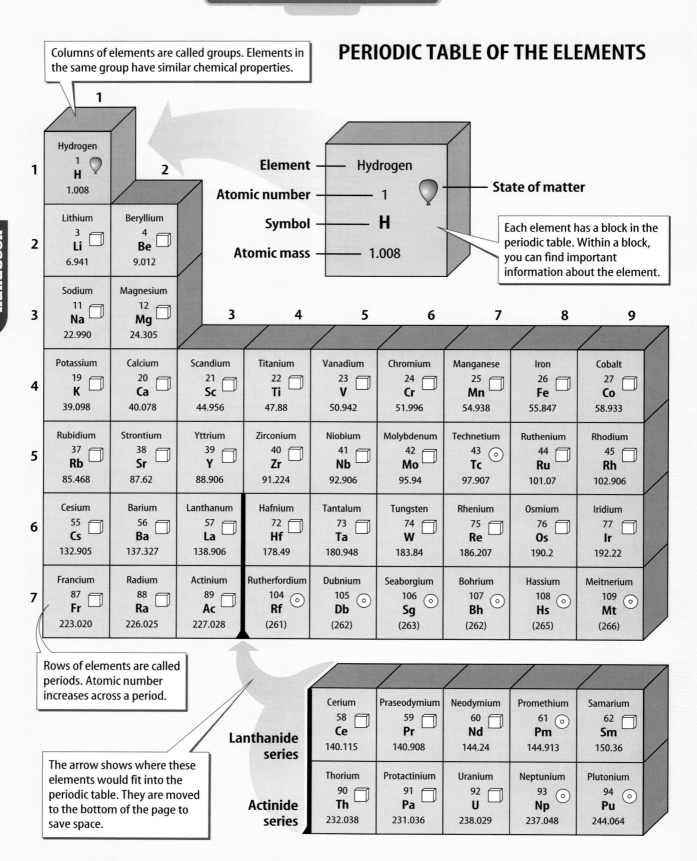

Element —— Hydrogen

Atomic number —— 1

Symbol —— **H**

Atomic mass —— 1.008

State of matter

Each element has a block in the periodic table. Within a block, you can find important information about the element.

Rows of elements are called periods. Atomic number increases across a period.

The arrow shows where these elements would fit into the periodic table. They are moved to the bottom of the page to save space.

Lanthanide series

Actinide series

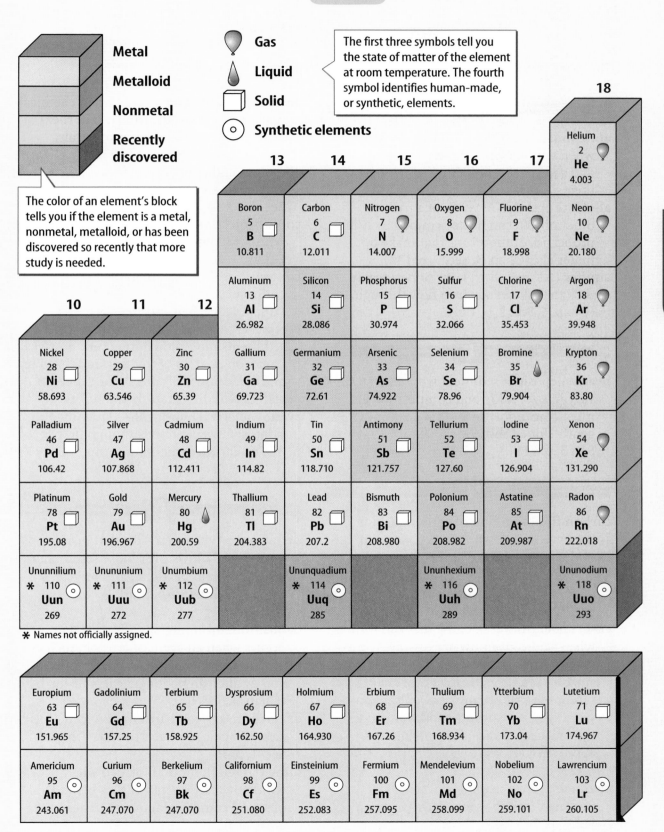

Metal

Metalloid

Nonmetal

Recently discovered

Gas

Liquid

Solid

⊙ Synthetic elements

The first three symbols tell you the state of matter of the element at room temperature. The fourth symbol identifies human-made, or synthetic, elements.

The color of an element's block tells you if the element is a metal, nonmetal, metalloid, or has been discovered so recently that more study is needed.

* Names not officially assigned.

Reference Handbook

English Glossary

This glossary defines each key term that appears in bold type in the text. It also shows the chapter, section, and page number where you can find the word used.

A

abrasion: a type of erosion that occurs when windblown sediments strike rocks and sediments, polishing and pitting their surface. (Chap. 3, Sec. 3, p. 76)

absolute age: age, in years, of a rock or other object; can be determined by using properties of the atoms that make up materials. (Chap. 5, Sec. 3, p. 139)

aquifer (AK wuh fur): layer of permeable rock that allows water to flow through. (Chap. 4, Sec. 2, p. 104)

B

beach: deposit of sediment whose materials vary in size, color, and composition and is most commonly found on a smooth, gently sloped shoreline. (Chap. 4, Sec. 3, p. 111)

C

carbon film: thin film of carbon residue preserved as a fossil. (Chap. 5, Sec. 1, p. 126)

cast: a type of body fossil that forms when crystals fill a mold or sediments wash into a mold and harden into rock. (Chap. 5, Sec. 1, p. 127)

cave: underground opening that can form when acidic groundwater dissolves limestone. (Chap. 4, Sec. 2, p. 107)

Cenozoic (sen uh ZOH ihk) **Era:** era of recent life that began about 66 million years ago and continues today; includes the first appearance of *Homo sapiens* about 400,000 years ago. (Chap. 6, Sec. 3, p. 174)

channel: groove created by water moving down the same path. (Chap. 4, Sec. 1, p. 94)

chemical weathering: occurs when chemical reactions dissolve the minerals in rocks or change them into different minerals. (Chap. 2, Sec. 1, p. 39)

climate: weather pattern that occurs in a particular area over many years. (Chap. 2, Sec. 1, p. 40)

conic projection: map made by projecting points and lines from a globe onto a cone. (Chap. 1, Sec. 3, p. 19)

contour line: line on a map that connects points of equal elevation. (Chap. 1, Sec. 3, p. 20)

creep: a type of mass movement in which sediments move downslope very slowly; common in areas of freezing and thawing, and can cause walls, trees, and fences to lean downhill. (Chap. 3, Sec. 1, p. 66)

cyanobacteria: chlorophyll-containing, photosynthetic bacteria thought to be one of Earth's earliest life-forms. (Chap. 6, Sec. 2, p. 163)

D

deflation: a type of erosion that occurs when wind blows over loose sediments, removes small particles, and leaves coarser sediments behind. (Chap. 3, Sec. 3, p. 76)

deposition: dropping of sediments that occurs when an agent of erosion, such as gravity, a glacier, wind, or water, loses its energy and can no longer carry its load. (Chap. 3, Sec. 1, p. 65)

drainage basin: land area from which a river or stream collects runoff. (Chap. 4, Sec. 1, p. 96)

dune (DOON): mound formed when windblown sediments pile up behind an obstacle; common landform in desert areas. (Chap. 3, Sec. 3, p. 79)

E

eon: longest subdivision in the geologic time scale that is based on the abundance of certain types of fossils and is subdivided into eras, periods, and epochs. (Chap. 6, Sec. 1, p. 155)

epoch: next-smaller division of geologic time after the period; is characterized by differences in life-forms that may vary regionally. (Chap. 6, Sec. 1, p. 155)

equator: imaginary line that wraps around Earth at 0° latitude, halfway between the north and south poles. (Chap. 1, Sec. 2, p. 14)

era: second-longest division of the geologic time scale; is subdivided into periods and is based on major worldwide changes in types of fossils. (Chap. 6, Sec. 1, p. 155)

erosion: process in which surface materials are worn away and transported from one place to another by agents such as gravity, water, wind, and glaciers. (Chap. 3, Sec. 1, p. 64)

F

fault-block mountains: mountains formed from huge, tilted blocks of rock that are separated from surrounding rocks by faults. (Chap. 1, Sec. 1, p. 12)

folded mountains: mountains formed when horizontal rock layers are squeezed from opposite sides, causing them to buckle and fold. (Chap. 1, Sec. 1, p. 11)

fossils: remains, imprints, or traces of prehistoric organisms that can tell when and where organisms once lived and how they lived. (Chap. 5, Sec. 1, p. 125)

G

geologic time scale: division of Earth's history into time units based largely on the types of life-forms that lived only during certain periods. (Chap. 6, Sec. 1, p. 154)

geyser: hot spring that erupts periodically and shoots water and steam into the air—for example, Old Faithful in Yellowstone National Park. (Chap. 4, Sec. 2, p. 101)

glaciers: large, moving masses of ice and snow that change large areas of Earth's surface through erosion and deposition. (Chap. 3, Sec. 2, p. 69)

groundwater: water that soaks into the ground and collects in pores and empty spaces; an important source of drinking water. (Chap. 4, Sec. 2, p. 103)

H

half-life: time it takes for half the atoms of an isotope to decay. (Chap. 5, Sec. 3, p. 140)

horizon: each layer in a soil profile—horizon A (top layer of soil), horizon B (middle layer), and horizon C (bottom layer). (Chap. 2, Sec. 2, p. 44)

humus (HYEW mus): dark-colored, decayed organic matter that supplies nutrients to plants and is found mainly in topsoil. (Chap. 2, Sec. 2, p. 44)

I

ice wedging: mechanical weathering process that occurs when water freezes in the cracks of rocks and expands, causing the rock to break apart. (Chap. 2, Sec. 1, p. 38)

impermeable: describes materials that water cannot pass through. (Chap. 4, Sec. 2, p. 104)

index fossils: remains of species that existed on Earth for a relatively short period of time, were abundant and wide-spread geographically, and can be used by geologists to assign the ages of rock layers. (Chap. 5, Sec. 1, p. 129)

L

latitude: distance in degrees north or south of the equator. (Chap. 1, Sec. 2, p. 14)

leaching: removal of minerals that have been dissolved in water. (Chap. 2, Sec. 2, p. 45)

litter: twigs, leaves, and other organic matter that help prevent erosion and hold water and may eventually be changed into humus by decomposing organisms. (Chap. 2, Sec. 2, p. 45)

loess (LOOS): windblown deposit of tightly packed, fine-grained sediments. (Chap. 3, Sec. 3, p. 79)

longitude: distance in degrees east or west of the prime meridian. (Chap. 1, Sec. 2, p. 15)

longshore current: current that runs parallel to the shoreline, is caused by waves colliding with the shore at slight angles, and moves tons of loose sediment. (Chap. 4, Sec. 3, p. 110)

M

map legend: explains the meaning of symbols used on a map. (Chap. 1, Sec. 3, p. 22)

map scale: relationship between distances on a map and distances on Earth's surface that can be represented as a ratio or as a small bar divided into sections. (Chap. 1, Sec. 3, p. 22)

mass movement: any type of erosion that occurs as gravity moves materials downslope. (Chap. 3, Sec. 1, p. 65)

meander (mee AN dur): broad, c-shaped curve in a river or stream, formed by erosion of its outer bank. (Chap. 4, Sec. 1, p. 97)

mechanical weathering: physical process that breaks rocks apart without changing their chemical makeup; can be caused by ice wedging, animals, and plant roots. (Chap. 2, Sec. 1, p. 37)

Mesozoic (mez uh ZOH ihk) **Era:** middle era of Earth's history, during which Pangaea broke apart, dinosaurs appeared, and reptiles and gymnosperms were the dominant land life-forms. (Chap. 6, Sec. 3, p. 170)

mold: a type of body fossil that forms in rock when an organism with hard parts is buried, decays or dissolves, and leaves a cavity in the rock. (Chap. 5, Sec. 1, p. 127)

moraine: large ridge of rocks and soil deposited by a glacier when it stops moving forward. (Chap. 3, Sec. 2, p. 71)

N

natural selection: process by which organisms that are suited to a particular environment are better able to survive and reproduce than organisms that are not. (Chap. 6, Sec. 1, p. 157)

O

organic evolution: change of organisms over geologic time. (Chap. 6, Sec. 1, p. 156)

outwash: material deposited by meltwater from a glacier. (Chap. 3, Sec. 2, p. 71)

oxidation (ahk sih DAY shun): chemical weathering process that occurs when metallic material is exposed to oxygen and water over time. (Chap. 2, Sec. 1, p. 40)

P

Paleozoic Era: era of ancient life, which began about 544 million years ago, when organisms developed hard parts, and ended with mass extinctions about 245 million years ago. (Chap. 6, Sec. 2, p. 164)

Pangaea (pan JEE uh): supercontinent formed at the end of the Paleozoic Era when sea-level dropped and continents came together to form one giant landmass. (Chap. 6, Sec. 1, p. 161)

period: third-longest division of geologic time; is subdivided into epochs and is characterized by the types of life that existed worldwide. (Chap. 6, Sec. 1, p. 155)

permeable (PUR mee uh bul): describes soil and rock with connecting pores through which water can flow. (Chap. 4, Sec. 2, p. 104)

permineralized remains: fossils in which the spaces inside are filled with minerals from groundwater. (Chap. 5, Sec. 1, p. 126)

plain: large, flat landform that often has thick, fertile soil and is usually found in the interior region of a continent. (Chap. 1, Sec. 1, p. 8)

plateau (pla TOH): flat, raised landform made up of nearly horizontal rocks that have been uplifted. (Chap. 1, Sec. 1, p. 10)

plucking: process that adds gravel, sand, and boulders to a glacier's bottom and sides as water freezes and thaws, breaking off pieces of surrounding rock. (Chap. 3, Sec. 2, p. 70)

Precambrian (pree KAM bree un) **time:** longest part of Earth's history, lasting from 4.0 billion to about 544 million years ago. (Chap. 6, Sec. 2, p. 162)

prime meridian: imaginary line that represents 0° longitude and runs from the north pole through Greenwich, England, to the south pole. (Chap. 1, Sec. 2, p. 15)

principle of superposition: states that in undisturbed rock layers, the oldest rocks are on the bottom and the rocks become progressively younger toward the top. (Chap. 5, Sec. 2, p. 132)

R

radioactive decay: process in which some isotopes break down into other isotopes and particles. (Chap. 5, Sec. 3, p. 139)

radiometric dating: process used to calculate the absolute age of rock by measuring the ratio of parent isotope to daughter product in a mineral and knowing the half-life of the parent. (Chap. 5, Sec. 3, p. 141)

relative age: the age of something compared with other things. (Chap. 5, Sec. 2, p. 133)

runoff: any rainwater that does not soak into the ground or evaporate but flows over Earth's surface; generally flows into streams and has the ability to erode and carry sediments. (Chap. 4, Sec. 1, p. 92)

S

sheet erosion: a type of surface water erosion caused by runoff that occurs when water flowing as sheets picks up sediments and carries them away. (Chap. 4, Sec. 1, p. 95)

slump: a type of mass movement that occurs when a mass of material moves down a curved slope. (Chap. 3, Sec. 1, p. 65)

soil: mixture of weathered rock, decayed organic matter, mineral fragments, water, and air that can take thousands of years to develop. (Chap. 2, Sec. 2, p. 42)

soil profile: vertical section of soil layers, each of which is a horizon. (Chap. 2, Sec. 2, p. 44)

species: group of organisms that reproduces only with other members of their own group. (Chap. 6, Sec. 1, p. 156)

spring: forms when the water table meets Earth's surface; often found on hillsides and used as a freshwater source. (Chap. 4, Sec. 2, p. 107)

T

terracing: farming method used to reduce erosion on steep slopes. (Chap. 2, Sec. 3, p. 53)

till: mixture of different-sized sediments that is dropped from the base of a retreating glacier and can cover huge areas of land. (Chap. 3, Sec. 2, p. 70)

topographic map: map that shows the changes in elevation of Earth's surface and indicates such features as roads and cities. (Chap. 1, Sec. 3, p. 20)

trilobite (TRI luh bite): organism with a three-lobed exoskeleton that was abundant in Paleozoic oceans and is considered to be an index fossil. (Chap. 6, Sec. 1, p. 154)

U

unconformity (un kun FOR mih tee): gap in the rock layer that is due to erosion or periods without any deposition. (Chap. 5, Sec. 2, p. 133)

English Glossary

uniformitarianism: principle stating that Earth processes occurring today are similar to those that occurred in the past. (Chap. 5, Sec. 3, p. 143)

upwarped mountains: mountains formed when blocks of Earth's crust are pushed up by forces inside Earth. (Chap. 1, Sec. 1, p. 12)

V

volcanic mountains: mountains formed when molten material reaches Earth's surface through a weak crustal area and piles up into a cone-shaped structure. (Chap. 1, Sec. 1, p. 13)

W

water table: upper surface of the zone of saturation; drops during a drought. (Chap. 4, Sec. 2, p. 104)

weathering: mechanical or chemical surface processes that break rocks into smaller and smaller pieces. (Chap. 2, Sec. 1, p. 36)

Este glosario define cada término clave que aparece en negrillas en el texto. También muestra el capítulo, la sección y el número de página en donde se usa dicho término.

A

abrasion / abrasión: tipo de erosión que ocurre cuando los sedimentos soplados por el viento golpean rocas y sedimentos, puliendo y dejando huecos en su superficie. (Cap. 3, Sec. 3, pág. 76)

absolute age / edad absoluta: edad, expresada en años, de una roca u otro material; se puede determinar usando las propiedades de los átomos que componen tales materiales. (Cap. 5, Sec. 3, pág. 139)

aquifer / acuífero: capa de roca permeable que permite la infiltración del agua. (Cap. 4, Sec. 2, pág. 104)

B

beach / playa: depósito de sedimentos cuyos materiales varían en tamaño, color y composición y que se halla comúnmente en un litoral liso y levemente inclinado. (Cap. 4, Sec. 3, pág. 111)

C

carbonaceous film / película carbonácea: fina película de residuo carbonoso preservada como fósil. (Cap. 5, Sec. 1, pág. 126)

cast / impresión fósil: tipo de fósil corporal que se forma cuando los cristales llenan un molde o cuando los sedimentos se asientan en un molde y se endurecen convirtiéndose en roca. (Cap. 5, Sec. 1, pág.127)

cave / caverna: abertura subterránea que se puede formar cuando las aguas subterráneas ácidas disuelven la piedra caliza. (Cap. 4, Sec. 2, pág. 107)

Cenozoic Era / Era Cenozoica: era de vida reciente que comenzó hace 66 millones de años aproximadamente y que continúa hoy en día; incluye la primera aparición del Homo sapiens hace unos 400,000 años. (Cap. 6, Sec. 3, pág. 174)

channel / cauce: surco creado por agua que corre hacia abajo del mismo sendero. (Cap. 4, Sec. 1, pág. 94)

chemical weathering / meteorización química: se presenta cuando las reacciones químicas disuelven los minerales de las rocas o los transforman en minerales diferentes. (Cap. 2, Sec. 1, pág. 39)

climate / clima: patrón meteorológico que ocurre en una región en particular durante muchos años. (Cap. 2, Sec. 1, pág. 40)

conic projection / proyección cónica: mapa que se hace proyectando puntos y líneas de un globo terráqueo a un cono. (Cap. 1, Sec. 3, pág. 19)

contour line / curva de nivel: línea en un mapa que conecta puntos con igual elevación. (Cap. 1, Sec. 3, pág. 20)

creep / corrimiento: tipo de movimiento de masas en el cual los sedimentos se mueven cuesta abajo paulatinamente; es común en áreas de congelamiento y derretimiento; puede hacer que las paredes, los árboles y las cercas se inclinen. (Cap. 3, Sec. 1, pág. 66)

cyanobacteria / cianobacterias: bacterias fotosintéticas que contienen clorofila y que se piensa son unas de las primeras

Spanish Glossary

formas de vida terrestre. (Cap. 6, Sec. 2, pág. 163)

D

deflation / deflacción: tipo de erosión que se presenta cuando el viento sopla sobre sedimentos sueltos, extrae micropartículas y deja atrás sedimentos más gruesos. (Cap. 3, Sec. 3, pág. 76)

deposition / depositación: acción de dejar caer los sedimentos, la cual ocurre cuando un agente erosivo, como la gravedad, un glaciar, el viento o el agua, pierde su energía y no puede seguir transportando su carga. (Cap. 3, Sec. 1, pág. 65)

drainage basin / cuenca hidrográfica: terreno del cual un río u otra corriente de agua recoge las aguas de escorrentía. (Cap. 4, Sec. 1, pág. 96)

dune / duna: montículo que se forma cuando los sedimentos arrastrados por el viento se acumulan detrás de una barrera; relieve común en las regiones desérticas. (Cap. 3, Sec. 3, pág. 79)

E

eon / eón: la subdivisión más larga de la escala del tiempo geológico, basada en la abundancia de ciertos tipos de fósiles; se subdivide en eras, períodos y épocas. (Cap. 6, Sec. 1, pág. 155)

epoch / época: la siguiente subdivisión de tiempo geológico que le sigue al período; se caracteriza por diferencias en formas de vida que pueden variar regionalmente. (Cap. 6, Sec. 1, pág. 155)

equator / ecuador: línea imaginaria que rodea la Tierra alrededor de 0° de latitud, equidistante del polo norte y el polo sur. (Cap. 1, Sec. 2, pág. 14)

era / era: segunda división mayor del tiempo geológico; se subdivide en períodos y se basa en cambios importantes a nivel mundial en los tipos de fósiles. (Cap. 6, Sec. 1, pág. 155)

erosion / erosión: proceso en el cual los materiales superficiales se desgastan y son transportados de un lugar a otro por agentes como la gravedad, el agua, el viento y los glaciares. (Cap. 3, Sec. 1, pág. 64)

F

fault-block mountains / montañas de bloques de falla: montañas que se forman de enormes bloques rocosos inclinados, pero separados de las rocas circundantes por fallas. (Cap. 1, Sec. 1, pág. 12)

folded mountains / montañas plegadas: montañas que se forman cuando las capas rocosas horizontales son comprimidas desde lados opuestos, lo cual hace que se encorven y se doblen. (Cap. 1, Sec. 1, pág. 11)

fossils / fósiles: restos, impresiones o trazas de organismos prehistóricos que pueden indicar cuándo y dónde los organismos vivieron y cómo vivieron. (Cap. 5, Sec. 1, pág. 125)

G

geologic time scale / escala del tiempo geológico: división de la historia de la Tierra en unidades cronológicas basadas en gran parte en los tipos de formas de vida que existieron solamente en ciertos períodos. (Cap. 6, Sec. 1, pág. 154)

geyser / géiser: manantial de agua caliente que brota periódicamente y lanza agua y vapor al aire. Un ejemplo es el Old Faithful en el parque nacional de Yellowstone. (Cap. 4, Sec. 2, pág. 101)

glaciers / glaciares: extensas masas de hielo y nieve en movimiento que cambian grandes regiones de la superficie terrestre, a través de la erosión y la depositación. (Cap. 3, Sec. 2, pág. 69)

groundwater / agua subterránea: agua que se filtra en el suelo y se junta en poros y espacios vacíos y la cual es una fuente importante de agua potable. (Cap. 4, Sec. 2, pág. 103)

H

half-life / media vida: tiempo que se demora en desintegrarse la mitad de los átomos de un isótopo. (Cap. 5, Sec. 3, pág. 140)

horizon / horizonte: cada capa del perfil del suelo: horizonte A (capa superior del suelo), horizonte B (capa intermedia) y horizonte C (capa inferior). (Cap. 2, Sec. 2, pág. 44)

humus / humus: materia orgánica negruzca y descompuesta que suministra nutrientes a las plantas y que se halla principalmente en la capa de suelo arable. (Cap. 2, Sec. 2, pág. 44)

I

ice wedging / grietas debido al hielo: proceso de meteorización mecánica que ocurre cuando el agua se congela en las grietas de las rocas y se expande, haciendo que la roca se fragmente. (Cap. 2, Sec. 1, pág. 38)

impermeable / impermeable: describe los materiales por los cuales el agua no puede filtrarse. (Cap. 4, Sec. 2, pág. 104)

index fossils / fósiles guía: restos de especies que existieron en la Tierra durante un período relativamente corto de tiempo, fueron abundantes y se extendieron geográficamente ; los geólogos pueden usar estos fósiles para determinar las edades de las capas rocosas. (Cap. 5, Sec. 1, pág. 129)

L

latitude / latitud: distancia en grados al norte o al sur del ecuador. (Cap. 1, Sec. 2, pág. 14)

leaching / lixiviación: extracción de minerales que se han disuelto en agua. (Cap. 2, Sec. 2, pág. 45)

litter / desechos orgánicos: ramitas, hojas y otras materias orgánicas que ayudan a evitar la erosión y que retienen agua y pueden, a la larga, convertirse en humus gracias a la acción de organismos descomponedores. (Cap. 2, Sec. 2, pág. 45)

loess / loess: depósito de sedimentos firmemente compactados y de granos finos que es arrastrado por el viento. (Cap. 3, Sec. 3, pág. 79)

longitude / longitud: distancia en grados al este o al oeste del primer meridiano. (Cap. 1, Sec. 2, pág. 15)

longshore current / corriente costera: corriente que corre paralela a la costa, producto de olas que chocan contra la costa haciendo ángulos leves y que mueven toneladas de sedimento suelto. (Cap. 4, Sec. 3, pág. 110)

M

map legend / leyenda de mapa: explica los símbolos que se usan en un mapa. (Cap. 1, Sec. 3, pág. 22)

map scale / escala de un mapa: relación entre la distancia en un mapa y la distancia real sobre la superficie terrestre, la cual se puede representar como una razón o como una pequeña barra dividida en secciones. (Cap. 1, Sec. 3, pág. 22)

mass movement / movimiento de masas: cualquier tipo de erosión que ocurre a medida que la gravedad mueve materiales cuesta abajo. (Cap. 3, Sec. 1, pág. 65)

meander / meandro: curva ancha y en forma de c en un río u otra corriente de agua, formada por la erosión de su ribera externa. (Cap. 4, Sec. 1, pág. 97)

mechanical weathering / meteorización mecánica: proceso físico que fragmenta rocas sin alterar su composición química; puede ser el resultado de las grietas debido al hielo, a la acción de los animales y a las raíces vegetales. (Cap. 2, Sec. 1, pág. 37)

Mesozoic Era / Era del Mesozoico: era intermedia de la historia de la Tierra, durante la cual se separó Pangaea, aparecieron los dinosaurios y los reptiles y las gimnospermas eran las formas de vida dominantes en tierra. (Cap. 6, Sec. 3, pág. 170)

mold / molde: tipo de fósil corporal que se forma en la roca cuando un organismo con partes duras se entierra, se descompone o se disuelve y deja una cavidad en la roca. (Cap. 5, Sec. 1, pág. 127)

moraine / morrena: extenso banco de rocas y suelo que un glaciar deposita cuando se detiene su movimiento. (Cap. 3, Sec. 2, pág. 71)

N

natural selection / selección natural: proceso por el cual los organismos que están adaptados a un entorno en particular son más capaces de sobrevivir y reproducirse que organismos que no lo están. (Cap. 6, Sec. 1, pág. 157)

O

organic evolution / evolución orgánica: cambio de organismos a través del tiempo geológico. (Cap. 6, Sec. 1, pág. 156)

outwash / derrubio: material depositado por el agua derretida de un glaciar. (Cap. 3, Sec. 2, pág. 71)

oxidation / oxidación: proceso de meteorización química que ocurre cuando cualquier material metálico se expone al oxígeno y al agua durante un período de tiempo. (Cap. 2, Sec. 1, pág. 40)

P

Paleozoic Era / Era Paleozoica: era de vida antigua, la cual comenzó hace unos 544 millones de años, cuando los organismos desarrollaron partes duras y terminó con extinciones en masa hace unos 245 millones de años. (Cap. 6, Sec. 2, pág. 164)

Pangaea / Pangaea: supercontinente que se formó al final de la era Paleozoica cuando bajó el nivel del mar y los continentes se juntaron para formar una gigantesca masa de tierra firme. (Cap. 6, Sec. 1, pág. 161)

period / período: tercera división mayor del tiempo geológico; se subdivide en épocas y se caracteriza por los tipos de vida que existieron por todo el planeta. (Cap. 6, Sec. 1, pág. 155)

permeable / permeable: describe el suelo y la roca con poros que se conectan y a través de los cuales puede correr el agua. (Cap. 4, Sec. 2, pág. 104)

permineralized remains / restos permineralizados: fósiles cuyos espacios interiores están llenos de minerales provenientes de aguas subterráneas. (Cap. 5, Sec. 1, pág. 126)

Spanish Glossary

plain / llanura: relieve enorme y plano que con frecuencia posee suelos gruesos y fértiles; por lo general se encuentra en las regiones interiores de un continente. (Cap. 1, Sec. 1, pág. 8)

plateau / meseta: relieve levantado formado principalmente de rocas casi horizontales que han sido levantadas. (Cap. 1, Sec. 1, pág. 10)

plucking / ablación: proceso mediante el cual se agrega grava, arena y piedras a las partes inferior y lateral de un glaciar conforme el agua se congela y derrite, rompiendo fragmentos de la roca circundante. (Cap. 3, Sec. 2, pág. 70)

Precambrian time / Era Precámbrica: la parte más larga de la historia de la Tierra, la cual duró de 4.0 billones hasta hace cerca de 544 millones de años. (Cap. 6, Sec. 2, pág. 162)

prime meridian / primer meridiano: línea imaginaria que representa 0° de longitud y corre desde el polo norte, atravesando Greenwich, Inglaterra, hasta el polo sur. (Cap. 1, Sec. 2, pág. 15)

principle of superposition / principio de sobreposición: establece que en capas rocosas inalteradas, las rocas más antiguas se encuentran en el fondo y las rocas más recientes se hallan en la parte superior. (Cap. 5, Sec. 2, pág. 132)

R

radioactive decay / desintegración radiactiva: proceso en el cual algunos isótopos se descomponen en otros isótopos y partículas. (Cap. 5, Sec. 3, pág. 139)

radiometric dating / datación radiométrica: proceso que se usa para calcular la edad absoluta de las rocas midiendo la razón del isótopo original al pro-

ducto descendiente en un mineral y conociendo la vida media del isótopo original. (Cap. 5, Sec. 3, pág. 141)

relative age / edad relativa: la edad de algo comparada con otras cosas. (Cap. 5, Sec. 2, pág. 133)

runoff / escorrentía: cualquier agua lluvia que no se filtra en el suelo o que no se evapora pero que corre por la superficie terrestre: por lo general, corre hacia corrientes de agua y tiene la capacidad de erosionar y transportar sedimentos. (Cap. 4, Sec. 1, pág. 92)

S

sheet erosion / erosión laminar: tipo de erosión hídrica de superficie causada por el agua de escorrentía que ocurre cuando el agua que fluye sobre capas extensas recoge sedimentos y los transporta. (Cap. 4, Sec. 1, pág. 95)

slump / desprendimiento: tipo de movimiento de masas que se presenta cuando una masa de material se mueve cuesta abajo por una pendiente curva. (Cap. 3, Sec. 1, pág. 65)

soil / suelo: mezcla de roca meteorizada, materia orgánica descompuesta, fragmentos minerales y aire; su formación puede tomar miles de años. (Cap. 2, Sec. 2, pág. 42)

soil profile / perfil del suelo: corte vertical de las capas del suelo, cada una de las cuales constituye un horizonte. (Cap. 2, Sec. 2, pág. 44)

species / especie: grupo de organismos que se reproduce sólo con otros miembros de su propio grupo. (Cap. 6, Sec. 1, pág. 156)

spring / manantial: se forma cuando el nivel hidrostático se junta con la superficie terrestre; a menudo se halla en las laderas de las colinas y se utiliza como una fuente de agua dulce. (Cap. 4, Sec. 2, pág. 107)

T

terracing / cultivo en terrazas: método de cultivo que se utiliza para reducir la erosión en laderas inclinadas. (Cap. 2, Sec. 3, pág. 53)

till / depositación glacial o morena: mezcla de sedimentos de diferentes tamaños que un glaciar en retirada deja caer de la base y que puede cubrir inmensas áreas de terreno. (Cap. 3, Sec. 2, pág. 70)

topographic map / mapa topográfico: mapa que muestra los cambios en elevación en la superficie terrestre e indica rasgos como caminos y ciudades. (Cap. 1, Sec. 3, pág. 20)

trilobite / trilobites: organismo con un exoesqueleto dividido en tres partes; existía en abundancia en los océanos del Paleozoico; se le considera un fósil guía. (Cap. 6, Sec. 1, pág. 154)

U

unconformity / discordancia: brecha en una capa rocosa provocada por la erosión o por períodos cuando no hubo depositación. (Cap. 5, Sec. 2, pág. 133)

uniformitarianism / uniformitarianismo: principio que establece que los procesos terrestres que suceden en la actualidad son semejantes a aquéllos que ocurrieron en el pasado. (Cap. 5, Sec. 3, pág. 143)

upwarped mountains / montañas plegadas anticlinales: montañas que se forman cuando los bloques de corteza terrestre son forzados a ascender por fuerzas internas de la Tierra. (Cap. 1, Sec. 1, pág. 12)

V

volcanic mountains / montañas volcánicas: montañas que se forman cuando el material fundido llega a la superficie terrestre a través de partes debilitadas de la corteza y se amontona en una estructura que tiene forma de cono. (Cap. 1, Sec. 1, pág. 13)

W

water table / nivel hidrostático o capa freática: nivel superior de la zona de saturación; disminuye durante una sequía. (Cap. 4, Sec. 2, pág. 104)

weathering / meteorización: procesos superficiales mecánicos o químicos que rompen las rocas en fragmentos cada vez más pequeños. (Cap. 2, Sec. 1, pág. 36)

The index for *The Changing Surface of Earth* will help you locate major topics in the book quickly and easily. Each entry in the index is followed by the number of the pages on which the entry is discussed. A page number given in boldfaced type indicates the page on which that entry is defined. A page number given in italic type indicates a page on which the entry is used in an illustration or photograph. The abbreviation *act.* indicates a page on which the entry is used in an activity.

Index

Index

Index

Index

Index

Art Credits

Glencoe would like to acknowledge the artists and agencies who participated in illustrating this program: Absolute Science Illustration; Andrew Evansen; Argosy; Articulate Graphics; Craig Attebery represented by Frank & Jeff Lavaty; CHK America; Gagliano Graphics; Pedro Julio Gonzalez represented by Melissa Turk & The Artist Network; Robert Hynes represented by Mendola Ltd.; Morgan Cain & Associates; JTH Illustration; Laurie O'Keefe; Matthew Pippin represented by Beranbaum Artist's Representative; Precision Graphics; Publisher's Art; Rolin Graphics, Inc.; Wendy Smith represented by Melissa Turk & The Artist Network; Kevin Torline represented by Berendsen and Associates, Inc.; WILDlife ART; Phil Wilson represented by Cliff Knecht Artist Representative; Zoo Botanica.

Photo Credits

Abbreviation Key: AA=Animals Animals; AH=Aaron Haupt; AMP=Amanita Pictures; BC=Bruce Coleman, Inc.; CB=CORBIS; DM=Doug Martin; DRK=DRK Photo; ES=Earth Scenes; FP=Fundamental Photographs; GH=Grant Heilman Photography; IC=Icon Images; KS=KS Studios; LA=Liaison Agency; MB=Mark Burnett; MM=Matt Meadows; PE=PhotoEdit; PD=Photo-Disc; PQ=PictureQuest; PR=Photo Researchers; SB=Stock Boston; TSA=Tom Stack & Associates; TSM=The Stock Market; VU=Visuals Unlimited.

Cover Jack Dykinga/Stone; **vi** PhotoTake NYC/PQ; **vii** Jim Hughes/PhotoVenture/VU; **viii** KS; **1** MM; **2** Charles Palek/ES; **3** (t)Tom Bean/Stone, (b)C. C. Lockwood/ES; **4** J.C. Marchak/AP/Wide World Photos; **5** (t)David Ulmer/SB, (b)MB; **6** David Weintraub/SB; **6-7** GSFC/NASA; **7** Dominic Oldershaw; **9** (t)Carr Clifton/Minden Pic- tures, (c)Alan Maichrowicz/Peter Arnold, Inc., (b)Stephen G. Maka/DRK; **10** (t)Tom Bean/DRK, (b)Liz Hymans/Stone; **11** John Lemker/ES; **12** (t)John Kieffer/Peter Arnold, Inc., (b)Carr Clifton/Minden Pictures; **13 16** Dominic Oldershaw; **21** (t)Rob & Ann Simpson, (c)Robert E. Pratt, (b)courtesy Maps a la Carte, Inc. and TopoZone.com; **26** John Evans; **27** Layne Kennedy/CB; **28** (l)Culver Pictures, (r)PD; **28-29** Pictor; **29** (t)PD, (bl)William Manning/TSM, (br)Kunio Owaki/TSM; **30** (l)William J. Weber, (r)AH; **31** (l)Tom Bean/DRK, (r)Marc Muench; **34** Mickey Gibson/ES; **34-35** Francois Gohier/PR; **35** Mary Kate Denny/PE; **36** MB; **37** (l)StudiOhio, (r)Tom Bean/DRK; **38** W. Perry Conway/CB; **39** Hans Strand/Stone; **40** (tl)Craig Kramer, (tr)A.J. Copley/VU, (bl br)John Evans; **41** (l)Runk/Schoenberger from GH, (r)William Johnson/SB; **43** (bkgd) Stephen R. Wagner, (t)James D. Balog, (c)Martin Miller, (b)Steven C. Wilson/Entheos; **44** (l)Bonnie Heidel/VU, (r)John Bova/PR; **49** MM; **50** (l)Gary Braasch/CB, (r)Donna Ikenberry/ES; **51** Chip & Jill Isenhart/TSA; **52** (t)Dr. Russ Utgard, (b)Denny Eilers from GH; **53** Georg Custer/PR; **54** (t)George H. Harrison from GH, (b)Bob Daemmrich; **55** KS; **56** Larry Hamill; **57** Courtesy Elvia Niebla; **58** (t)Adam Jones/Masterfile, (c)Barry L. Runk from GH, (b)Tom Bean/DRK; **59** (l)Tom Bean/DRK, (r)David M. Dennis/ES; **60** MB; **62** Victor Englebert; **62-63** Robert Holmes/CB; **63** MM; **64** Robert L. Schuster/USGS; **65** Martin G. Miller/VU; **66** (tl)Atwood/USGS, (bl)Sylvester Allred/VU, (br)Tom Uhlman/VU; **67** AP/Wide World Photos; **68** D. Newman/VU; **70** James N. Westwater; **71** (t)Michael Marten/Science Photo Library/PR, (b)Tom Bean/CB; **72** John Gerlach/VU; **73** Gregory G. Dimijian/PR; **74** Mark E. Gibson/VU; **75** Timothy Fuller; **76** Galen Rowell/CB; **77** Jerry Howard/SB; **78** Fletcher & Baylis/PR; **79** (t)John D. Cunningham/VU, (b)file photo; **80** (tl)Stephen J. Krasemann/PR, (tr)Steve McCurry, (c)Breck P.

Kent/ES, (b)Wyman P. Meinzer; **81** Georg Gerster/PR; **82** (t)Greg Vaughn/TSA, (b)MM; **84** (t)Yann Arthus-Bertrand/CB, (b)Curt Schieber; **85** (t)AP/Wide World Photos, (b)World Class Images; **86** (t)David Cavagnaro/VU, (c)MB/PR, (b)David Weintraub/PR; **87** (l)David Hosking/PR, (r)AP/Wide World Photos; **90** NASA; **90-91** William Manning/TSM; **91** AH; **92** (l)Michael Busselle/Stone, (r)David Woodfall/ DRK; **93** Tim Davis/Stone; **94** (t)GH, (b)KS; **96** Panoramic Images; **98** (bkgd) Stephen R. Wagner, (inset)CB/PQ; **99** (l)Harald Sund/The Image Bank, (r)Loren McIntyre; **100** C. Davidson/Comstock; **101** James L. Amos/CB; **102** (l)Wolfgang Kaehler, (r)Nigel Press/Stone **103** First Image; **105** CB; **106** file photo; **107** Barbara Filet/Stone; **108** Chad Ehlers/Stone; **109** Steve Lissau; **110** Macduff Everton/The Image Bank; **111** (tl)Steve Bentsen, (tr)SuperStock, (bl)Runk/Schoenberger from Grant Heilman Photography, (br)Breck P. Kent/ES; **112** Bruce Roberts/PR; **114 115** KS; **116** Jack Dermid/BC; **117** (l)David Alan Harvey/National Geographic, (r)Gary Bogdon/CB Sygma; **118** (l)Tom Bean/DRK, (r)David W. Hamilton/The Image Bank; **119** (l)Todd Powell/Index Stock, (r)J. Wengle/DRK; **122** James L. Amos/PR; **122-123** Larry Ulrich/DRK; **123** MM; **124** (t)Mark E. Gibson/VU, (b)A.J. Copley/VU; **125** Jeffrey Rotman/CB; **126** (t)Dr. John A. Long, (b)Martin Land/PR; **128** (t)PhotoTake NYC/PQ, (bl br)Louis Psihoyos/Matrix; **130** David M. Dennis; **131** (l)Gary Retherford/PR, (r)Fred McConnaughey/ PR; **132** AH; **135** (tl)IPR/12-18 T. Bain, British Geological Survey/NERC, (tr)Tom Bean/CB, (b)Lyle Rosbotham; **136** Jim Hughes/PhotoVenture/VU; **137** (l)Michael T. Sedam/CB, (r)Pat O'Hara/ CB; **139** AH; **141** James King-Holmes/ Science Photo

Library/PR; **142** (t)Breck P. Kent/ES, (b)Kenneth Garrett; **143** WildCountry/CB; **144** (t)A.J. Copley/VU, (b)MM; **145** Lawson Wood/CB; **146-147** Jacques Bredy; **147** (t c)CMN Archives/Dinofish, (b)Norbert Wu; **148** (t)Francois Gohier/PR, (c)from Journal of Ecology 2000, 88, pp. 45-53. Photo courtesy Michigan Technological University, (b)Tom Bean/DRK; **149** (tl)Francois Gohier/PR, (tr)Mark E. Gibson/DRK, (b)Sinclair Stammers/PR; **152** CB; **152-153** Reuters New Media Inc./CB; **153** KS; **154** Tom & Therisa Stack/TSA; **156** (l)Gerald & Buff Corsi/VU, (r)John Gerlach/AA; **158** (t)Mark Boulron/PR, (others)Walter Chandoha; **159** Jeff Lepore/PR; **163** (l)Mitsuaki Iwago/Minden Pictures, (r)R. Calentine/VU; **165** J.G. Gehling/Discover Magazine; **166** Gerry Ellis/ENP Images; **169** MM; **172** (l)David Burnham/Fossilworks, Inc., (r)Francois Gohier/PR; **174** Michael Andrews/ES; **175** Tom J. Ulrich/VU; **176** David M. Dennis; **177** MB; **178** Bridgeman Art Library; **180** (l)Adam Jones/PR, (r)Ken Lucas/VU; **181** (l)E. Webber/VU, (r)Len Rue, Jr./AA; **183** John Cancalosi/SB; **184** Maresa Pryor/ES; **185** (tl)Joyce Photographics/PR, (tr)M. Deeble/Stone/OSF/ES, (b)Jeff Foott/DRK; **186-187** PD; **188** Townsend P. Dickinson/The Image Works; **189** (tl)Townsend P. Dickinson/ The Image Works, (tr)A.J. Copley/VU, (bl)Stephen J. Krasemann/DRK, (br)Ken Lucas/VU; **190** (tl) Sinclair Stammers/Science Photo Library/PR, (tr)Townsend P. Dickinson/The ImageWorks, (bl)John Elk III/SB, (br)James L. Amos/PR; **192** Michell D. Bridwell/PE; **196** David Young-Wolff/ PE; **198** Kaz Chiba/PD; **199** Dominic Oldershaw; **200** StudioOhio; **201** MM; **203** (tl tr c)Mark Steinmetz, (bl)Elaine Shay, (br)Brent Turner/BLT Productions; **206** Paul Barton/TSM; **209** AH.

PERIODIC TABLE OF THE ELEMENTS

Columns of elements are called groups. Elements in the same group have similar chemical properties.

Element — Hydrogen
Atomic number — 1
Symbol — **H**
Atomic mass — 1.008
State of matter

Each element has a block in the periodic table. Within a block, you can find important information about the element.

1

1
Hydrogen
1
H
1.008

2

2
Lithium
3
Li
6.941

Beryllium
4
Be
9.012

3
Sodium
11
Na
22.990

Magnesium
12
Mg
24.305

3 | **4** | **5** | **6** | **7** | **8** | **9**

4
Potassium
19
K
39.098

Calcium
20
Ca
40.078

Scandium
21
Sc
44.956

Titanium
22
Ti
47.88

Vanadium
23
V
50.942

Chromium
24
Cr
51.996

Manganese
25
Mn
54.938

Iron
26
Fe
55.847

Cobalt
27
Co
58.933

5
Rubidium
37
Rb
85.468

Strontium
38
Sr
87.62

Yttrium
39
Y
88.906

Zirconium
40
Zr
91.224

Niobium
41
Nb
92.906

Molybdenum
42
Mo
95.94

Technetium
43
Tc
97.907

Ruthenium
44
Ru
101.07

Rhodium
45
Rh
102.906

6
Cesium
55
Cs
132.905

Barium
56
Ba
137.327

Lanthanum
57
La
138.906

Hafnium
72
Hf
178.49

Tantalum
73
Ta
180.948

Tungsten
74
W
183.84

Rhenium
75
Re
186.207

Osmium
76
Os
190.2

Iridium
77
Ir
192.22

7
Francium
87
Fr
223.020

Radium
88
Ra
226.025

Actinium
89
Ac
227.028

Rutherfordium
104
Rf
(261)

Dubnium
105
Db
(262)

Seaborgium
106
Sg
(263)

Bohrium
107
Bh
(262)

Hassium
108
Hs
(265)

Meitnerium
109
Mt
(266)

Rows of elements are called periods. Atomic number increases across a period.

The arrow shows where these elements would fit into the periodic table. They are moved to the bottom of the page to save space.

Lanthanide series
Cerium
58
Ce
140.115

Praseodymium
59
Pr
140.908

Neodymium
60
Nd
144.24

Promethium
61
Pm
144.913

Samarium
62
Sm
150.36

Actinide series
Thorium
90
Th
232.038

Protactinium
91
Pa
231.036

Uranium
92
U
238.029

Neptunium
93
Np
237.048

Plutonium
94
Pu
244.064